Reducing Carbon Footprint

Reducing Carbon Footprint

Sustainable Tourism Initiatives Worldwide

RAFEAL MECHLORE

WSM Publisher

CONTENTS

INDEX 1

INTRODUCTION 3

Chapter 1 17

Chapter 2 34

Chapter 3 52

Chapter 4 69

Chapter 5 83

Chapter 6 99

Chapter 7 114

Chapter 8 134

Chapter 9 150

Chapter 10 168

INDEX

Introduction

1. The Significance of Sustainable Tourism
2. Overview of the Carbon Footprint Challenge
3. Purpose and Scope of the Book
4. Structure of the Book

Chapter 1: Understanding Sustainable Tourism
1.1 Definition and Principles of Sustainable Tourism
1.2 The Environmental Impact of Tourism
1.3 The Role of Tourism in Local Economies
1.4 The Sociocultural Aspects of Sustainable Tourism

Chapter 2: Measuring Carbon Footprint in Tourism
2.1 Carbon Emissions in the Tourism Industry
2.2 Methods of Carbon Footprint Measurement
2.3 The Carbon Emission Assessment Process
2.4 Carbon Offset Mechanisms

Chapter 3: Sustainable Tourism Practices
3.1 Eco-friendly Accommodations
3.2 Sustainable Transportation Options
3.3 Sustainable Dining and Food Sourcing
3.4 Reducing Waste and Promoting Recycling

Chapter 4: Sustainable Destinations
4.1 The Role of Destination Management Organizations
4.2 Sustainable Destination Certification Programs

Chapter 5: The Role of Technology in Sustainable Tourism

5.1 Advancements in Green Technology
5.2 Digital Platforms for Sustainable Travel Planning
5.3 The Influence of Artificial Intelligence and Big Data

Chapter 6: Community Engagement and Empowerment
6.1 Community-Based Tourism Initiatives
6.2 The Importance of Local Engagement
6.3 Economic Empowerment Through Sustainable Tourism

Chapter 7: Challenges and Barriers to Sustainability
7.1 Economic and Commercial Challenges
7.2 Policy and Regulatory Hurdles
7.3 Social and Cultural Complexities
7.4 The Global Context: Climate Change and Its Impacts

Chapter 8: Success Stories from Around the World
8.1 Lessons Learned and Best Practices
8.2 Innovations and Collaborations Driving Change

Chapter 9: Policies and Regulations Promoting Sustainable Tourism
9.1 Global and National Initiatives
9.2 Environmental Legislation and Agreements
9.3 Public and Private Sector Partnerships

Chapter 10: The Future of Sustainable Tourism
10.1 Emerging Trends and Technologies
10.2 The Role of Sustainable Tourism in Mitigating Climate Change
10.3 Building Resilience and Preparedness

INTRODUCTION

The imperative to reduce carbon footprints has moved beyond the sphere of academic debate and become a global call to action in a society that is confronted by the urgent and complex challenge of climate change. At this crucial juncture in history, where the protection of the environment is of the utmost importance, "Reducing Carbon Footprint: Sustainable Tourism Initiatives Worldwide" emerges as a beacon of hope, casting light on the transforming power of sustainable tourism.

The importance of implementing environmentally friendly policies has never been higher as our global society struggles to come to terms with the negative effects that travel and tourism have on the environment, society, and the economy. This book takes the reader on an adventure of investigation and discovery as it travels through the complex landscapes of sustainable tourism initiatives that are transforming the way in which we experience the globe.

Long ago, a fork in the road appeared before the tourism sector, which plays a significant role in shaping cultures, economies, and even our entire perception of the world. It has the ability to improve people's lives and communities, but if it is allowed to continue uncontrolled, it also has the potential to wreak havoc on our world. We investigate the revolutionary potential of sustainable tourism while acknowledging the hurdles that lie in its way in our article titled "Reducing Carbon Footprint," which delves deep into the core of this duality.

This book has two goals: the first is to provide readers with a full grasp of the principles of sustainable tourism; the second is to fire a profound call to action, motivating individuals and organizations to embark on the journey toward responsible travel. Both of these goals will be accomplished if the reader completes this book. It is not only a documentation of sustainable tourism activities; rather, "Reducing Carbon Footprint" is an irresistible invitation to a greener, more conscientious, and more responsible exploration of the globe.

In the next chapters, we will explore the various aspects of sustainable tourism, such as the calculation of carbon footprints, the use of eco-friendly hotels, the function of technology in environmentally responsible travel, and the influence that tourism has on local communities. We will investigate the joint efforts of locations all over the world that have embraced sustainability, and we will unearth the success stories that highlight the transforming impact of environmentally friendly activities.

"Reducing Carbon Footprint" is not an individual activity; rather, it is a symphony of voices and deeds from sustainable pioneers, industry leaders, and responsible travelers who share a collective vision for a more harmonious cohabitation with our planet. This symphony of voices and actions is what we mean when we talk about "reducing carbon footprint." It is a strong cry to make every journey one that is responsible and eco-conscious, a testament to the incredible progress that has been done, and an investigation of the present and future of environmentally responsible tourism.

Join us on this fascinating journey as we unravel the magnificent tapestry of sustainable tourism initiatives that is altering our planet and learn how you can be a part of it. We are able to go on a journey of discovery together, not only of the wondrous things that the earth has to offer, but also of the transforming power of environmentally responsible behaviors. This book extends a call to adventure, education, and action with the overarching purpose of lowering our collective carbon footprints and ensuring that future generations can continue to enjoy the natural splendor of our planet.

1. **The Significance of Sustainable Tourism**
   Since the dawn of time, tourism in all its guises has been an essential component of human existence, serving as a medium through which people can engage in activities such as discovery, adventure, and the sharing of cultural traditions. However, it is impossible to deny that the expansion of the tourist sector, particularly over the course of the most recent few decades, has resulted in the emergence of a number of problems. These problems include the destruction of the natural environment, the disturbance of cultural traditions, and the existence of social inequalities. The idea of sustainable tourism has evolved as a significant paradigm shift as a response to the issues that have been presented. It tries to strike a balance between the indisputable economic benefits of travel and tourism and the imperatives of preserving cultural heritage, protecting the environment, and improving the well-being of host communities. This article dives into the significance of sustainable tourism, investigating its guiding principles, the consequences it has had, and the promise for radical change that it carries for the future.
   Recognizing the Importance of Sustainable Tourism
   Sustainable tourism, also known as responsible tourism or eco-tourism, is a concept and approach to tourism that places utmost priority on the long-term well-being of destinations, as well as the well-being of the surroundings in which they are located and the communities that inhabit those destinations. It

acknowledges that tourism can have both positive and negative effects, and it works to enhance the former while reducing the latter as much as it can.

Principles Crucial to an Ecologically Sound Tourism Industry:
Conservation of the Environment: Ecosystems, Biodiversity, and Natural Resources Sustainable tourism places a high priority on preserving natural resources and biodiversity. It encourages the adoption of methods that lessen the impact that tourism and travel have on the surrounding ecosystem.

Preserving Culture: Preserving cultural heritage is an essential component of environmentally responsible tourism. Its purpose is to honor and maintain the traditions, customs, and overall cultural authenticity of the communities that host it.

Economic Benefits The practice of sustainable tourism aims to deliver economic advantages that are just and equitable to the communities that it visits. It places an emphasis on community participation in tourism-related businesses as well as community ownership of those businesses.

Responsibility Towards Society Both social equality and being responsible for one's actions are essential components of sustainable tourism. Its goals are to improve the quality of life for local residents, to encourage inclusiveness, and to reduce any negative social repercussions that may be caused by tourism.

Education and Awareness: Education and awareness-raising are two of the most important aspects of sustainable tourism, both for tourists and the communities they visit. It creates a knowledge of the natural and cultural significance of the locations that are visited, as well as urges travelers to behave responsibly while they are away.

The Importance of Ecotourism to the Tourism Industry
Conservation of the Natural Environment:
The function that sustainable tourism plays in the protection of the environment is probably the aspect of its relevance that is the most immediate and pressing. Tourism activities that are not environmentally responsible can result in the destruction of habitat, pollution, and the depletion of natural resources. Sustainable tourism, on the other hand, is tourism that does not negatively impact the natural environment and actively works to protect biodiversity and promote eco-friendly business practices.

For instance, the creation of national parks and marine reserves, which are frequently backed by programs for sustainable tourism, offers a safe haven for delicate ecosystems and the wildlife that resides inside them, so ensuring that they will be around for future generations.

Economic Expansion and Work Opportunities:
In many areas, sustained tourism may be a driving force behind increased economic activity. It does this by providing local communities with possibilities to earn cash and work, which can have a substantial impact on people's ability

to make a living in regions where there are few other economic prospects. Travelers make a contribution to the overall economic growth of a destination when they select environmentally friendly lodging, patronize independently owned and operated companies, and participate in tourism activities that are rooted in the community. The practice of sustainable tourism is a potent instrument for the alleviation of poverty as well as the expansion of economic opportunities.

Protecting Our Cultural Heritage:

The value of ecotourism can't be overstated, and cultural preservation is an essential part of that. It gives the host communities the opportunity to preserve their cultural identity and pass along their traditions to subsequent generations. Travelers can develop a more profound appreciation for the places they visit by participating in native ceremonies, exchanging cultural experiences, and learning about the region's traditions.

Visitors are able to engage in traditional activities, communicate with residents, and obtain a deeper understanding of the cultural significance of the area when participating in cultural heritage programs, which are frequently a component of sustainable tourism projects.

Empowerment of the Community:

The focus of sustainable tourism should always be on the local community. It fosters an environment that is conducive to the active participation of local communities in the tourism business. Residents have the opportunity to have a direct interest in the benefits generated by the tourism industry by taking ownership of tourism-related enterprises and experiences through the implementation of community-based tourism projects.

It is more probable that communities will support and safeguard their natural and cultural assets when they are enabled to make decisions and benefit from tourism. This helps build a sense of pride and responsibility among the community members.

Carbon Footprint That Is Significantly Lower

Carbon emissions caused by tourism are another environmental concern that can be mitigated by the practice of sustainable tourism. It encourages the use of environmentally responsible behaviors, such as the minimization of waste, energy-efficient lodging, and low-impact modes of transportation, among other things.

Travelers who choose to reduce their impact on the environment by engaging in environmentally responsible behaviors, like as taking public transportation, limiting their use of water and electricity, and discarding waste in an efficient manner, contribute to a smaller carbon footprint left by their trips. This not only helps the environment, but it also demonstrates responsible behavior that others can follow.

Responsibility to the Community and Fairness:
Sustainable tourism encourages social responsibility by addressing the negative social repercussions that tourism can bring, such as overcrowding, gentrification, and the exploitation of vulnerable population groups. This type of tourism can be defined as "green" or "eco-friendly."
Sustainable tourism attempts to promote social equality and guarantee that all stakeholders profit from tourism by, among other things, encouraging fair labor practices, supporting local artisans and companies, and respecting the rights of the communities who act as hosts for tourists.

Education and a Consciousness of the Facts:
Education and awareness are essential parts of tourism that does not harm the environment. Travelers who participate in behaviors that are environmentally friendly become ambassadors for responsible tourism and create awareness about the importance of preserving cultural and natural resources.
In addition, sustainable tourism efforts frequently include educational components, which provide visitors the opportunity to gain a deeper understanding of the ecological and cultural significance of the locations they visit. Because of this, there is a stronger connection formed between travelers and the locations they visit.

Both Resilience and Adaptability are Required:
The significance of environmentally responsible tourism extends to its function in developing resilience and adaptability in response to external pressures. This became particularly clear during the COVID-19 pandemic, when locations with a history of sustainable tourism shown a greater capacity for adaptation and resilience in the face of the crisis.
Destinations can become more resilient to the effects of external shocks and adapt to shifting market dynamics if they diversify their tourism offers and place a greater emphasis on environmental responsibility.
It is impossible to exaggerate how important it is to practice sustainable tourism. It symbolizes an essential step on the path toward bringing into balance our desire to travel and gain experience in new places with our obligation to preserve the natural world. A commitment to the protection of the natural environment, the maintenance of cultural traditions, the promotion of social justice, and the expansion of economic opportunity are all essential components of sustainable tourism. It gives local communities more influence, encourages education, and encourages travelers to behave responsibly in their travels.
When tourists, companies, and government officials embrace the concepts of sustainable tourism, they contribute to a future in which the advantages of the tourism industry are fairly distributed, cultural heritage is maintained, and the environment is safeguarded for future generations. The transformative

potential of sustainable tourism is what gives it its relevance as an industry. This is the possibility for the tourism industry and the world as a whole to have a future that is more responsible, inclusive, and environmentally conscientious.

2. **Overview of the Carbon Footprint Challenge**

The issue of carbon footprint has arisen as one of the most important environmental challenges of our day, which is a reflection of the quickly changing world we live in today. The effect that this has had on the climate system of the Earth is becoming more and more obvious as human activities continue to contribute to the accumulation of greenhouse gases in the atmosphere. The term "carbon footprint," which refers to the total amount of greenhouse gases generated directly or indirectly by human activities, has garnered a large amount of interest in recent years, particularly in the fields of environmental science, policymaking, and public debate. This article provides a detailed overview of the challenge posed by carbon footprints by examining its primary components, implications, and the necessity of collaborative action to address this urgent worldwide concern.

Acquiring Knowledge of One's Carbon Footprint

The amount of greenhouse gases, mostly carbon dioxide, that are emitted into the atmosphere can be used as a measurement of the impact that human activities have on the environment. This impact can be measured using a concept called the "carbon footprint." It takes into consideration not only the direct emissions from sources such as industrial processes and transportation but also the indirect emissions from the full lifespan of products and services, which includes the manufacture, delivery, and disposal of such items and services.

Components that make up a carbon footprint are as follows:

Emissions That Are Direct:

Emissions from sources that are owned or controlled by an entity are included in this category. For example, emissions caused by the combustion of fossil fuels for the purpose of heating a building or powering a vehicle fall into this category.

Emissions That Are Not Direct:

These are emissions that are created as a result of the actions of the entity, but those emissions come from sources that are owned or controlled by a third party. For instance, the emissions that are produced as a result of the generation of the power that is used by a corporation would be considered to be indirect emissions.

Emissions under Scope 1, 2, and 3:

Emissions are divided into three different scopes according to the Greenhouse Gas Protocol. Scope 1 addresses direct emissions, Scope 2 addresses indirect emissions resulting from the entity's purchase and use of electricity, and Scope

3 addresses additional indirect emissions, such as those resulting from the supply chain, business travel, and waste disposal.

Effects of Attempting to Reduce One's Carbon Footprint

The Influence of Climate:

The most significant effect that the carbon footprint dilemma has is the contribution that it makes to climate change. Greenhouse gases, which include carbon dioxide, cause heat to be trapped within the atmosphere of the Earth, which in turn causes an increase in average temperatures around the globe, changes in weather patterns, and a variety of other environmental disruptions.

Loss of Biological Diversity:

Loss of biodiversity is one of the unintended consequences of climate change, which is made worse by the difficulty of reducing one's carbon footprint. Changes in temperature and the patterns of the weather can have a destabilizing effect on ecosystems, which can result in the loss of habitat, the extinction of species, and imbalances within ecological systems.

Deterioration of the Environment:

Excessive carbon emissions are a contributor to many different types of environmental degradation, such as pollution of the air and water, loss of forest cover, and degradation of the soil. These factors not only have an effect on the natural ecosystems, but they also pose risks to the health and well-being of humans.

Disruptions in Social and Economic Systems:

The implications of the challenge posed by one's carbon footprint are not exclusive to the natural environment. They also include socioeconomic disruptions, such as a lack of access to food and water, the relocation of people as a result of natural disasters, and economic instability as a result of the effects of climate change on businesses such as agriculture and tourism.

Taking up the Challenge of Reducing Our Carbon Footprint

Transition to Renewable Energy Sources:

Changing our energy system so that we no longer rely on fossil fuels and instead use renewable sources of power is one of the most important steps we can take to reduce our carbon footprint. This includes the implementation of renewable energy sources like solar, wind, and hydroelectric power, all of which have the potential to drastically cut carbon emissions from the generation of energy.

Measures to Improve Energy Efficiency:

It is absolutely necessary to implement energy-efficient techniques in industrial, commercial, and residential settings if one want to reduce their overall energy consumption and, as a direct result of this, their carbon emissions. This may involve the utilization of appliances that are more friendly to the environment, the improvement of insulation, or the optimization of transportation infrastructure.

Solutions for a More Sustainable Transportation System:
The difficulty of reducing one's carbon footprint caused by transportation can be helped in part by encouraging electric automobiles, advocating for increased use of public transportation, and making investments in infrastructure that facilitates walking and biking. The implementation of these strategies has the potential to drastically cut down on the emissions produced by the transportation industry.

Waste Minimization and Resource Management :
The implementation of efficient waste management measures, such as recycling, composting, and the conversion of trash into energy, can lead to a significant reduction in the emissions of greenhouse gases. These techniques help reduce the quantity of methane that is released into the atmosphere as a result of the breakdown of organic waste because they reduce the amount of waste that is delivered to landfills.

Offsetting Carbon Emissions and Storing It:
Carbon offsetting programs entail investing in projects that reduce or remove carbon emissions. These projects may include forestry initiatives or projects involving renewable energy. Carbon sequestration, on the other hand, refers to the process of removing carbon dioxide from the atmosphere and storing it in underground reservoirs. This can be accomplished through either natural or technical means.

Interventions of Policy and Regulatory Measures:
The implementation of laws and regulations by governments that provide financial incentives for
reducing carbon emissions is one of the most important roles that governments play in addressing the challenge of reducing their carbon footprint. This can involve the establishing of targets to reduce emissions, the implementation of mechanisms for pricing carbon, and the provision of subsidies for environmentally friendly activities and technologies.

The Absolute Necessity of Collaborative Effort
Taking on the challenge of reducing one's carbon footprint will need concerted action on the part of individuals, organizations, and governments at all levels. Due to the gravity of the problem, it is necessary to take preventative actions, participate in cooperative endeavors, and make a joint commitment to sustainability and environmental stewardship. We can collectively work toward minimizing the carbon footprint challenge and guaranteeing a sustainable and resilient future for generations to come if we embrace sustainable practices, advocate for legislative reforms, and invest in innovative technologies. This will allow us to ensure a sustainable future for future generations.

3. **Purpose and Scope of the Book**
In the ever-changing landscape of literature and knowledge, the purpose and

scope of a book serve as its guiding principles, illuminating the road it carves through a domain of information and ideas. In other words, the aim of a book is to illuminate the way it carves through a realm of information and ideas. In addition to serving as a compass for both the author and the reader, the "Purpose and Scope of the Book" section also serves as a declaration of intent and a guide to the intellectual trip that lies ahead. This article's goal is to clarify the scope and aim of the book, so laying the groundwork for the investigation that is still to come.

The Reason Behind Writing This Book

Every book has a significant reason for existing, known as its raison d'être, which is what drives its production and determines what it will contain. The goal of writing a book may take many shapes, but at its core, it is to communicate information, perspectives, and tales in a way that educates, motivates, or stimulates thought in the reader. The word "Purpose" serves as the central support for the entire framework of the book, dictating both the path it travels and the kind of influence it aspires to have.

There are many different goals that can be included under the umbrella of "purpose of a book," some of which are as follows:

Providing Information and Education:

A great number of books are written with the primary intention of enlightening and informing the people who read them. The reader is intended to gain knowledge, facts, and insights from these types of publications, regardless of whether the book in question is a non-fiction work, an academic textbook, or a reference guide.

Both Interesting and Captivating:

Books of fiction, poetry, and creative non-fiction frequently have the goals of entertaining and engaging the reader. These books take readers to other realms, stimulate their imaginations, and provide them with emotional experiences.

Motivating and a Source of Inspiration:

Books that fall into the categories of self-help, motivational, and inspirational writing all have the same goal: to encourage and inspire readers to make positive changes in their lives, whether those changes pertain to personal development, job advancement, or overall well-being.

Inspiring Difficulty and Mind-Blowing Contemplation:

Some novels are written with the express intention of upending the reader's assumptions and encouraging them to engage in introspective contemplation. These writings inspire readers to challenge preexisting standards and open their minds to alternative points of view.

The Acts of Preserving and Recording:

A great number of books are written with the intention of preserving and recording information pertaining to history, culture, or individual experiences.

Memoirs, historical reports, and archival records are all examples of this type of material.

Advancing the Cause of Change While Also Activating It:

Books have the potential to be influential change agents and advocates. These works are written with the intention of inspiring readers to take action, whether it be in the form of a call to protect the environment, fight for social justice, or alter political institutions.

The author's interests, expertise, and driving forces behind writing a book are inextricably bound up with the book's ultimate goal. It acts as the primary impetus behind the creation of the book and its subsequent publication, firmly establishing it inside a certain literary category, subject matter, or narrative framework.

The Ranging Ambitions of the Book

The scope of a book outlines the limits and bounds of the subject matter, substance, and themes that the book will cover. It determines what will be included and, just as importantly, what will not be included in the game, so establishing the playing field. The scope of the book serves as a guide for the author's exploration and helps to maintain the book's concentration as well as its overall cohesion. The "territory" of the book is essentially defined by its scope.

Some of the factors that determine the overall scope of a book are as follows:

Object of Discussion:

One of the key aspects that determines the scope of a book is the subject matter that it covers. For example, a book titled "Sustainable Tourism Initiatives" will go into a variety of themes, including those pertaining to tourism, environmental protection, community involvement, and more.

Target Group:

The scope of a book is significantly impacted by the readers for whom it was written. A book that is created for academics and specialists in a certain field will cover a wider range of topics and delve into more specific information, in contrast to a book that is published for a general audience, which will adopt an approach that is more user-friendly.

Both in depth and in scope:

The extent of the coverage, both in terms of breadth and depth, is a critical component in establishing the scope of a book. In some books, the goal is to provide extensive coverage of a topic, while in others, the focus is narrower, and the reader is given a thorough examination of a particular facet of the topic.

The Time Period:

There are sometimes time constraints placed on reading books. They may zero in on a specific era, historical event, or time period, narrowing their attention in order to provide a more in-depth perspective on the time period in question.

Boundaries Defined by Geography:

The scope of a book may be constrained by its geographical setting. A book with a regional concentration, on the other hand, may restrict its geographic scope to a particular region, but a book on "sustainable tourism initiatives worldwide" would have a scope that extended to a global perspective.

Approach That Draws From Different Disciplines:

Some books take an interdisciplinary approach, which enables them to cover more ground by relying on the findings of a variety of academic disciplines in order to present a more complete picture of the subject matter.

Forms of Narration and Types of Stories:

The narrative mode and category of a book are additional factors that contribute to its overall scope. The purpose of a novel might be to tell a story that is led by a particular character inside a certain location, whereas the purpose of a textbook might be to cover a topic area in an organized manner.

Author Knowledge and Available Resources:

The author's knowledge and experience, as well as the resources and research materials that are at their disposal, all play a key part in determining the breadth. The author's access to data, archives, and expertise can either broaden or restrict the range of topics that can be covered in the book.

Finding Your Way Around the Objectives and the Scope

The goal of writing a book and determining its scope are inextricably linked concepts, with the former providing context for the latter. While the purpose lays forth the overall goal to be accomplished, the scope of the project outlines the parameters within which that goal can be accomplished. The authors need to align their purpose with a manageable scope that can be adequately explored within the limitations of the book in order to successfully navigate these components, as doing so demands a delicate balance.

In order for readers to make educated decisions about what to read and how to engage with the material of a book, it is vital for readers to grasp the purpose and scope of the book.

It gives readers the ability to choose whether a book meets their interests, requirements, and expectations before reading it.

4. **Structure of the Book**

The architecture of a book, which acts as the framework that governs the flow of information, ideas, and narratives, directs readers through a logical and well-organized investigation of the topic at hand. The content of the book is easier to comprehend, more interesting to engage with, and easier to remember when the structure has been thoughtfully planned to create a logical development. This article looks into the complexities of the structure of a book, highlighting its numerous components and the roles that they play in generating a reading experience that is unified and compelling.

A Brief Exposition of the Organization

The format of a book is like to a map in that it outlines the path that the reader will take from the beginning to the end of the text and ensures that every stage along the route makes a significant contribution to the story as a whole. It defines the reader's expectations for the book as a whole, sets the tone for what they can expect from it, and introduces them to the thematic contours that will develop as they continue to read.

A book with strong structure often has a logical progression that can be broken down into chapters, sections, and subsections, each of which fulfills a distinct function within the overarching framework of the story. The framework has been meticulously crafted to provide a smooth transition from one topic to the next. This enables readers to easily browse through the content and get a better understanding of how the many ideas offered are connected to one another.

Principal Elements that Make Up the Structure

A Look at the Table of Contents:

The table of contents is the first point of reference for readers, as it provides an outline of the content of the book along with the titles of the chapters and the page numbers. It acts as a preliminary road map to the organization of the book and gives a quick reference for readers to identify specific sections of the book that are of interest to them.

In the beginning...

The introduction establishes the tone for the remainder of the book by providing a synopsis of the subject matter, the author's goals, and the range of the narrative in a concise manner. It lays forth the primary ideas, principles, and goals that will be covered throughout the paper, providing the reader with a foundational comprehension of what to anticipate and the significance of the subject matter.

The Main Part:

The primary content of the book is contained within the book's main body, which is broken up into chapters or sections that go into greater depth regarding certain areas of the subject matter. Generally speaking, each chapter or section will concentrate on a specific subsidiary subject, researching that subject in depth and presenting exhaustive insights, analysis, and supporting data.

Concluding remarks:

The conclusion serves as the book's climax, bringing together all of the most important topics, findings, and arguments that were discussed throughout the course of the narrative. It provides a comprehensive synthesis of the book's primary ideas and insights, and it frequently includes recommendations, consequences, or possible directions for further investigation.

Supplementary and Additional Materials: Appendices

The primary body of the book is supplemented by appendices and other materials, which, if present, provide additional information, data, or resources that are relevant to the topic at hand. These may take the form of graphs, charts, tables, or expanded analyses that offer a more in-depth context for the primary topics of the book or provide support for them.

A Glossary For:

When present, a glossary offers readers definitions of important terminology, topics, and jargon that are discussed throughout the work. It acts as a point of reference for readers, ensuring that specialized vocabulary that a general readership may not be familiar with is clear and easily understood by that audience.

Bibliography, often known as the Reference List:

The bibliography or reference list provides a detailed compilation of the sources, texts, and materials that are mentioned or referred to throughout the entirety of the book. It is helpful for further research and investigation because it gives readers the opportunity to investigate the primary and secondary sources that have informed the author's research and ideas.

Index of:

The index provides a comprehensive listing, organized alphabetically, of the subjects, persons, and important concepts that are mentioned in the book, together with the page numbers that correlate to each entry. It is an extremely helpful tool for researchers, scholars, and others who are looking for certain data or references, as it enables readers to rapidly discover specific information within the book.

Developing an Efficient Plan for the Building

The successful creation of an effective structure for a book necessitates meticulous planning and organization, as well as thorough consideration of the aims and target audience. The author is responsible for determining the most effective and interesting manner to communicate the material in the book, while also ensuring that the structure is in line with the book's main purpose and the flow of the narrative.

The following are important factors to take into account while constructing an efficient structure:

Continuing in a Logical Manner:

It is essential, in order to sustain the reader's interest and ensure comprehension of the material, to make sure that the concepts and themes presented in the book proceed in a logical manner. Building upon the groundwork that was established in earlier chapters, each succeeding chapter or section should flow naturally into the one that comes after it.

Transparency and Consistency:

It is crucial to keep the structure of the book clear and coherent if one wishes to facilitate understanding and memory retention of the material contained therein. The reader will have an easier time navigating the material and understanding the connections between the many subjects if the headings, subheadings, and section divisions are crystal clear.

Harmony and progression:

A well-rounded and interesting reading experience is mostly influenced by the author's ability to strike a balance between the breadth and depth of content provided, as well as to keep the information presented at an appropriate pace. The key to preserving the interest of the reader is to avoid overwhelming them with information and to make sure there is a consistent flow of content.

Participation of the Reader:

You may improve the structure of the book and make the information more relatable and captivating for the audience by incorporating components that drive reader engagement, such as case studies, stories, images, and interactive exercises. This will make the book more interesting to read.

Accessibility and User-Friendliness:

When the layout of the book places an emphasis on usability and accessibility, it assures that readers will have an easy time navigating the content and gaining access to the information they require. A user-friendly reading experience is characterized by features such as clear formatting and styling, consistent formatting, and intuitive arrangement.

By giving careful attention to these concerns, authors are able to construct a structure that optimally fulfills the requirements and expectations of their readers, so producing a story that is consistent and effective and that resonates with their audience.

The Importance of Having a Book That Is Well-Organized

It is necessary to have a book that is well structured in order to offer a narrative that is consistent and impactful, one that successfully communicates the author's message and thoughts. Not only does a structure that has been thoughtfully created make it easier for readers to engage with and grasp the material, but it also improves the whole reading experience and makes the material more approachable and interesting.

The reader is able to easily traverse the book thanks to its clear and well-organized structure, which also makes it possible for them to follow the author's arguments, ideas, and tales without any difficulty. It provides the reader with the ability to connect with the subject matter on a deeper level, encouraging a sense of intellectual immersion as well as discovery.

In addition, a book that is organized effectively can help an author establish their credibility and authority in their field by demonstrating their level of knowledge, research skills, and overall mastery of the material being discussed. Earning the readers' confidence and respect requires presenting information in a way that is logical and easy to understand, and a structure that has been meticulously designed reveals that the author is dedicated to doing so.

Chapter 1

Understanding Sustainable Tourism

Tourism is a powerful force that has a significant impact on the global economy, the trade of cultures, and the contact of people. On the other hand, it is a double-edged sword, meaning that it has the potential to be beneficial to the environment as well as harmful to the communities that live there. The concept of sustainable tourism was developed as a response to the need to strike a balance between the socio-economic benefits of travel and the preservation of ecosystems, cultural heritage, and local livelihoods. Sustainable tourism seeks to achieve this balance. In the course of this in-depth investigation of sustainable tourism, we will talk about the concept of sustainable tourism, its guiding principles, the obstacles that stand in its way, and the bright future that it has in a world that is becoming more concerned with environmental issues.

The Meaning of the Term "Sustainable Tourism"

The idea of sustainable tourism, which is sometimes referred to as ecotourism, responsible tourism, or green tourism, is one that attempts to maximize the positive effects that tourism may have on both the environment and the cultures that are visited, while at the same time minimizing the adverse effects that tourism can have on these areas. The purpose of this is to bring about a harmonious interaction between the tourism sector and the natural and cultural elements that are attractive to tourists.

Principles Crucial to an Ecologically Sound Tourism Industry:

The basic goal of environmental conservation is to safeguard and ensure the survival of natural ecosystems as well as its constituent parts. This involves lowering pollution levels, conserving energy, and supporting environmentally friendly habits like recycling and cutting down on trash.

Respect for Culture: Sustainable tourism is defined by its ability to respect and support the cultural identity and customs of the community that it visits. It fosters interaction between tourists and natives in a way that is beneficial to both parties, so everyone benefits.

Economic Benefits This type of tourism ought to be beneficial to the local economy in that it ought to create job opportunities, support local businesses, and contribute to the community's general economic development.

Participation of Local Communities: In order for tourism to be sustainable, it is necessary for local communities to take an active role in the decision-making processes that are associated with tourism development. Their opinions and requirements are taken into consideration.

The Significance of Ecotourism in Today's World

1. **The protection of our earth's natural resources**
   The reduction of negative effects that tourism operations have on the surrounding environment is one of the key objectives of sustainable tourism. It does this by encouraging actions that are responsible, which helps conserve the natural resources that are necessary for the continued health of our world. This includes safeguarding fragile ecosystems as well as species and lowering the amount of pollution in the environment.
2. **The protection of cultural heritage**
   The cultural history of many popular tourist locations is extensive. Promoting relationships between tourists and local people that are courteous and responsible helps to achieve the goal of sustainable tourism, which is to save and maintain these cultural assets. This not only helps to maintain cultural customs but also facilitates cross-cultural communication and understanding.
3. **The Promotion of Economic Growth**
   In areas where the economy is heavily dependent on tourist, sustainable tourism has the potential to be a key economic growth engine. It fosters the growth of local enterprises, which in turn helps communities produce cash and provides employment possibilities. It is possible for it to contribute to the decrease of poverty as well as an improvement in living standards when it is managed effectively.
4. **Spreading Knowledge and Being Aware**
   People can be effectively educated about the significance of protecting the natural world and maintaining cultural variety through the use of tourism as a potent educational tool. Travelers' awareness is raised and they are inspired to be more responsible global citizens through the participation in educational activities that are frequently a part of sustainable tourism experiences.
5. **The Standard of Living**

Local populations may see an improvement in their quality of life if tourism is managed in a sustainable manner.

People who live in tourist locations may experience an improvement in their quality of life if their communities are cleaner, more work possibilities are available, and there is a strong cultural scene.

The Obstacles and Problems Facing a Sustainable Tourism Industry

1. **Excessive tourism**
   When attractive sites are inundated with a greater number of visitors than they can sensibly accommodate, this is an example of overtourism. This can result in a rise in both pollution and overcrowding, as well as the destruction of both natural and cultural resources. Promoting less-traveled locations and responsible vacationing are two aspects of sustainable tourism that are intended to help solve this problem.
2. **The practice of "greenwashing"**
   Greenwashing is a form of deceptive marketing in which a company fraudulently asserts that it is environmentally benign or sustainable. This has the potential to mislead travelers and lessen the impact of real initiatives to promote sustainable tourism. Clear certification and labeling methods are required in order to put an end to the practice of greenwashing.
3. **The Changing Climate**
   Because of the volume of energy and transportation that it requires, the tourism industry is a substantial contributor to the emission of greenhouse gases. The goal of decreasing the carbon footprint of travel should be the primary emphasis of efforts to promote sustainable tourism. This can be accomplished by encouraging eco-friendly transit options and energy-efficient hotels.
4. **The Commercialization of Culture**
   It is possible for tourism to result in the commercialization of culture in certain instances. This happens when local customs and rituals are performed simply for the purpose of entertaining tourists. This can cause the culture's authenticity to suffer, as well as damage the feeling of identity held by the host community.
5. **An Absence of Conscience**

The fundamental tenets of sustainable tourism are unknown to the majority of travelers. It's possible that they are unaware of the potential effects that their actions can have on the surrounding populations and the environment. The promotion of responsible travel among tourists is an essential component of tourism that does not damage the environment.

The Prospects for Ecotourism in the Future

1. **Technological Advancement and Creative Effort**
   The development of technology will play an important part in the promotion of environmentally responsible tourism. Apps and websites that provide

information on environmentally friendly accommodations, responsible tour operators, and solutions for travel that have a low impact on the environment will become increasingly common.

2. **Involvement of the Government**
A growing number of national governments are acknowledging the significance of ecotourism and are putting into effect laws and guidelines designed to encourage responsible vacationing. This includes taking precautions to safeguard natural resources as well as cultural and historical artifacts.

3. **Cooperative effort**
To maintain a sustainable tourism industry, it is sometimes necessary for a variety of stakeholders, including governments, local communities, businesses, and individual tourists, to work together. An increase in collaboration may result in tourism practices that are more efficient and environmentally responsible.

4. **Proceed With Caution**
The idea of "slow travel" lays an emphasis on staying in one location for an extended period of time rather than racing to see as many different locations as quickly as possible. This way of doing things lessens the toll that travel takes on the environment and opens the door to richer cultural encounters.

5. **Lodging Options That Are Kind to the Environment**
There is an increasing desire for environmentally responsible lodging options, such as eco-lodges, sustainable hotels, and vacation rentals that have earned their green certifications. These choices are available for vacationers who are interested in reducing their impact on the local ecosystem.

6. **Behavior Befitting a Responsible Traveler**
The future of environmentally responsible tourism will rely heavily on the actions of individual tourists. People are becoming more aware of the influence they have on the areas they visit and are looking for methods to lessen that impact, help the communities they visit, and safeguard the environment.

7. **Spreading Knowledge and Being Aware**

Education regarding environmentally responsible vacationing will remain a top priority. Travelers will seek out more information on responsible travel practices and increasingly select places and businesses that are congruent with their morals and beliefs.

The idea of sustainable tourism is an important one that strives to find a middle ground between the positive aspects of traveling and the protection of our natural resources and cultural history. It has the ability to change the travel and tourism sector into a force that is more responsible and sustainable, contributing to the well-being of our planet and the wealth of local communities. The future of environmentally responsible tourism appears to be bright as tourists are becoming more conscientious of the decisions they make and as governments and businesses adopt environmentally responsible practices. In spite of this, it is absolutely necessary for all parties involved to cooperate in order to surmount the obstacles and make certain that the tenets of sustainable tourism continue to be respected in the years to come.

1.1 Definition and Principles of Sustainable Tourism

Tourism has evolved into a substantial global sector that has a positive impact on economic growth, the dissemination of cultural experiences, and individual satisfaction. However, growing concerns about tourism's effects on the environment and other aspects of society and culture have been brought about by its rapid expansion. The concept of sustainable tourism, which is also known as ecotourism and responsible tourism, has recently surfaced as a potential solution to these problems. Within the scope of this paper, we shall investigate the meaning of "sustainable tourism" as well as its guiding principles.

The Meaning of the Term "Sustainable Tourism"

Reduces Harm to the ecosystem One of the goals of sustainable tourism is to minimize the damage that traditional tourist can cause to the local ecosystem. This involves taking steps to reduce pollution, preserve natural resources, and guard delicate ecosystems. It promotes the use of environmentally friendly modes of transportation, establishments that are efficient with energy, and the minimization of trash.

It recognizes the significance of preserving and enhancing the cultural legacy of the host community and acts on this acknowledgment with respect and support for the culture. The goal of sustainable tourism is to prevent the commodification of culture, which occurs when visitors reduce local customs to mere entertainment for themselves. Instead, it encourages courteous relationships between tourists and people of the area, which opens the door to cultural exchange and contributes to the enrichment of both parties.

Benefits the Local Economy Sustainable tourism isn't just about preserving the environment and the culture; it also tries to help the local economy thrive.

This involves increasing the number of available jobs, providing assistance to existing local firms, and making a contribution to the community's general economic development.

It supports the active participation of local communities in decision-making processes that are relevant to tourism development, which results in increased community engagement. Their perspectives and requirements are taken into consideration, and they are given opportunities to participate in the process of planning and managing tourism-related activities.

The core notion behind sustainable tourism is that it should promote a healthy interaction between the tourism sector, the natural environment, cultural assets, and the local people. These principles are a reflection of that fundamental idea.

The Fundamentals of Responsible and Sustainable Tourism

1. **Protection of the Natural Environment**
   Impacts on the Environment Being Minimized One of the primary goals of sustainable tourism is to reduce the adverse effects that tourism activities have on the surrounding environment. This includes lowering the amount of pollution in the air and water as well as conserving energy, as well as responsibly managing garbage.
   Protection of Ecosystems: Sustainable tourism activities frequently take place in or close to sensitive ecosystems. Protecting these ecosystems should be a top priority because they are necessary for the conservation of biodiversity as well as the provision of ecosystem services.
   Encouragement of Sustainable Practices: One essential component of this guiding principle is the promotion of sustainable practices, which may include recycling, reusing, and cutting down on waste. Destinations with a sustainable tourism model typically encourage visitors and locals alike to engage in environmentally responsible activities.
2. **Showing Respect for Culture**
   Avoiding the Commodification of Culture Sustainable tourism discourages the practice of cultural commodification, which occurs when local customs and practices are exhibited purely for the purpose of entertaining visitors. Instead, it encourages encounters between tourists and local populations that are genuine and respectful of both parties.
   Contributing to the Preservation of Cultural Landmarks Sustainable tourism frequently includes efforts to preserve and publicize cultural landmarks. This may include the preservation of historical sites, local traditions, as well as traditional arts and practices.
   Exchange of Cultures: One of the main goals of sustainable tourism is to promote cultural exchange, which not only gives visitors the opportunity to learn about the customs and traditions of the communities they visit, but also gives locals the chance to become more globally educated.
3. **Advantages to the Economy**
   The creation of jobs is one of the most important benefits that can accrue to host communities from environmentally responsible tourism. This might involve a wide variety of vocations, such as working as a tour guide or as a member of the hospitality staff. It can also include working as an artist or as a farmer providing items acquired locally.
   Contributing to the Growth of the Local Economy Sustainable tourism frequently emphasizes the utilization of locally sourced goods and services, which is beneficial to the local economy and contributes to the expansion of existing enterprises.
   Overall Contribution to Economic Growth The overall economic growth of a place may be helped along by the revenue that is created from ecotourism that is

managed responsibly. This might result in upgrades to the area's infrastructure, healthcare system, and educational opportunities, which would ultimately improve the citizens' quality of life.
4. **Participation in the Community**

Participatory decision-making occurs when communities at the local level take an active role in the deliberation and implementation of policies for the expansion of tourism in their region. This can involve activities such as generating tourism items, establishing rules, and designing infrastructure.

Benefit Sharing: Sustainable tourism guarantees that local communities benefit from tourism operations by sharing the benefits generated by tourism with those communities. This can be accomplished by the distribution of a portion of the profits, the provision of employment opportunities, and several other types of community participation.

Engagement of the local community is another factor that contributes to the preservation of cultural traditions. When it comes to preserving and advancing their cultural legacy, local communities frequently play an important role.

Problems Associated with the Application of Sustainable Tourism Principles

1. **Excessive tourism**
   When popular sites are swarmed with a greater number of visitors than they are able to sustainably accept, this is an example of overtourism. This can result in a rise in both pollution and overcrowding, as well as the destruction of both natural and cultural resources. Through the promotion of less-traveled destinations and appropriate travel behavior, sustainable tourism works toward the goal of finding a solution to this problem.
2. **The practice of "greenwashing"**
   Greenwashing is a form of deceptive marketing in which a company fraudulently asserts that it is environmentally benign or sustainable. This has the potential to mislead travelers and lessen the impact of real initiatives to promote sustainable tourism. There is a need for transparent certification and labeling systems that can accurately reflect the sustainable operations of a company in order to prevent the practice of greenwashing.
3. **The Changing Climate**
   Because of the volume of energy and transportation that it requires, the tourism industry is a substantial contributor to the emission of greenhouse gases. The goal of decreasing the carbon footprint of travel should be the primary emphasis of efforts to promote sustainable tourism. This can be accomplished by encouraging eco-friendly transit options and energy-efficient hotels.
4. **The Commercialization of Culture**
   It is possible for tourism to result in the commercialization of culture in certain

instances. This happens when local customs and rituals are performed simply for the purpose of entertaining tourists. This can cause the culture's authenticity to suffer, as well as damage the feeling of identity held by the host community. Sustainable tourism seeks to achieve harmony by emphasizing mutually beneficial cultural interaction rather than exploitative practices.

5. **An Absence of Conscience**

The fundamental tenets of sustainable tourism are unknown to the majority of travelers. It's possible that they are unaware of the potential effects that their actions can have on the surrounding populations and the environment.

It is a key component of responsible and sustainable tourism to educate tourists on responsible travel practices; nonetheless, this remains a struggle.

The Prospects for Ecotourism in the Future

1. **Technological Advancement and Creative Effort**
   The development of technology will play an important part in the promotion of environmentally responsible tourism. Apps and websites that provide information on environmentally friendly accommodations, responsible tour operators, and solutions for travel that have a low impact on the environment will become increasingly common. Through improvements in both modes of mobility and energy efficiency, technology can also play a role in lowering the carbon footprint left by human travel.

2. **Involvement of the Government**
   A growing number of national governments are acknowledging the significance of ecotourism and are putting into effect laws and guidelines designed to encourage responsible vacationing. This involves actions to preserve natural resources and cultural history, in addition to initiatives to lessen the damage tourism does to the surrounding ecosystem.

3. **Cooperative effort**
   To maintain a sustainable tourism industry, it is sometimes necessary for a variety of stakeholders, including governments, local communities, businesses, and individual tourists, to work together. An increase in collaboration may result in tourism practices that are more efficient and environmentally responsible.

4. **Proceed With Caution**
   The idea of "slow travel" lays an emphasis on staying in one location for an extended period of
   time rather than racing to see as many different locations as quickly as possible. This way of doing things lessens the toll that travel takes on the environment and opens the door to richer cultural encounters. Traveling at a slower pace allows visitors to become more ingrained in the culture of the area they are

visiting, which results in a greater level of comprehension and appreciation for the location.
5. **Lodging Options That Are Kind to the Environment**
There is an increasing desire for environmentally responsible lodging options, such as eco-lodges, sustainable hotels, and vacation rentals that have earned their green certifications. These choices are catered to vacationers who are interested in reducing their impact on the surrounding environment while yet enjoying a comfortable and responsible place to stay.
6. **Behavior Befitting a Responsible Traveler**
The future of environmentally responsible tourism will rely heavily on the actions of individual tourists. People are becoming more aware of the influence they have on the areas they visit and are looking for methods to lessen that impact, help the communities they visit, and safeguard the environment. A responsible traveler will make decisions including reducing their waste output, using environmentally friendly modes of transportation, and showing respect for the traditions and norms of the places they visit.
7. **Spreading Knowledge and Being Aware**

Education regarding environmentally responsible vacationing will remain a top priority. Travelers will seek out more information on responsible travel practices and increasingly select places and businesses that are congruent with their morals and beliefs. Travelers can be empowered to make decisions that promote the ideals of sustainable tourism by receiving the education necessary to do so.

The notion of sustainable tourism is an important one that aims to strike a balance between the positive aspects of tourism and the protection of the area's natural resources, cultural traditions, and community structures. A foundation for responsible and environmentally conscious travel is provided by its guiding principles, which include the protection of natural resources, appreciation of diverse cultures, pursuit of economic advantage, and participation in local communities. The future of environmentally responsible tourism appears to be bright as tourists are becoming more conscientious of the decisions they make and as governments and businesses adopt environmentally responsible practices. In spite of this, it is absolutely necessary for all parties involved to cooperate in order to surmount the obstacles and make certain that the tenets of sustainable tourism continue to be respected in the years to come. Sustainable tourism provides a way toward a more responsible and mutually beneficial approach to travel in a world where the environment and cultural variety are becoming increasingly vulnerable.

1.2 The Environmental Impact of Tourism

Tourism is a massive industry all over the world because millions of people go on vacation to various locations all over the world in the hopes of finding excitement, relaxation, and new cultural experiences. The tourism industry is responsible for a sizeable amount of environmental damage in addition to the creation of new jobs and a big amount of annual money. This essay investigates the myriad ways in which tourism impacts the environment, both favorably and badly, and highlights the techniques and projects that are intended to mitigate the consequences of tourism on the environment.

The tourism industry has positive effects on the surrounding environment.

1. **Initiatives Regarding Conservation**
   There are a great number of natural beauties that serve as tourist sites, such as national parks, wildlife reserves, and marine sanctuaries. The protection and upkeep of these locations is frequently dependent on the cash generated from tourism. Entrance fees and programs designed for ecotourism can help pay vital conservation activities, thereby contributing to the protection of biodiversity and ecosystems.
2. **The Replanting of Forests and the Repair of Damaged Habitats**
   In regions where deforestation or habitat degradation has occurred, tourism can provide financial assistance for programs to restore habitats and replant trees. These measures are absolutely necessary in order to safeguard wildlife and maintain the natural beauty of the environment. Ecotourism excursions typically include activities such as tree planting and habitat rehabilitation.
3. **The protection of cultural heritage**
   The protection of cultural traditions can benefit from tourism's involvement. Communities that rely heavily on tourism frequently take proactive measures to preserve their history, cultural practices, and architectural landmarks. Because of this, cultural and historical items that could have otherwise deteriorated can now be maintained for future generations.
4. **Education Regarding the Environment**
   People can be taught a lot about the need of protecting their natural surroundings and the environment through the use of tourism as an effective teaching tool. Educative programs, guided tours, and instructional materials are offered at many tourist attractions across the world. These offerings are designed to educate visitors about local ecosystems, species, and conservation activities.
5. **Financial Support for Conservation Lands and Areas**

Tourism results in the generation of revenue, which can then be reinvestment in the maintenance and administration of protected areas. This cash can contribute to the financing of the salaries of park guards, the maintenance of infrastructure, and efforts to combat poaching.

The Tourism Industry's Harmful Effects on the Environment

1. **Excessive urbanization**
   The construction of tourism infrastructure frequently results in the degradation of habitats, the loss of open areas, and the cutting down of trees. The establishment of new roads, resorts, and hotels in an area can have a significant impact on the ecosystems of that area.
2. **The problem of pollution**
   The tourism industry is a contributor to the pollution of air, water, and land. The transportation of tourists, including automobiles, buses, and airlines, contributes to the emission of greenhouse gases and other pollutants into the atmosphere. In addition, the disposal of garbage from tourists, which can include waste made of plastic as well as sewage, can contaminate water bodies and cause damage to the ecosystem.
3. **The amount of water used**
   Many popular vacation spots are plagued by water shortages, which are only made worse by the high water requirements of attractions like hotels, golf courses, and swimming pools. The overexploitation of water resources for the sake of tourism can result in the depletion of local water supplies, which in turn has a negative impact on the ecosystems and communities in the surrounding area.
4. **Utilization of Available Energy**
   The primary consumers of energy in tourist lodgings and infrastructure are the heating, ventilation and air conditioning systems, followed by the lighting systems. An increase in energy use not only adds to an increase in carbon emissions but also places a strain on the power networks of local communities, which has the potential to impair the dependability and sustainability of energy supply.
5. **Congestion caused by Heavy Traffic**
   Popular destinations see an increase in the number of vehicle trips because of tourism. Congestion in the roads not only leads to air pollution but also has a bad impact not just on the environment but also on the overall experience that visitors have there.
6. **The deterioration of land**
   Tourism activities, particularly in ecosystems that are already vulnerable, might hasten the process of land degradation.
   Off-road driving and trampling on sensitive landscapes are two examples of activities that can cause long-term damage to the ecosystem. These problems can result in the loss of flora and soil erosion.
7. **A Disturbance to the Wildlife**

It's possible that tourism will have a negative effect on the local wildlife in popular destinations. Activities such as making an excessive amount of noise, coming into close contact with humans, and feeding wildlife can all cause disruptions in natural behaviors and put a strain on local animal populations. In addition, the building of tourist infrastructure can sometimes interfere with the natural habitats of local animals.

Sustainable Tourism: Reducing the Impacts of Unwanted Activities

1. **Planning for Tourism in a Responsible Manner**
   To develop tourism that is environmentally and socially responsible, one must first engage in extensive planning that takes into account the economic, social, and environmental factors of a particular location. Overdevelopment and the degradation of habitat can be mitigated with the implementation of appropriate zoning, land-use rules, and construction guidelines.
2. **Infrastructure that is Friendly to the Environment**
   The concept of sustainability should be incorporated into the planning and construction of tourist hotels and infrastructure. It is possible for tourism infrastructure to have a substantially smaller impact on the surrounding environment if green building methods, energy-efficient technologies, and waste reduction initiatives are implemented.
3. **Travel Options That Include Public Transportation and Other Alternatives**
   In order to alleviate traffic congestion and cut down on the emissions that are caused by tourist travel, it is helpful to encourage the use of public transportation, biking, walking, and carpooling. Tourists benefit from well-planned public transit networks because they offer more convenient options while simultaneously reducing their impact on the environment.
4. **The Management of Waste**
   For tourism to be sustainable, it is essential to implement practices that effectively manage garbage. The introduction of recycling programs, the reduction of single-use plastics, and improved waste management can all contribute to a lower level of environmental damage caused by tourism.
5. **Environmental Accreditation and Labeling**
   Certification schemes, such as Green Key and EarthCheck, make it easier for tourists to choose lodgings and tour operators that are respectful to the environment. These certifications offer some level of assurance that a company is committed to maintaining a sustainable relationship with the environment.
6. **Tourism with Respect for the Animals**
   In order to promote responsible wildlife tourism, it is necessary to adhere to ethical norms when observing animals. This includes keeping appropriate distances from animals, avoiding disrupting the natural habits of animals, and avoiding engaging in activities that put wildlife under unnecessary stress.
7. **Participation in the Community**
   It is absolutely necessary, in order to achieve sustainability, to involve the local communities in the planning and development of tourism. These communities

frequently have insightful knowledge on the local environment and culture, and their participation helps ensure that tourism is beneficial to both the local economy and the cultural heritage of the area.
8. **Raise People's Awareness and Educate Them**

Education is an essential component of tourism that does not harm the environment. Tourists have a responsibility to be educated about environmentally friendly travel practices as well as the cultural and historical relevance of the locations they visit. In a similar vein, local communities and businesses ought to continually educate both themselves and the people that visit them.

When it comes to the effects that it has on the surrounding ecosystem, tourism is a double-edged sword. On the one hand, it has the ability to fund conservation activities, encourage cultural preservation, and increase consciousness about environmental issues. On the other side, it is possible that it might raise awareness about environmental issues. On the other hand, it might result in excessive growth, pollution, the destruction of habitat, and human interference with wildlife.

In order to move forward, sustainable tourism, which places an emphasis on responsible design, environmentally friendly infrastructure, public transit, trash management, and community engagement, is one solution. Even while difficulties still exist, a continuous commitment to sustainability can help ensure that tourism will continue to be a source of delight and enlightenment while also reducing the amount of damage it causes to the environment. In a world where maintaining a healthy equilibrium between tourism and environmental protection is difficult but essential for our collective future, responsible tourism is not merely a preference but a requirement.

1.3 The Role of Tourism in Local Economies

The tourism business operates on a global scale and makes a considerable contribution to the overall economic growth of countries as well as regions. On the other hand, its effects are likely to be felt most strongly at the local level. In this essay, we will investigate the varied role that tourism plays in local economies, focusing on its potential to contribute to the creation of jobs, the diversification of economic activity, and the growth of communities.

Creating New Jobs

1. **Jobs Involved Directly With Tourism**
   Positions in the tourism industry that directly involve the sale of goods or provision of services to visitors are referred to as direct tourism occupations. The staff of hotels, restaurants, and transportation companies are included in this category. Also included are tour guides. As a result of the fact that many of these occupations are entry-level roles, the tourist industry is an excellent source of employment for people with a wide range of degrees of education and professional experience.

2. **Jobs Supported by Tourism Indirectly**
Jobs in industries that provide goods and services to the tourism sector are examples of indirect employment opportunities in the tourism industry. Included in this category are companies that provide hotels and restaurants with food, equipment, and construction materials. As a result of the requirement for support workers and resources, firms that provide these services create indirect jobs, which in turn assist promote the wider local economy.
3. **Jobs That Were Induced**

Tourism employees who spend their paychecks on goods and services offered in the surrounding community are responsible for the creation of induced jobs. For instance, when employees of hotels, tour companies, or restaurants spend their wages on things like lodging, groceries, and entertainment, they are contributing to the creation of induced jobs in those industries. This recirculation of cash contributes to the maintenance of a wide variety of jobs within the community.

In areas that are short on other employment opportunities, the contribution that the tourism industry may make to job development is of critical importance. It does this by creating employment possibilities for those living in the area, which in turn lowers the rate of unemployment and raises the overall quality of life.

Diversification of the Economic System
By lessening a community's reliance on just one sector of the economy, tourism has the potential to make a major contribution to the process of economic diversification. Because it lessens a company's reliance on the performance of a single industry, diversification is one of the most important factors in determining an economy's ability to withstand adverse economic conditions. When a single industry, like manufacturing or agriculture, has a downturn, it can have a serious impact on the economy of a community that relies primarily on that industry. In many situations, these areas might face severe economic hardships.

The incorporation of tourism into the economy can contribute to the diversification of the economy by offering a new source of revenue. A community can benefit from the tourist dollar, which is frequently less subject to economic swings, in addition to the traditional industries that the community is known for.

The discovery by residents of chances to supply services and products that are geared toward tourists is another positive side effect of diversification, which increases the activity of business owners. Craft stores, artisanal food manufacturers, outdoor adventure activities, and guided tours are some examples of the types of businesses that fall under the category of entrepreneurial endeavors.

In addition, tourism can assist in the maintenance and propagation of traditional cultural activities and handicrafts, which, in turn, can help to support local economies. Authentic cultural experiences are frequently of interest to vacationers, which can result in an increased demand for traditional arts and crafts as well as cultural gatherings. Local artists and cultural practitioners may be able to profit from these opportunities.

The cultivation of the community

1. **The Construction of New Facilities**
   The requirement to provide accommodations for tourists frequently serves as a driving force behind the construction of new infrastructure, including roadways, airports, public transportation systems, and recreational facilities. This infrastructure has the potential to assist the local population by increasing connectivity and accessibility. As a result, it will be much simpler for locals to gain access to the various services and amenities that are available.
2. **The Rejuvenation of Our Rich Cultural Heritage**
   The protection and dissemination of a community's cultural heritage is frequently prompted and supported by tourism.
   Many local communities take great delight in exhibiting their distinct customs and histories in an effort to draw in visitors. The community's feeling of self-identity and pride can be bolstered by putting more emphasis on the preservation of its cultural traditions.
3. **The Promotion of Learning and Professional Abilities**
   The expansion of learning opportunities and professional capabilities can be fostered by tourism. Residents of the area may perhaps learn new skills that would allow them to work in the tourism industry or start new business enterprises that would cater to tourists. Additionally, the local community can be educated through cultural exchanges and experiences with tourists, which can increase their understanding of the diversity that exists across the world.
4. **Responsible Management of the Environment**
   Communities that rely heavily on tourism are frequently motivated to preserve the natural environment that surrounds them. The protection of the natural environment not only makes a destination more alluring to visitors, but it also helps to ensure that tourism will continue to be an important economic driver in the area.
5. **An overall better quality of life**

A strong tourism industry almost always results in an improvement in the quality of life for the population of the surrounding area. The economic benefits of tourism can be used to fund improvements in areas such as education, healthcare, and other public services. These improvements are geared on catering to tourists, but they also provide advantages for the native community.

It is essential to keep in mind that the connection between tourism and community development does not exist in a vacuum free of difficulties. Communities have a responsibility to find a middle ground between economic development and the protection of their traditions and surroundings. When tourism is not handled in a sustainable manner and with the best interests of the community in mind, some of the negative outcomes that can emerge include overtourism, the monetization of cultural traditions, and environmental damage.

The creation of jobs, the stimulation of economic diversity, and the contribution to community development are all important aspects of the role that tourism plays in local economies. The money brought in by tourism can be put toward the improvement of infrastructure, the maintenance of cultural landmarks, the provision of educational opportunities, and the protection of natural resources. However, in order to ensure that the economic benefits of tourism are realized without damaging the cultural or natural integrity of the location, it is vital to approach tourism with careful planning and sustainable methods. When this is done, local communities have the opportunity to take advantage of tourism's potential as a tremendous engine of both economic and social well-being.

1.4 The Sociocultural Aspects of Sustainable Tourism

The protection of the natural environment is only one aspect of sustainable tourism; it also takes into account the sociocultural facets of vacationing in different places. It tries to strike a balance between the economic benefits of tourism and the maintenance and improvement of the communities and cultures that are found locally. Within the confines of this brief discussion of three hundred words, we will investigate the social facets of ecotourism.

Protecting Our Cultural Heritage:

The protection of historical artifacts and buildings is accorded a high priority in sustainable tourism. This encompasses both visible assets such as historical buildings, monuments, and architecture, in addition to intangible characteristics such as traditions, language, and ways of life. There are many locations that rely on their cultural assets to attract tourists, and it is essential that these resources be managed in a responsible manner in order to ensure that they retain their originality and are available to future generations.

The Exchange of Cultures:

Sustainable tourism fosters deeper, more meaningful cultural exchanges between visitors and the communities that they visit. Tourists are not merely passive observers but rather active participants who engage with the local people, as well as their rituals and traditions. This interaction benefits both parties by increasing their knowledge of one another's culture, as well as cultivating tolerance and respect for one another's beliefs and practices.

Interaction that is Respectful:

Tourism has the potential to result in the commercialization of culture, in which local customs and rituals are transformed into performances for the benefit of tourists. This is something that sustainable tourism aims to prevent by fostering interactions that are courteous and genuine. It instills in tourists an appreciation for cultural diversity while discouraging them from imposing their own beliefs, attitudes, or ways of behaving.

Empowerment of the Community:

Sustainable tourism relies heavily on the participation of local people as stakeholders. They ought to receive immediate financial benefits from tourism revenues and have an active part in the decision-making process. Communities gain power from sustainable tourism because it generates new employment possibilities, boosts the economy of local businesses, and engages locals in the process of planning and managing tourist-related activities.

The Education of Cultures:

Many times, educational components are a part of sustainable tourism. These components aim to increase awareness among tourists regarding the significance of cultural preservation as well as societal responsibility. These learning opportunities can help travelers become more aware of their place in the world and more respectful of its inhabitants.

Honoring the Richness of Differences:

When it is done so in a way that does not harm the environment, tourism is a way of honoring the complex fabric that is human culture. When people travel, they experience a wide variety of different cultures, languages, and traditions. This diversity fosters an awareness for the vast array of cultures that can be found around the globe and encourages people to work toward the preservation of cultural traditions.

Chapter 2

Measuring Carbon Footprint in Tourism

Many different businesses, including tourism, are coming under growing scrutiny for the amount of carbon footprint they leave behind. Concerns about climate change and the long-term viability of the environment are continuing to intensify. It is vital to measure the carbon footprint of the tourist sector in order to understand the influence that the industry has on the environment and to put into place effective policies to lower the industry's overall ecological footprint. In this in-depth investigation, we will delve into the difficulties of measuring the carbon footprint in the tourism sector. Specifically, we will investigate the methodology, obstacles, and implications of these measures on the industry's efforts to become more environmentally sustainable.

A Better Understanding of Tourism's Carbon Footprint

1. **An Explanation of the Carbon Footprint**
   The total amount of greenhouse gases, principally carbon dioxide, that are created directly and indirectly by the travel and hospitality activities of tourists is referred to as tourism's "carbon footprint." It takes into account emissions produced by modes of transportation, lodging, the provision of food, activities, and any other services linked with travel. The assessment of the environmental impact of tourism is aided by the measurement of the carbon footprint, which also contributes to the creation of initiatives to lessen the severity of these impacts.
2. **The Range of the Measurement of the Carbon Footprint**

When calculating the tourism industry's carbon footprint, it is necessary to take into account both direct and indirect sources of emissions. Direct emissions are those that are produced by activities within the tourism industry, such as transportation and the use of energy on-site. Indirect emissions are those that are produced by other means. On the other hand, indirect emissions are those that are related with the supply chain. This includes the manufacturing of goods and services that visitors consume, such as food, construction materials, and other facilities. Indirect emissions are a significant contributor to global warming.

Techniques for Determining the Tourism Industry's Impact on the Environment

1. **The Life Cycle Analysis (also known as LCA)**
   An evaluation of a product, service, or activity's impact on the environment is called a life cycle assessment, and it is a procedure that takes into account all aspects of that evaluation throughout its entirety. In the context of tourism, life cycle assessment (LCA) contributes to the measurement of the carbon footprint by taking into account the emissions caused by all aspects of the trip, such as the mode of transportation, the lodging, the activities, and the disposal of trash.
2. **An investigation of inputs and outputs**
   Another method that can be used to measure the tourism industry's carbon impact is the input-output analysis. It does this by calculating the direct and indirect carbon emissions that are related with the activity of each sector of the economy as well as analyzing the interconnection of the various economic sectors. This method sheds light on the more far-reaching financial repercussions of carbon emissions within the tourism sector.
3. **Instruments for Carbon Accounting**
   Carbon accounting tools are specialized pieces of software that are created with the purpose of measuring and controlling carbon emissions. These tools assist tourism firms and organizations in tracking their carbon footprint, locating areas in which they can improve, and putting policies into place to reduce their carbon output. Tools for carbon accounting offer a methodical strategy for monitoring and reporting data on emissions, which enables organizations to make educated decisions concerning the influence they have on the environment.
4. **Calculations Regarding Carbon Offsetting**

Calculations for carbon offsetting require first estimating the quantity of carbon emissions created by tourism activities and then offsetting these emissions by investing in projects that reduce or capture an equivalent amount of carbon dioxide in another location. Through the use of a practice known as carbon offsetting, individuals and enterprises in the tourism industry are able to make amends for the impact of their activities on the environment by contributing to the funding of projects in areas such as sustainable agriculture, forestry, and renewable energy.

Problems Associated with Determining Tourism's Impact on the Environment

1. **The Availability of Accurate Data and Its Accuracy**
   The availability of accurate data presents one of the most significant obstacles

when attempting
to calculate the carbon footprint of the tourism industry. It can be difficult to acquire complete data on emissions from a variety of sources within the tourism industry, particularly in places that do not have well-established mechanisms for the collecting of data. This can be especially problematic.

2. **Intricate Networks of Supply**
It can be difficult to track down the source of carbon emissions over the entirety of a vacation experience because tourism frequently involves intricate supply chains that involve several stakeholders. The correct measurement of the carbon footprint presents a number of key issues, including the management and coordination of the data gathering across the various stakeholders.

3. **The Unpredictability of Travel Behaviors**
The ways in which tourists travel might vary greatly, which in turn can cause changes in the amount of carbon emissions. The total carbon footprint is affected by a variety of factors, including the mode of transportation taken, the type of lodging selected, and the activities engaged in by tourists. Developing standardized procedures for monitoring carbon emissions in the tourism industry is made more difficult by the necessity of taking into account these differences.

4. **The absence of any sort of standardization**
Comparison and evaluation of carbon footprint data across a variety of locations and companies is made difficult by the absence of defined measurement techniques and reporting frameworks for the tourism industry. The development of established norms and benchmarks is absolutely necessary in order to conduct an accurate assessment of the effect tourism has on the surrounding environment.

5. **The Repercussions for the Economy**

Businesses who are involved in the tourism industry may face financial repercussions as a result of the implementation of carbon footprint monitoring and reduction methods. Especially for smaller and medium-sized businesses, the financial burden of the expenditures connected with the implementation of carbon reduction initiatives, such as the adoption of environmentally friendly technologies or the modification of operating procedures, can be difficult to bear.

Measurement of a Destination's Carbon Footprint and Its Implications for Tourism

1. **Methods of Environmentally Friendly Tourism**
The tourism sector can benefit from the adoption of more environmentally responsible practices by measuring the carbon footprint of the industry. Tourism businesses can undertake programs to reduce their carbon emissions, improve

energy efficiency, and minimize their total ecological footprint if they first understand the impact their actions have on the environment and then understand how to lessen those impacts.

2. **Raising Awareness and Educating Customers**
A consumer's understanding of the environmental impact of their transportation decisions can be increased by the transparent reporting and communication of data regarding their carbon footprint. When it comes to the planning of their journeys, tourists can be empowered to make decisions that are more informed and sustainable if they are educated about the carbon footprint of the various travel options.

3. **The Formulation of Regulations and Policies**
The gathering of useful information through the measurement of tourism's carbon footprint enables policymakers and regulatory authorities to more effectively formulate and put into practice environmental policies and regulations. The tourism industry can be encouraged to adopt more environmentally responsible practices if governments establish targets for carbon emission and implement incentives for the reduction of carbon emissions.

4. **Initiatives to Offset Carbon Emissions**
It is possible for the measurement of carbon footprints in the tourism industry to stimulate the development of efforts to offset carbon emissions. Businesses and individuals involved in the tourism industry as well as tourists themselves have the ability to take an active role in offsetting their emissions by providing financial assistance to initiatives that cut levels of carbon dioxide emissions in other industries and so contribute to the fight against global warming.

5. **Advantage over Other Businesses**

It is possible for tourism enterprises to obtain a competitive edge if they actively measure and work to reduce their carbon footprint. Many vacationers are looking for sustainable and environmentally friendly solutions, and businesses that adopt green practices have a better chance of attracting clients who are environmentally sensitive.

Understanding the environmental impact of the tourism sector and developing strategies to reduce that impact starts with accurately measuring the business's carbon footprint. Methods as diverse as life cycle assessments, input-output analyses, carbon accounting tools, and carbon offsetting calculations are used in the process of measuring the carbon emissions that are caused by activities related to tourism. Carbon footprint measurement in tourism holds significant implications for sustainable tourism practices, consumer awareness, policy development, carbon offsetting initiatives, and competitive advantage, despite the challenges related to the accuracy of the data, the complexity of the supply chains, and the lack of standardization. In a world that is more focused on sustainability and climate action, this is an essential component in the promotion of ecologically responsible travel and the reduction of the ecological footprint left by the tourism industry.

2.1 Carbon Emissions in the Tourism Industry

The tourism industry is a large contributor to global carbon emissions, despite the fact that it has positive effects on the economy and promotes the sharing of other cultures. There is a carbon footprint connected with every facet of the tourism experience, including travel, lodging, and the many different kinds of activities that tourists participate in. In the following paragraphs, we will investigate the many different sources of carbon emissions in the tourism business, as well as the environmental repercussions of these emissions and the methods that can be used to lessen their influence.

The Tourism Industry's Contributing Factors to Carbon Emissions

1. **Means of conveyance**
   Within the tourism industry, one of the most significant contributors of carbon emissions comes from transportation. Because of the significant amount of fuel that airplanes require, air travel in particular is a substantial contribution to the release of carbon dioxide. In addition, road travel, which includes automobiles, buses, and any other modes of ground transportation used by visitors, is a considerable contributor to the carbon footprint, particularly in locations where there are few options for public transportation.

2. **Make Arrangements for**
   The consumption of energy by hotels, resorts, and other types of lodgings for the purposes of heating, cooling, lighting, and heating water contributes to the production of carbon emissions. The greater the size of the property and the higher the quality of the amenities, the higher the overall energy consumption and, as a result, the carbon footprint. In addition, a significant number of lodging establishments continue to increase their carbon emissions by making use of non-renewable forms of energy.

3. **Activities Enjoyed by Vacationers**
   Numerous tourist pursuits, such as sightseeing tours, outings, and recreational activities, are all potential contributors to the release of carbon dioxide. These activities frequently include the utilization of transportation, energy, and resources, which leads to a rise in the overall carbon footprint of the experience that one has while on vacation. Off-road tours and other activities that include the use of motorized vehicles, such as recreational vehicles, can have a substantial negative influence on the quality of the air in the surrounding area and contribute to carbon emissions.

4. **Services for Consumables and Drinks**
   Carbon emissions are caused by the manufacturing of food, delivery of that food, and the management of waste generated by food and beverage services.

These services include restaurants, cafes, and catering services. Carbon emissions are produced during the production and delivery of food items, particularly those that are sourced from faraway regions. Inefficient waste management techniques further compound the negative impact that these activities have on the environment.

5. **The Creation of New Infrastructure**

The construction of tourist infrastructure, which may include hotels, resorts, airports, and recreational facilities, frequently results in the release of a considerable amount of carbon dioxide. The process of construction, which involves the use of heavy machinery, the transportation of materials, and procedures that need a lot of energy, contributes to the carbon footprint left by the industry as a whole. Additionally, the use of building materials and technology that require a significant amount of energy to operate further exacerbates the negative effects that tourism infrastructure has on the surrounding ecosystem.

Carbon Emissions and Their Effects on the Environment in Relation to Tourism

1. **The changing climate**
   The carbon emissions produced by the tourist industry contribute to the warming of the planet's climate, which in turn causes a number of unfavorable impacts, including an increase in average world temperature, changes in weather patterns, and an intensification of the occurrence of extreme weather. These shifts have the potential to have significant repercussions for ecosystems, biological diversity, and human livelihoods, in particular in vulnerable regions and people who are dependent on natural resources for their survival.
2. **Pollution of the Air and Water**
   Air and water pollution are caused in part by carbon emissions produced by transportation and energy use in the tourism industry. This results in a decline in the quality of the air we breathe, as well as acid rain and the contamination of aquatic bodies. This pollution not only has an effect on the natural environment, but it also poses hazards to human health and the well-being of local populations. This is especially true in major tourist locations, which are under great demand on their environmental resources.
3. **The destruction of habitats**
   The construction of tourist infrastructure frequently results in the deterioration of natural habitats and the disappearance of ecosystems. The establishment of hotels, resorts, and other types of amenities can lead to the clearing of forests, the deterioration of land, and the fragmentation of habitats, all of which pose a risk to the continued existence of the local flora and wildlife. This reduction in biodiversity may have far-reaching repercussions for the provision of

ecosystem services and the continued viability of the natural environment over the long run.

4. **The exhaustion of resources**
   The tourist industry is responsible for contributing to the depletion of natural resources such as water, land, and energy due to its extremely high energy consumption and resource-intensive business methods. This depletion can lead to increasing rivalry for resources between the tourism sector and local residents, which has the potential to make the resource scarcity and socio-environmental problems that already exist much worse.
5. **Deterioration of the World's Heritage**

The negative effects of carbon emissions on the environment caused by the tourism sector can also result in the erosion of cultural assets and the discontinuation of long-standing activities. Destruction of habitat, pollution, and development that is not sustainable can have a severe impact on cultural places, artifacts, and indigenous knowledge, which can lead to the erosion of cultural identity and the displacement of local inhabitants.

Strategies for Reducing Tourism's Contribution to Greenhouse Gas Emissions

1. **Transportation that is Environmentally Friendly**
   A large reduction in the carbon footprint of the tourism industry is possible through the encouragement of environmentally responsible modes of mobility such as electric automobiles, public transit, and cycling. The tourism industry's reliance on transportation that generates a lot of carbon dioxide can be reduced by encouraging tourists to utilize methods of transportation that are less harmful to the environment and by supporting the construction of an efficient infrastructure for public transportation.
2. **Methods That Are Efficient In Utilizing Energy**
   It is possible for the tourism industry to leave a smaller carbon footprint if energy-efficient
   technology and practices are implemented in tourist lodgings and other types of tourist infrastructure. This involves the utilization of renewable energy sources, energy-efficient appliances, and intelligent building designs that prioritize energy conservation and minimize the impact that they have on the environment.
3. **Responsible Handling of Waste and Recycling**
   It is possible to reduce carbon emissions and the amount of pollution in the environment by putting into practice efficient waste management and recycling procedures in tourist lodgings and destinations. The efforts that are being made by the industry to reduce its negative impact on the environment can be considerably aided by the adoption of sustainable waste management systems,

the promotion of recycling activities, and a reduction in the use of single-use plastics.
4. **Accreditation for Ecotourism and Responsible Travel**
It is possible to help encourage ecologically responsible practices and reduce the carbon emissions produced by the tourism sector by encouraging firms involved in the industry to earn sustainable tourism certifications. Certifications for sustainable tourism give a framework for enterprises to conform to certain environmental norms and principles, which helps to develop openness and responsibility in the organizations' respective efforts to promote sustainability.
5. **Participation in the Community and Educational Opportunities**

Fostering a culture of environmental stewardship and empowering communities to actively participate in projects to reduce carbon emissions can be accomplished by involving local communities in environmentally responsible tourist activities and providing educational programs. A sense of shared responsibility can be developed and sustainable tourism practices can be promoted at the local level by involving local stakeholders in decision-making processes and raising awareness about the environmental effects of tourism.

Carbon emissions from the tourism industry have substantial environmental repercussions, including a contribution to climate change, pollution of the air and water, destruction of habitat, depletion of resources, and loss of cultural heritage. These environmental issues are interconnected and mutually reinforcing. However, the tourism industry is capable of efficiently mitigating its carbon footprint and lessening its negative impact on the environment if it implements sustainable transportation, energy-efficient procedures, waste management and recycling, sustainable tourism certification, and community participation and education. All of these measures are interconnected.

The tourist industry has the potential to make a significant contribution to global efforts to battle climate change and to promote a more sustainable and resilient future for both the environment and the communities that it serves if it places a higher priority on environmental sustainability and implements comprehensive plans for the reduction of carbon emission.

2.2 Methods of Carbon Footprint Measurement

The determination of a household's, an industry's, or a nation's carbon footprint is now an essential component of sustainability efforts across a wide range of spheres, from individual households to industries and nations. A person's, company's, product's, or activity's "carbon footprint" is the sum of all greenhouse gas emissions (GHG), predominantly carbon dioxide (CO_2), that are related with that person, organization, product, or activity. In the course of this in-depth investigation, we will investigate the strategies and procedures that are utilized to quantify carbon footprints, focusing on their significance, accuracy, and the practical uses to which they can be put.

Measurement of carbon footprints is becoming increasingly important.

Measurement of carbon footprints offers a method for holding individuals, organizations, and businesses accountable for the role they play in the production of greenhouse gases through the provision of a means to do so. This accountability is essential for tracking progress toward emission reduction goals and comprehending the impact that particular actions or activities have on the environment.

Developing Efficient Mitigation methods Relies on Accurate Carbon Footprint Measurements Accurate carbon footprint measurements are used to design effective mitigation methods. Stakeholders can more effectively aim their efforts to reduce greenhouse gas emissions and minimize the impact these emissions have on the environment if they first identify the key sources of emissions.

Policy Making: When it comes to formulating and enforcing climate policies and regulations, governments and regulatory organizations rely heavily on the data provided by carbon footprint measurements. These programs intend to bring about a transition to an economy with lower carbon emissions and more sustainability.

Consumer Education Labeling and reporting on a product's or service's carbon footprint gives customers the ability to make educated decisions about the goods or services they purchase. Customers who are aware of the carbon footprint of a certain item have the ability to select alternatives that are better for the environment, which in turn encourages businesses to cut back on their emissions.

Measurement and public disclosure of a company's carbon footprint are two essential components of its corporate social responsibility obligations. Companies are becoming more aware of the significance of minimizing the environmental impact of their operations in order to satisfy the expectations of stakeholders and to protect their reputations.

Agreements on a Global Scale Regarding Climate Change Participating countries in international climate agreements, such as the Paris Agreement, are required to declare their levels of emissions of greenhouse gases. When it comes to monitoring compliance and making headway toward emission reduction goals, having accurate measurements of one's carbon footprint is absolutely necessary.

Measurement Strategies That Are Commonly Employed for Carbon Footprints

1. **An analysis of the life cycle, also known as an LCA:**
   The evaluation of the environmental impact of a product, service, or activity across its entire life cycle (from the extraction of raw materials to the disposal of waste at the end of its useful life) is the purpose of the comprehensive process known as life cycle assessment (LCA). The life cycle assessment takes into account every stage, from manufacture to transit to use to disposal. The carbon

footprint is a subset of the life cycle assessment (LCA) that focuses on emissions of greenhouse gases. The LCA is especially helpful when examining complicated systems that consist of several stages and processes, such as the manufacturing or transportation industries.

2. **Analysis of Inputs and Outputs:**
The measurement of carbon footprints can be done economically through the use of input-output analysis. It does this by calculating the direct and indirect carbon emissions that are related with the activity of each sector of the economy as well as analyzing the interconnection of the various economic sectors. This strategy not only sheds light on the broader economic ramifications of carbon emissions, but it also has the potential to be useful in gaining a knowledge of how economic activities contribute to emissions.

3. **Instruments for Carbon Accounting:**
Carbon accounting tools, also known as carbon calculators or carbon footprint calculators, are
specialized software applications that are meant to quantify and control carbon emissions. Other names for carbon accounting tools include carbon calculators and carbon footprint calculators. Organizations frequently make use of these tools in order to monitor their carbon footprint, locate areas in which they may make improvements, and publish statistics regarding emissions. Carbon accounting systems provide a methodical approach to the processes of data collection, evaluation, and reporting of emissions.

4. **Calculations Regarding Carbon Offsetting:**
Calculations for carbon offsetting consist of calculating the quantity of carbon emissions produced by a particular activity or company and then offsetting those emissions by investing in initiatives that reduce or capture an equivalent amount of carbon dioxide in another location. Offsetting carbon emissions is a common strategy for mitigating the impact of emissions that cannot be avoided entirely. Reforestation, initiatives including renewable energy sources, and methane absorption from landfills are examples of possible projects.

5. **Emission Factors That Are Specific to a Sector:**

Some companies or sectors have their own unique emission variables, which makes it possible to obtain a more accurate measurement of their carbon footprint. Emission factors are numerical numbers that are used to describe the typical level of emissions of greenhouse gases that are caused by a certain action, product, or process. For instance, the automobile industry may make use of emission factors in order to estimate the emissions that are caused by the various types of vehicles and the amounts of gasoline they consume.

Labeling of carbon emissions and reporting on them:

The practice of displaying the carbon footprint of a good, service, or activity in order to educate consumers about that thing's effect on the environment is known as "carbon labeling." This practice is quite prevalent in product labeling, and it enables customers to obtain information that might help them make environmentally responsible decisions. Carbon reporting is quite similar to this, but its primary focus is on the documentation and disclosure of emission data for businesses and other organizations in order to encourage openness and responsibility.

Measurement of the Carbon Footprint Faces Difficulties

Access to Accurate and Complete Data on Emissions Sources Having access to accurate and complete data on emissions sources can be a considerable difficulty. It may be difficult to compute carbon footprints accurately because certain data may be sensitive, inaccessible, or subject to issues about confidentiality. These factors may combine.

Accuracy of the Data The quality of the data sources and the measuring procedures used both have a role in determining the accuracy of the data on emissions. Estimates of a carbon footprint might be rendered erroneous if the data used are inaccurate or incomplete.

Determining the Scope and bounds of an evaluation It can be difficult to determine the scope and bounds of an evaluation of a carbon footprint. The decision of what to include and what to leave out of the evaluation might have a considerable influence on the findings.

Systems That Are Often Interconnected Emissions of carbon can be found in many different locations, and adjustments in one area can have an effect on emissions in other places. Because of this intricacy, it can be difficult to determine the entire amount to which particular actions or adjustments will have an impact.

Standards: The absence of standards in the measuring of carbon footprints might make it more difficult to compare and benchmark the performance of various entities. The lack of standardized techniques can result in reporting that is fraught with misunderstanding and inconsistent with itself.

Complex Systems: Carbon footprint assessment may be difficult to do in certain businesses due to the presence of complex systems. These industries include those with very convoluted supply chains. These systems could include a large number of stakeholders and complicated procedures, making them challenging to monitor.

Measurement of Carbon Footprints Put to Use in Various Situations

Corporate Sustainability: Measurement of a company's carbon footprint allows businesses to determine the extent of their impact on the surrounding environment and formulate plans to cut emissions. It is an essential component of sustainability measures undertaken by businesses and of environmental reporting.

Labeling of items Consumers can learn about the emissions related with the manufacture and usage of items by looking at the carbon footprint labels that are attached to such products. The information presented here assists customers in making decisions that are better for the environment.

Analysis of the Supply Chain Businesses do supply chain analyses to determine the carbon footprint of their supply chains in order to locate opportunities for lowering emissions, enhancing efficiency, and optimizing transportation.

Policy Development: Governments and regulatory organizations utilize data on carbon footprints to plan and implement climate policies, establish objectives for reducing emissions, and monitor compliance with these policies.

Carbon Footprint Data Can enhance Consumer knowledge Carbon footprint data can enhance consumer knowledge about the environmental impact of their decisions, which in turn can encourage more sustainable behaviors.

Carbon Offsetting: Companies and individuals can assess their environmental effect by

measuring their carbon footprint and then investing in carbon offsetting projects in order to reduce the amount of harmful emissions they produce.

The determination of an individual's, organization's, product's, or activity's carbon footprint is an essential step in comprehending and resolving the environmental impact of that individual, organization, product, or activity. It has a tremendous impact on accountability, sustainability, policy formulation, consumer awareness, and stewardship of the environment. Even while it presents difficulties in terms of data availability, quality, and standardization, its relevance in reducing the effects of climate change and encouraging responsible behavior toward the environment cannot be overestimated. Measurements of a company's carbon footprint that are accurate and trustworthy will continue to be at the forefront of sustainability programs across a wide variety of industries as the fight against climate change heats up.

2.3 The Carbon Emission Assessment Process

The evaluation of carbon emissions, which is also commonly known as a carbon footprint evaluation, is an essential stage in the process of comprehending and regulating the impact that a variety of entities, ranging from individuals and organizations to products and activities, have on the surrounding environment. Calculating and analyzing the emissions of greenhouse gases, principally carbon dioxide (CO_2), that are caused by a certain organization or activity is an important step in this process. In this section, we will go over the fundamental steps that make up the carbon emission assessment method.

1. **Define the Aims and Boundaries of the Project:**
   The first thing that needs to be done in order to conduct an evaluation of carbon emissions is to precisely identify the scope and bounds of the study. This requires deciding what will be counted toward the assessment and what won't be counted toward it. For instance, in the context of a corporation's carbon footprint, the boundaries could include direct emissions from company-owned

facilities, emissions from purchased electricity, and certain categories of business travel, but they would not include emissions from employee commuting or products manufactured by suppliers. The extent to which these limitations are defined is an essential factor in determining how complete the evaluation will be.

2. **Compile the Information:**
The process of evaluating carbon emissions begins with the collecting of data as its foundational stage. It entails collecting data on different sources of emissions that fall within the parameters of the designated scope. This information can originate from a wide variety of places, such as utility bills, records of fuel usage, manufacturing figures, and transportation records. It is crucial to verify that the data is correct and thorough, and in order to do so, it may be necessary to collaborate with multiple departments or stakeholders within a company.

3. **Classify the Emissions as Follows:**
Scope 1 refers to emissions that come directly from sources that are owned or controlled by the firm. For example, emissions from company-owned automobiles or emissions from on-site combustion operations fall under this category.
Scope 2 refers to emissions that are produced indirectly as a result of using purchased electricity, heating, and cooling systems. Even when the emissions take place in another location, they are nevertheless counted as part of the entity's carbon footprint.
Scope 3: These are indirect emissions that are a result of the actions of the business, but they come from sources that are not owned or controlled by the entity. These emissions are a consequence of the activities. Emissions from supply chains, corporate travel, and staff commuting are all included in the scope 3 category of emissions.
The process of classifying emissions is useful for determining where to concentrate our efforts to reduce emissions.

4. **Figure Out Your Emissions:**
After data has been gathered and organized, the following step is to compute the amount of emissions produced. The specific procedures that are used to calculate emissions can differ from one business or activity to another, depending on which is being evaluated. For instance, emissions from the use of energy can be determined by utilizing emission factors (the amount of CO_2 produced per unit of energy), whereas emissions from transportation may need calculations depending on parameters such as the driving distance, the kind of fuel used, and the fuel efficiency of the vehicle. In order to simplify and expedite these calculations, specialized software and tools are frequently utilized.

5. **Transform Your Emissions Into CO2 Equivalents:**
In addition to carbon dioxide (CO_2), other greenhouse gases including methane (CH_4) and nitrous oxide (N_2O) also have a role in the warming of the planet. The emissions from these gases are converted to CO_2 equivalents (CO_2e) based

on their capacity to contribute to the warming of the planet in order to make them comparable to CO2 emissions. This conversion enables a more in-depth knowledge of the role that a particular entity plays in the process of climate change.

6. **Describe and Share the Obtained Results:**
The process of determining a company's carbon emission levels relies heavily on communication and transparency.
When the results of the assessment are reported, stakeholders, including internal teams, regulatory authorities, and the general public, are given a clear picture of the environmental impact that the business has. As part of their attempts to comply with the requirements of corporate social responsibility, a lot of companies choose to produce sustainability reports or disclose their carbon emissions.

7. **Determine Your Reduction Goals and Come Up with Strategies:**
The second phase, which comes after the emissions have been measured and reported, is to establish reduction targets and to devise strategies for achieving those targets. These targets may include explicit goals for reducing emissions, improvements in energy efficiency, or commitments to shift to renewable energy sources. When it comes to minimizing an entity's negative influence on the environment, one of the most important steps is the formulation of reduction plans.

8. **Put into Practice and Keep an Eye on:**
Following the establishment of reduction targets and the development of plans, the entity is obligated to put these strategies into action and regularly monitor progress. This may require investments in energy-efficient equipment, shifts in operating processes, and continuous data collecting to monitor emissions over the course of time.

9. **Involve Relevant Stakeholders:**
Participation from relevant stakeholders is a necessary component of the process for assessing carbon emissions. Employees, customers, investors, and local communities are examples of different types of stakeholders. The most effective forms of engagement include communication and collaboration, with the goals of increasing knowledge about efforts to reduce emissions and gaining support for sustainability programs.

10. **Examine and Bring Up to Date:**

The very last thing that has to be done is to routinely check the carbon emission assessment and bring it up to date. It is vital to reassess the evaluation at regular intervals to ensure that it continues to be accurate and is matched with the most recent emissions when new plans are put into place and new data becomes available. Continuous development in sustainability initiatives is enabled by conducting regular evaluations and keeping track of relevant information.

The process of evaluating carbon emissions is an essential element of both responsible management of the environment and long-term sustainability.

It entails a series of steps, such as defining the scope and boundaries, collecting data, classifying emissions, calculating emissions, converting them to CO_2 equivalents, reporting and communicating, establishing targets, formulating strategies, putting them into action, monitoring, involving stakeholders, and performing ongoing reviews and updates. Entities are able to get insights into their impact on the environment and take action to reduce the amount of carbon emissions they produce as a result of this process, which contributes to a more sustainable and environmentally responsible future.

2.4 Carbon Offset Mechanisms

Carbon offset mechanisms are an essential component in the fight against climate change. These mechanisms make it possible for individuals, organizations, and governments to make amends for the greenhouse gas emissions they are responsible for by funding initiatives in other locations that either capture or reduce an equivalent quantity of carbon dioxide (CO_2) or other greenhouse gases. In this in-depth study, we will investigate a variety of mechanisms for offsetting carbon emissions, as well as the relevance of these mechanisms, the difficulties they present, and the potential impact they have on reducing climate change.

The Importance of Carbon Offset Mechanisms in Today's World

The capacity of carbon offset mechanisms to contribute to global efforts to mitigate climate change in several critical ways is what gives these mechanisms their significance in the fight against climate change.

Emissions Reduction: Carbon offsetting programs, including reforestation, renewable energy, and methane capture, directly reduce or eliminate emissions of greenhouse gases. It is possible for entities to reduce their carbon footprint and begin taking immediate action to address the environmental impact they have by providing support for these projects.

Numerous carbon offsetting projects offer both economic and social benefits to the communities in which they are situated. This is one of the most important aspects of these initiatives. These initiatives have the potential to provide new employment opportunities, give a boost to the economies of the surrounding areas, and enhance the quality of life for the people who live there, making them a tool for sustainable development.

Cooperative Efforts on a worldwide Scale In the battle against climate change, carbon offset methods foster cooperative efforts on a worldwide scale. They promote equality and shared responsibility in the process of tackling climate challenges by providing a mechanism through which entities in wealthy nations can assist projects aimed at reducing emissions in developing countries.

Innovation and the Transfer of Technology: Carbon offsetting operations frequently require the implementation of forward-thinking technologies and procedures that are adaptable to and replicable in a variety of geographical locations. The transfer of this technology has the potential to speed up the transition to an economy with lower levels of carbon emissions.

Carbon Neutrality: Many businesses and people have the goal of reaching carbon neutrality, which means that their total net carbon emissions have been brought down to zero through a combination of emission cuts and offsetting efforts. Mechanisms for offsetting carbon emissions are an essential component of carbon neutrality achievement for entities.

Mechanisms Used Commonly in the Fight Against Carbon

1. **Deforestation, Reforestation, and Afforestation:**
   Afforestation is the process of establishing new forests on land that has not been covered in trees for an extended amount of time, whereas reforestation is the process of planting trees in areas that have been previously deforested or converted to purposes other than those associated with forests. Because trees are able to remove and store carbon from the air, reforestation and afforestation efforts can be quite effective in bringing down overall levels of CO_2 in the environment.
2. **Projects Involving Renewable Energy:**
   Electricity can be generated from renewable energy sources such as wind farms, solar power plants, and hydroelectric dams, all of which do not release any greenhouse gases during the process. Carbon offset mechanisms make it possible for businesses to invest in projects that either eliminate or significantly cut down on the demand for energy sources that are based on fossil fuels.
3. **Initiatives to Improve Energy Efficiency:**
   Putting money into projects that improve energy efficiency helps cut down on overall energy usage and, as a result, on emissions of greenhouse gases. Depending on the nature of the project, it may involve retrofitting buildings with energy-efficient technologies, improving industrial workflows, or developing and implementing solutions for more energy-efficient transportation.
4. **The Capture and Utilization of Methane:**
   Methane is a strong greenhouse gas that can be emitted into the atmosphere by a variety of different sources, including landfills and agricultural operations. Projects that capture methane and put it to use in energy production do two things: they cut down on the amount of that gas that is released into the atmosphere and they provide electricity that is less polluting.
5. **Carbon Capture and Storage in Soils:**
   Carbon sequestration in soils can be improved through the implementation of specific agricultural and land management strategies, such as no-till farming and the planting of trees on marginal lands. Because of these techniques, the soil's

capacity to hold carbon is increased, which in turn reduces the overall carbon footprint.

6. **Projects That Convert Waste Into Energy:**
Putting organic waste materials, such as biomass or biodegradable trash, through a process that generates electricity is what is known as a waste-to-energy project. This procedure helps cut down on waste while also producing clean energy, which contributes to a reduction in emissions.

7. **Initiatives to Increase Access to Clean Cookstoves and Energy**

Traditional cooking methods that are high in carbon emissions, such as burning wood or biomass, can be phased out in developing regions thanks to the increased availability of efficient cookstoves and other clean-cooking technology. This helps reduce the amount of pollution that is released into the indoor air.

Disputes and Obstacles to Overcome

1. **The additionality of this:**
The question of whether or not a carbon offset project leads to reductions in emissions that would not have occurred without the project itself is one of the most important and contentious issues. Additionality refers to this question. It can be difficult to verify that the actions that are being counted as "offsets" are indeed additional and do not merely represent "business as usual" operations.

2. **Unchangingness:**
Projects that aim to offset carbon emissions are susceptible to a variety of dangers, including the loss of carbon storage in soils and forests. It is a big problem to ensure that reductions in emissions will remain permanent over the long term.

3. **The leaking:**
The term "leakage" refers to the phenomenon that happens when emissions are lowered in one region but raised in another due to shifts in the economic activity taking place. For instance, a carbon offset project might avoid deforestation in one region, but this might result in deforestation in another region.

4. **Counting Something Twice:**
It is necessary to avoid double counting of emission reductions. This means ensuring that emission reductions are not claimed by both the company developing the project and the organization buying the offsets.

5. **Accreditation and Professional Standards:**
There is not a common certification or set of quality standards in place for the carbon offset industry. It can be difficult to compare and judge the overall quality of offset initiatives due to the variety of standards and verification techniques that are used.

6. **The effect of the rebound:**

Because of the perceived availability of carbon offsets, some persons or entities may choose to increase their emissions in other areas, which will counteract the positive effects that are supposed to result from the initiatives.

Supporting the Development of High-Quality Carbon Offsets

Verification by a Third Party: A significant number of offset initiatives go through the process of having their additionality, permanence, and conformity to quality standards verified by a third party. Building trust in offset programs requires verification from established organizations with a good reputation.

Standards for Certification: The establishment of standards for certification, such as the Verified Carbon Standard (VCS) and the Gold Standard, provides a framework for evaluating and certifying the quality of offset programs.

Systems of Registries: Registries, such as the Climate Action Reserve and the Clean Development Mechanism (CDM) registry, assist in the monitoring and management of carbon offset projects, thereby improving both transparency and accountability.

Participation of Stakeholders: Participation of stakeholders, such as local communities and indigenous peoples, in the design and execution of offset projects can assist in addressing issues around additionality, leakage, and social repercussions.

Continuous Improvement: It is essential to regularly examine and update carbon offset techniques and standards in order to handle the constantly shifting difficulties and debates that are being brought up.

Carbon offset methods are key tools in the battle against climate change because they enable individuals, businesses, and governments to compensate for the greenhouse gas emissions they have caused by funding programs that reduce or eliminate emissions. These mechanisms not only provide communities with economic and social benefits, but also present a path toward achieving carbon neutrality. But in addition to that, they face issues of additionality, permanence, leakage, double counting, and standards. It is possible to improve the efficiency and credibility of carbon offset mechanisms, which will lead to a more sustainable and resilient future. This can be accomplished through the promotion of high-quality carbon offsets, which can be verified by a third party, have certification standards, registry systems, stakeholder engagement, and continuous improvement.

Chapter 3

Sustainable Tourism Practices

The term "sustainable tourism practices" refers to the guiding principles, policies, and strategies that are put into place by the tourism industry in order to reduce the industry's negative impact on the environment, encourage the preservation of natural and cultural heritage, and foster the economic and social prosperity of the communities that are directly affected by tourism activities. The idea of sustainable tourism is gaining popularity as people all around the world become more conscious of the problems facing our planet and the significance of protecting the rich cultural diversity that exists in it. Within the context of this in-depth study, we will investigate sustainable tourism practices in great detail, analyzing their relevance, central principles, and obstacles, as well as the part they play in the process of building a tourism industry that is more responsible and ethical.

Recognizing the Importance of Sustainable Tourism
The Significance of Ecotourism in Today's World

The ability of sustainable tourism to advance the cause of environmental preservation, to safeguard cultural heritage, and to make a positive contribution to the socioeconomic growth of local communities is what gives the industry its relevance. Tourism practices that are sustainable are essential to preserving the ecological balance of natural ecosystems, safeguarding biodiversity, and avoiding the negative consequences of climate change. In addition, they play a significant part in the promotion of cultural interchange, the maintenance of indigenous traditions, and the emancipation of local people through the creation of economic possibilities and sustainable means of subsistence.

The Fundamentals of Responsible and Sustainable Tourism

Conservation of the Environment: Tourism practices that are environmentally sustainable put an emphasis on the protection and preservation of natural resources, such as ecosystems, biodiversity, and landscapes. They emphasize how important it is to have as little of an influence as possible on the environment, to reduce pollution, and to conserve energy and water resources.

Respect and Preservation of Culture: Sustainable tourism is characterized by respect for, and preservation of, the cultural history and customs of the communities that it visits.

It encourages tourists to participate in cultural activities that contribute to the preservation of native arts, languages, and traditions as well as fosters cross-cultural understanding, mutual respect, and cross-cultural understanding.

Community Engagement and Empowerment: Sustainable tourism practices place a priority on the engagement of local communities in decision-making processes and tourism development projects. These practices also emphasize the empowerment of local communities. They want to achieve this by establishing new economic opportunities, providing assistance to existing local enterprises, and fostering community-based tourist initiatives that are designed to be of direct benefit to the local populace.

Economic Viability Sustainable tourism practices attempt to produce economic advantages for local communities while also guaranteeing the long-term viability of the tourism industry. These practices are referred to as "green" tourism. They advocate for responsible and ethical business practices in the marketplace, which in turn contribute to the economic growth and general well-being of the communities in which they operate.

Education and Awareness of Visitors: Sustainable tourism practices place a strong emphasis on the necessity of teaching visitors about the ecological and cultural significance of the locations they visit. During their travels, they encourage travelers to engage in responsible behavior, respect local customs, and support programs that promote sustainable tourism.

Initiatives Towards a Sustainable Tourism Industry
Ecotourism

Ecotourism is a major form of sustainable tourism that places a focus on responsible vacationing in natural regions with the goals of preserving the natural environment and enhancing the quality of life for the people who live there. Activities associated with ecotourism frequently include encounters with nature, participation in programs designed to preserve animals, and educational opportunities designed to increase awareness of the importance of protecting biodiversity and the environment.

Tourism that is Based on Communities

Local communities are given more agency when they are included in the planning, development, and management of tourism activities through community-based tourism programs. Through the provision of tourism-related services like homestays, guided tours, and cultural performances, these programs help to preserve the local cultural heritage, stimulate community engagement, and create sustainable livelihoods for local residents.

Hotel Operations That Are More Eco-Friendly

Implementing environmentally friendly measures like as water conservation initiatives, waste reduction and recycling programs, energy-efficient lighting, and trash reduction and recycling programs, as well as the use of eco-friendly building materials, are all examples of sustainable hotel practices. Numerous hotels participate in community development projects, offer their support to regional suppliers, and promote cultural heritage by incorporating regional arts and crafts into their establishments.

Tourism with Respect for the Wildlife

Initiatives geared toward responsible wildlife tourism place a high priority on the humane treatment of animals as well as the protection of their natural habitats. They teach visitors on the significance of wildlife conservation and preservation, advocate for the protection of endangered species, and promote ethical viewing techniques.

Tourism based on cultural heritage

The preservation of cultural traditions, as well as the establishment of cultural sites and monuments, is the primary aim of cultural heritage tourism efforts. They encourage tourists to participate in culturally immersing activities, such as going to historical places, taking part in traditional festivities, and purchasing goods made by local artisans and craftsmen.

Transportation That Is Ecologically Sound

projects that promote environmentally friendly modes of transportation, such as electric vehicles, public transit, and cycling, are some examples of sustainable transportation projects that try to lessen the negative effects of travel on the environment. These programs additionally advocate for the development of effective transportation infrastructure and the incorporation of environmentally friendly mobility solutions inside tourist areas.

The Obstacles Faced When Attempting to Put Sustainable Tourism Practices Into Action

Lack of Awareness and Education: A lack of sustainable tourism practices awareness and understanding among tourists and industry stakeholders can be a barrier to the widespread implementation of sustainable projects.

Inadequate infrastructure, particularly in developing regions, can provide obstacles to the implementation of sustainable tourism practices. These obstacles can include a lack of waste disposal facilities as well as inefficient water and electricity systems.

Policy and Regulatory Frameworks: Inconsistent or insufficient policy and regulatory frameworks related to sustainable tourism have the potential to inhibit the successful implementation of sustainable practices. When it comes to ensuring industry compliance and accountability, having clear norms and laws is quite necessary.

Economic Pressures: Economic concerns and budgetary restrictions may lead certain tourism operators to prioritize short-term economic benefits above long-term sustainability, resulting in unsustainable practices that harm the integrity of the environment and the culture. This can be a problem because economic gains can be made quickly.

Engagement of the Community A lack of community engagement and participation in the planning and decision-making processes of tourism can be a barrier to the effective implementation of sustainable tourism initiatives. It is absolutely necessary, in order to advance sustainable development, to establish solid alliances and to encourage collaboration between local communities and those involved in the tourism industry.

Striking a Balance Between Conservation and Tourism: Striking a balance between conservation efforts and the promotion of tourism activities can be tough, particularly in ecologically sensitive places where tourism development may harm natural habitats and biodiversity. However, it is possible to achieve this balance.

What Role Does Technology Play in Encouraging More Eco-Friendly Tourism?
knowledge and Education in Digital Form The advancement of technology has created new avenues for the dissemination of knowledge and education concerning environmentally responsible tourism activities. Tourists can gain useful knowledge into environmentally friendly travel options and ethical conduct through the use of websites, apps, and social media platforms.

Digital Booking and Reservation Systems: Online booking systems enable travelers to select environmentally friendly activities, modes of transportation, and hotels. They also make it possible for tourism firms to sell their environmentally friendly services and products to a larger audience.

Energy and Resource Management: Hotels and other types of lodgings can lower their overall energy consumption and their negative impact on the environment by implementing smart technology. These technologies include energy-efficient lighting, heating, and cooling systems.

Solutions for trash Management Technology plays an important role in the effective management of trash by providing novel solutions for recycling, waste reduction, and disposal practices that are less harmful to the environment.

Mobility applications provide users with access to environmentally responsible modes of mobility, such as electric vehicle rentals, public transit routes, and bike-sharing services.

Monitoring and Saving the Environment Technology helps in environmental monitoring activities by providing data on climate change, biodiversity protection, and the health of ecosystems. The use of environmental sensors, remote sensing technology, and geospatial analysis all contribute to the efficiency of conservation initiatives.

Cultural Preservation and Heritage documenting: Digital technologies, such as 3D modeling and virtual reality, help in the preservation and documenting of cultural heritage places. These technologies also enable tourists to experience historical landmarks while simultaneously limiting the amount of physical damage that they have.

The adoption of tourist policies and practices that are friendly to the environment, respectful of cultural traditions, and beneficial to the well-being of the communities in which they are located is absolutely necessary. These practices are governed by a set of principles that place an emphasis on ecological responsibility, cultural sensitivity, community empowerment, economic viability, and educational opportunities for tourists. Although sustainable tourism initiatives such as ecotourism, community-based tourism, and responsible wildlife tourism have been gaining steam, obstacles such as knowledge gaps, constraints in infrastructure, and economic pressures continue to exist.

Technology plays a significant role in the promotion of sustainable tourism as a means of overcoming these challenges. This is accomplished through the technology's facilitation of information dissemination, digital booking and reservation systems, energy and resource management, waste solutions, sustainable transportation apps, environmental monitoring, and the preservation of cultural heritage. The tourist sector is well positioned to become more responsible and ethical if it adopts techniques that are environmentally friendly and makes more use of technology. The world as a whole is increasingly recognizing the need of sustainability, which bodes well for the industry's prospects.

3.1 Eco-friendly Accommodations

In a time marked by an increasing awareness of the environment and the critical need to address climate change, eco-friendly accommodations have emerged as a ray of hope in the hospitality business. These facilities are the ones that are leading the way for ethical and sustainable travel, providing guests with a guilt-free and environmentally friendly place to stay while on their vacations. In this essay of 1000 words, the notion of eco-friendly accommodations, as well as their relevance, important features, and benefits, as well as the role they play in encouraging a more sustainable and eco-conscious style of traveling, are investigated.

The Meaning of the Term "Eco-Friendly Accommodations"

Eco-friendly accommodations, also known as green hotels, sustainable lodgings, or eco-hotels, are hospitality establishments that are constructed and maintained with a strong dedication to decreasing their impact on the environment. Other names for these types of hotels are green hotels, sustainable lodgings, and eco-hotels. These lodging establishments implement a number of different measures in order to reduce their carbon footprint, save resources, and encourage more sustainable business practices. These efforts span all element of their business, from the architecture and construction of their buildings to the day-to-day activities they offer and the amenities they provide for their guests.

The Characteristics That Set Apart Eco-Friendly Lodgings

Architecture & Design that Are Friendly to the Environment:

Most of the time, environmentally friendly accommodations adhere to ecologically sustainable design principles when constructing their structures. This involves the utilization of renewable materials, efficient insulation, and innovative architectural solutions that harness natural light and ventilation in order to reduce overall energy usage.

REDUCING CARBON FOOTPRINT

Resources d'énergie renouvelables :

The utilization of renewable energy sources, such as solar panels, wind turbines, and geothermal heating systems, is one of the most distinguishing characteristics of environmentally friendly lodging options. These establishments drastically reduce their reliance on fossil fuels by greatly reducing their reliance on clean energy which they harness.

Efficiency in the Use of Energy:

In order to reduce the amount of energy that is used within the lodging, it is usual practice to install energy-efficient appliances, LED lighting, and intelligent HVAC systems. Additionally, through a variety of programs, such as room key card systems that control electricity, guests are encouraged to be careful of the amount of energy that they are using.

The Practice of Conserving Water:

Low-flow showerheads, dual-flush toilets, and rainwater harvesting systems are examples of

water-saving technologies that are commonly seen in eco-friendly hotels. Additionally, they encourage water conservation among visitors by requesting that they reuse towels and linens while they are staying at the hotel.

Reduce Your Waste and Recycle What You Can:

A commitment to waste reduction is one of the defining characteristics of environmentally friendly lodging. They are quite active in promoting recycling programs, composting, and reducing the usage of plastics that are only intended for one use. To reduce the amount of trash generated from packing, many in-room amenities are provided in refillable containers or bulk dispensers.

Transportation that is Kind to the Environment:

In order to lessen the impact that the visitors' various modes of mobility have on the environment, many of these lodging establishments include amenities such as bicycle rentals, charging stations for electric vehicles, and shuttle services.

Food that is both Local and Organic:

The procurement of locally sourced, organic, and ethically produced food for restaurants and in-room dining should be a top priority at eco-friendly hotels. This not only lessens the negative effects on the environment that are caused by the transportation of food, but it also helps local farmers and craftspeople.

The Advantages of Staying in Eco-Friendly Lodging

Conservation of the Natural World:

These lodging establishments make a considerable contribution to the protection of the environment through the implementation of sustainable practices. They limit the amount of energy and water that is consumed, as well as the emissions of greenhouse gases, and they cut down on the trash that is produced, which helps to safeguard natural resources and ecosystems.

Savings on Costs:

Long-term returns on investments in energy-saving technologies and resource conservation are common for businesses that are committed to operating in an environmentally responsible manner. Significant cost savings can be realized as a result of reduced utility expenditures and reduced maintenance costs.

Attracting Travelers Who Are Concerned About the Environment

Accommodations that are sympathetic to the environment attract tourists that are environmentally aware. These customers are willing to spend more for a stay that is in line with their core beliefs and values, which translates to higher occupancy rates and greater profitability for the businesses that cater to their values and principles.

Enhancement of One's Reputation:

Hotels and lodges that make a significant effort to reduce their environmental impact generally have a more positive reputation among both their guests and their peers in the hospitality sector. They are praised for their environmentally friendly practices and may even be presented with awards as a result.

Maintaining Conformity with Regulations:

To encourage businesses in the hospitality industry to become more environmentally conscious, the governments of some areas have passed legislation and provided financial incentives. Keeping a leading position in the field of sustainability guarantees that these lodging options continue to meet the ever-evolving requirements set by the environmental community.

An Experience That Considers the Whole Guest:

Accommodations that are friendly to the environment offer their visitors an experience that is holistic and fulfilling. These lodgings provide a respite that nourishes both the body and the soul in a variety of ways, from the relaxing use of natural materials in room design to the cuisine that is fresh and made with local ingredients.

The Contribution That Eco-Friendly Lodging Can Make Towards the Promotion of Sustainable Travel

The promotion of environmentally responsible travel activities is significantly aided by eco-friendly lodging options. They serve as models of responsible tourism and set a benchmark that other businesses might aspire to achieve. These types of lodgings encourage guests to make decisions that are more respectful of the natural world by bringing attention to the issue and demonstrating in a concrete way what is feasible. The following are some of the ways in which they contribute to the effort to make travel more environmentally friendly:

Education and a Consciousness of the Facts:

In many cases, eco-friendly motels will interact with its visitors by providing them with educational materials, such as brochures or in-room displays, in order to teach them about the environment and the green initiatives that the institution participates in. Having this understanding gives travelers the ability to incorporate comparable behaviors into their day-to-day life.

Providing Evidence That It Is Feasible:

These accommodations demonstrate that environmentally conscious policies and procedures may be easily incorporated into the hospitality business in a way that does not jeopardize guests' sense of comfort or luxury. This example is essential to disproving the notion that sustaining the environment is difficult or impossible to do practically.

Increasing the Adoption of Sustainable Behaviors:
Guests who stay in hotels that provide an eco-friendly experience are more likely to take the green behaviors they observe during their trip home with them. This includes practices like as conserving water and energy as well as recycling materials, all of which may be incorporated into their typical travel routine.

Efforts Made to Raise Industry Standards:
The success of environmentally friendly lodgings compels other types of establishments to take notice and modify their practices. This rivalry to be more sustainable is beneficial to the entire sector, and by extension, it is beneficial to the world.

The tourism sector needs to take considerable steps toward becoming more environmentally sensitive and sustainable, and eco-friendly lodgings are one of those steps. These institutions are paving the way by implementing a wide variety of ecologically friendly measures, ranging from water conservation and waste reduction to sustainable architecture and renewable energy sources. Their dedication to sustainable practices not only helps the environment, but it also improves their bottom line, which in turn helps them build a better reputation and attract more tourists who are environmentally sensitive.

Eco-friendly accommodations provide a look into a more sustainable future for the hospitality business in a world where climate change and environmental degradation are important concerns. They motivate guests to make decisions that are better for the environment and encourage other lodging establishments to follow their lead, which ultimately results in a world that is more sustainable and environmentally friendly for everyone.

3.2 Sustainable Transportation Options

It has never been more important to have access to environmentally friendly modes of transportation than it is in this day and age, which is characterized by the effects of climate change, air pollution, and urban congestion. Not only is the manner in which we travel from one location to another a reflection of our way of life, but it is also one of the most important factors in determining the extent of the damage we do to the natural world. It is becoming more widely acknowledged that conventional modes of mobility, such as automobiles fueled by gasoline, cannot be maintained indefinitely and pose a threat to the health of the planet as well as individuals.

As a direct consequence of this, people all around the world are experiencing a paradigm shift toward alternate modes of transportation that are better for the environment and more effective. In the following paragraphs, we will discuss a variety of environmentally friendly modes of transportation that are paving the way toward a greener future.

1. **Battery-Powered Vehicles (BPVs):**
   The movement toward more environmentally friendly modes of transportation is being led by electric automobiles. They are powered by electricity, thus they do not produce any emissions from their tailpipes and they considerably cut emissions of greenhouse gases. The development of new battery technologies has helped speed the rise of electric vehicles (EVs) by making these vehicles more accessible and inexpensive. Tesla, Nissan, and other major automakers are currently manufacturing a variety of electric vehicles that are designed to appeal to a wide variety of customers. The adoption of electric vehicles is being encouraged by governments all over the world through the provision of various financial incentives, such as tax credits and refunds.
   In addition, electric vehicles present the opportunity for the development of vehicle-to-grid (V2G) technology. This technology enables electric vehicles to operate as energy storage units and even feed electricity back into the grid during times of peak demand, which further contributes to the efficiency of energy use and the stability of the grid.

2. **Transportation Systems:**
   In order to maintain a sustainable urban lifestyle, it is necessary to have public transit systems that are both effective and widespread. Public transportation options such as buses, subways, light rail, and commuter trains are efficient ways to cut down on the number of private automobiles on the road. This helps to ease the burden of gridlock and lowers the amount of pollution produced. Public transportation has the potential to become even more environmentally friendly if it runs on renewable energies such as electricity or alternative fuels such as natural gas.
   Those who would rather not drive have access to an environmentally friendly option in the form of public transportation, which helps them reduce the amount of carbon dioxide emissions related with their daily trips. It is essential to make investments in updating and extending public transit networks in order to increase the use of these networks, which will in turn reduce the dependency on private automobiles.

3. **Infrastructure that is accessible to pedestrians and cyclists:**
   One more environmentally responsible method of transportation is to encourage walking and cycling. As a result of their low energy consumption and absence of pollutants, bicycles are ideally suited for journeys of short to medium distance. To encourage more people to adopt this environmentally beneficial mode of transportation, cities all over the world are investing in cycling infrastructure, such as bike lanes, racks, and bike-sharing programs. Walking is

encouraged by pedestrian-friendly urban planning, which also includes well-maintained sidewalks and urban green spaces. This planning helps reduce the need for short automobile trips, which in turn helps reduce overall greenhouse gas emissions.

4. **Ridesharing and carpooling to save money:**
Initiatives such as carpooling and ridesharing encourage the sharing of resources and cut down on the number of automobiles on the road. This idea has gained popularity thanks to businesses such as Uber and Lyft, which have made it simpler for consumers to share trips and split the cost of such rides. Carpooling apps like BlaBlaCar connect drivers and passengers for long-distance travels, thus decreasing the negative impact that individual vehicle use has on the environment.

5. **Alternate sources of fuel:**
In comparison to conventional diesel fuel, biodiesel is a cleaner and more sustainable alternative because it is produced from renewable resources such as vegetable oil and animal fat.
Compressed natural gas (CNG) and liquefied natural gas (LNG) are two forms of natural gas that burn more cleanly than traditional gasoline and diesel, making them viable solutions for buses, trucks, and even some passenger vehicles.
Hydrogen Fuel Cells: As a possible alternative to gasoline and diesel, hydrogen fuel cells are now being researched and examined. Hydrogen fuel cells create electricity to power vehicles and emit only water vapor as a byproduct.
Ethanol: Ethanol, a byproduct of plants such as corn and sugarcane, is an alternative fuel that can be used in place of gasoline to reduce emissions of greenhouse gases.
Propane: Propane is another alternative fuel that can be used to power automobiles. Compared to gasoline and diesel, propane's emissions of harmful pollutants are far lower.

6. **Maglev Trains and Other High-Speed Rail Systems:**
The introduction of high-speed rail and magnetic levitation (maglev) trains are two examples of innovative approaches to environmentally responsible intercity transportation. They provide an alternative mode of transportation that is both quicker and friendlier to the environment in comparison to flying for shorter distances and driving for longer ones. Trains like these are more environmentally friendly than cars, emit fewer emissions per passenger mile traveled, and help alleviate traffic on highways and in airports.

7. **Planning for a Greener City:**
When we talk about sustainable mobility, we should not only be talking about the vehicles themselves, but also about the way that we organize and build the urban environments around us. Planning cities with a focus on people rather than automobiles is an essential component of environmentally responsible

green urban planning. The capacity to stroll, bike, and get around on foot, the provision of green space, and the operation of public transportation effectively are essential components. Implementation of these principles may result in less reliance on automobiles, lowered levels of traffic congestion, and decreased levels of pollution.

8. **Vehicles that Drive Themselves and Are Connected:**

Autonomous vehicles, often known as AVs, have the potential to bring about a revolution in environmentally friendly transportation by enhancing the flow of traffic and lowering the number of accidents. Because of their smoother driving patterns and better routes, they may also be more efficient in terms of energy use. Electric vehicles are an option for autonomous vehicles, which further cuts pollution. In addition, linked vehicles that are able to interact with one another as well as with the surrounding infrastructure have the potential to enhance traffic management, thereby lowering both congestion and pollution.

Concerns and Things to Take Into Account:
Even while environmentally friendly modes of transportation have a great deal of potential, there are still a number of obstacles and factors to take into account.

1. Investments in system The creation of a transportation system that is both sustainable and efficient demands large investments. Building and maintaining electric charging stations, public transit networks, bicycle lanes, and other infrastructure requires financial investment from both public and private groups, including governments.
2. **Affordability:** The high starting price of electric automobiles, high-speed rail, and other environmentally friendly transportation solutions may prevent their widespread use. Incentives and subsidies are absolutely necessary in order to make these options more accessible to a greater number of people.
3. worries Regarding the Vehicle's Range Electric vehicles still confront worries regarding the vehicle's range constraints and the charging infrastructure, despite the fact that these issues are continually being addressed and improved.
4. Modification of Behaviour Changing one's conduct may be required in order to make the transition from private automobiles to environmentally friendly alternatives. People may find it easier to make the change with the assistance of educational and awareness efforts.
5. **Integration and Accessibility:** Methods of environmentally friendly transportation should be easily included into the development of cities and the operation of transportation networks. In order for them to have any real impact, they need to be available to people of all different ages and backgrounds.

The search for a greener and healthier future offers a glimmer of hope in the form of alternative modes of transportation that are environmentally friendly. There are a variety of approaches that may be taken to lessen the negative effects that our day-to-day travel has on the environment. Some of these include the use of electric automobiles, efficient public transit, cycling, and green urban planning. However, in order to successfully transition to these alternative methods, a concentrated effort is required not just from businesses and governments, but also from individuals. It is easy to see the benefits, which include enhanced public health, less congestion in the roads, lower emissions of gases that contribute to global warming, and cleaner air. If we want to pave the path to a greener and more sustainable future for our planet and the generations that will come after us, sustainable mobility can't just be an option; it has to be a must.

3.3 Sustainable Dining and Food Sourcing

In this day and age, the manner in which we consume food and determine where it comes from has significant repercussions for the environment. The global food sector is a substantial contributor to a number of environmental problems, including biodiversity loss, climate change, and deforestation. As a consequence of this, there is a growing trend toward sustainable dining and food sourcing, which not only attempts to promote better eating but also aims to lessen the impact that humans have on the environment. In this paper, we are going to investigate the meaning behind the notion of sustainable eating and food sourcing, as well as the steps that may be taken to put it into practice.

Acquiring Knowledge of Sustainable Dining:

A dedication to dining in a manner that is environmentally responsible, socially just, and economically feasible is what we mean when we talk about sustainable dining. It requires taking into consideration not just where our food comes from, but also how it is produced, as well as the effect that this has on local ecosystems, communities, and our own bodies.

When we eat in a way that is more sustainable, we are able to make decisions that are beneficial to the well-being of the environment, our communities, and ourselves.

The Importance of Eating Sustainably and Using Locally Sourced Food:

Reducing Our Impact On The Environment The food sector is a major contributor to the emission of greenhouse gases, the destruction of forests, and the degradation of soil. Eating in a sustainable manner promotes behaviors that lessen the impact that our meals have on the environment, such as selecting foods that are grown or raised locally and eating less meat overall.

Preserving Biodiversity Unsustainable methods of farming and fishing can lead to the destruction of ecosystems and put species in risk, hence it is important that these methods be avoided. The goal of getting food in a sustainable manner is to preserve and improve biodiversity so that future generations will have access to a wide variety of delicious foods.

Buying locally produced food is a great way to help support small-scale farmers and local communities, which in turn supports the local economy. This not only boosts the economy of the surrounding areas, but it also lowers the environmental impact of carrying food over great distances.

When it comes to health and nutrition, sustainable dining typically places an emphasis on whole, unprocessed meals, which have proven to be better for our bodies. A diet and way of life that place a greater emphasis on fresh, locally grown food and cereals in their entire form may be more healthful.

Methods That Can Be Implemented Immediately for More Environmentally Responsible Dining and Food Sourcing:

Consume Food Produced Locally One of the easiest methods to practice sustainable dining is to consume food products grown locally and in season. Both the local farmers and the reduction in carbon emissions associated with long-distance transportation benefit from this practice. If it is at all possible, you should try to cultivate your own food, shop at farmer's markets, or participate in a community-supported agriculture (CSA) program.

Reduce Your Intake of Meat The meat business is a key contribution to the environmental challenges that we face today. You may dramatically lessen your impact on the environment by altering your diet to include more plant-based meals and by selecting meat alternatives that were farmed in a sustainable manner or that were made from plants.

When you go grocery shopping, keep an eye out for labels such as "organic," "Fair Trade," and "Rainforest Alliance" on the goods you buy. The presence of one of these labels on a product usually denotes that it was manufactured using processes that were less harmful to the environment and more responsible to society.

Reduce Your Food Waste: Food waste is a significant problem for the environment. To cut down on food waste, make a meal plan, get creative with how you use leftovers, and compost any food scraps. When eating somewhere, instead of leaving behind your leftovers, take them with you to enjoy at home.

Choose seafood that is sourced in a sustainable manner by consulting organizations such as the Marine Stewardship Council (MSC) and the Seafood Watch program offered by the Monterey Bay Aquarium. This will help support sustainable fishing practices. These materials offer direction on which types of seafood can be consumed while minimizing their impact on the environment.

Reduce the use of single-use plastics since the disposal of plastic trash is a significant problem for the environment. When eating out, you should try to avoid using straws, cutlery, and water bottles that are made of single-use plastic. Bring reusable alternatives with you and support local businesses that are working to reduce the amount of trash plastic they produce.

To advocate for change and support policies and initiatives that promote sustainable eating and food sourcing at both the local and national levels, see "Supporting

Policies and Initiatives That Promote Sustainable Dining and Food Sourcing." To advocate for food production methods that are more environmentally friendly, get involved in the conversations happening in your town, write to your elected officials, and read what others have to say.

In a world in which the environmental and health implications of our food choices are becoming increasingly clear, sustainable dining and food sourcing are not just buzzwords; rather, they are vital practices that must be implemented. We are able to contribute to a food system that is more sustainable and equitable if we make deliberate choices regarding the foods that we consume and the origins of those foods. These selections not only lessen our impact on the environment by supporting local economies and reducing our carbon footprint, but they also encourage better eating and safeguard the irreplaceable ecosystems of our planet. Dining in a way that is good for the environment and for future generations is more than simply a passing fad; it is an essential and significant step toward nourishing both ourselves and the earth.

3.4 Reducing Waste and Promoting Recycling

In a world characterized by unchecked consumption and waste, the need to cut down on waste and increase recycling efforts has never been more pressing than it is today. The environmental, economic, and social benefits of trash reduction and recycling are becoming increasingly apparent as the world population continues to expand and as our consumption patterns continue to deplete the planet's resources. In this essay, we will discuss the significance of lowering trash production and the vital part that recycling plays in the movement toward a future that is more sustainable and responsible toward the environment.

The Challenge of Waste:

In recent decades, the amount of waste generated has ballooned to astounding levels. The so-called "throwaway culture" that has taken root in many different cultures has led to the accumulation of mountains of trash that overburden landfills, contaminate ecosystems, and release greenhouse gasses. The environmental repercussions are extremely severe, and they include the destruction of habitats, pollution of both air and water, and climate change. However, this is not just an environmental issue; it also has economic and societal repercussions.

The handling of waste is expensive. The process of collecting, transporting, and disposing of trash requires a significant investment of resources on the part of governments and municipalities. These costs, which are frequently shouldered by taxpayers, take money away from other important public services that could be provided with those dollars instead. The quest for garbage disposal solutions is becoming increasingly difficult as landfills continue to fill up and as worries about air quality make incineration a less appealing choice.

However, recycling presents an opportunity to break free from this cycle, which cannot be maintained indefinitely

The Significance of Reusing and Recycling:

Recycling helps preserve precious natural resources like metals, paper, and plastics by reusing and repurposing materials that would otherwise be thrown away. Recycling procedures, which do not include the extraction of virgin materials, lower the demand for raw resources, which in turn minimizes the amount of habitat degradation and energy consumption.

Recycling has the ability to create cash through the sale of recyclable materials, which is one of the economic benefits of recycling. This cash could be put back into programs that encourage recycling or into other public initiatives that need funding.

The production of goods from raw materials typically needs more energy than recycling, which results in energy savings. Recycling metal, for instance, can save up to 95% of the energy that would have been required to produce the same quantity of aluminum from bauxite ore.

Recycling helps cut down on the emissions of greenhouse gases because it lowers the amount of carbon that is produced during the processes of resource extraction, production, and trash disposal. Because of this, it is a significant tactic in the overall effort to combat climate change.

The recycling business provides employment opportunities in a variety of fields, including collecting, processing, and manufacture. It has the potential to energize local economies and make a contribution to employment that is secure over time.

Recycling helps preserve the environment by easing the burden placed on landfills, which in turn lessens the need for new trash disposal sites and mitigates the environmental concerns connected with these sites.

The Obstacles Standing in the Way of Recycling and Waste Reduction:

Lack of Awareness There are a lot of people and communities that do not have a complete understanding of the positive effects that recycling may have on the economy and the environment. To affect a change in behavior, public education and awareness efforts are absolutely necessary.

Inadequate Infrastructure Recycling programs are dependent on having appropriate infrastructure for collection and processing of recyclables. Recycling activities are hampered in many locations because the requisite infrastructure and services are lacking.

Contamination: The presence of contamination in recyclable materials can reduce the efficiency of recycling activities. To ensure that recyclable materials retain their high quality over time, it is necessary to sort them and dispose of them in the appropriate manner.

Some recycling programs have a difficult time competing economically with programs that use cheaper virgin materials. It is possible that recycling-related businesses require financial aid in the form of subsidies or incentives.

Legislation and Regulation: Recycling regulations that are either inconsistent or lax might be a barrier to progress. For change to occur, we need recycling regulations that are both all-encompassing and rigorously policed.

Strategies That Can Be Put Into Practice to Decrease Waste and Increase Recycling:
Reduce the amount of garbage you produce and look for ways to reuse what you already have as the first step in waste reduction. You can accomplish this by purchasing items that have less packing, reusing stuff, and adopting a "zero-waste" mindset that places an emphasis on responsible consumption.

Recycling initiatives: Be a part of and show your support for your community's recycling initiatives. Find out what kinds of materials can be recycled in your region, and make sure you follow the rules for sorting and throwing away waste the right way.

Engage with local governments and policymakers to lobby for improved recycling infrastructure, comprehensive recycling regulations, and public education efforts. This can be accomplished by advocating for change.

Choosing products manufactured from recycled materials is a great way to show your support for the recycling industry and save money at the same time. This results in an increased demand for recyclable materials and motivates producers to utilize these resources in the production of their goods.

Audits of Waste Conduct waste audits either at your house or at your place of employment to determine areas in which there is potential for waste reduction. Conduct a waste stream analysis to identify potential areas for recycling and reduction of the source of the trash.

Composting is an efficient method for lowering the amount of organic waste produced and producing nutrient-dense soil that may be used for gardening. Additionally, it lessens the amount of methane that is produced as a result of the decomposition of food waste in landfills.

Recycling of Electronic trash (e-Waste): An environmentally responsible way to dispose of electronic trash is to recycle outdated electronic devices. The majority of electronic devices have valuable metals inside of them that may be extracted and recycled for new uses.

Participate in the Circular Economy: Give your financial backing to companies that subscribe to the ideas of the circular economy, which holds that goods and resources should be created with the intention of being reused, recycled, or repurposed.

The move toward a manner of living that is more sustainable and responsible requires a number of important initiatives, including the reduction of waste and the promotion of recycling. We can contribute to a healthier planet and more successful communities by limiting the economic costs of waste management, lowering our environmental imprint, and preserving resources. In doing so, we will also reduce the amount of waste we produce. The hurdles that stand in our way of attaining universal recycling and reducing waste are enormous; nevertheless, if we work together, raise awareness, and advocate for change, we can overcome these challenges and make the world a cleaner and more sustainable place for both the generations living now and those who will come after them. Recycling is not merely a choice; rather, it is an obligation that each of us must do in order to contribute to a better and more environmentally friendly future.

Chapter 4

Sustainable Destinations

It is reflective of a growing awareness of the environmental, social, and economic implications of travel that the concept of sustainable destinations has acquired substantial popularity in the worldwide tourist sector. Concerns regarding the protection of natural ecosystems, cultural heritage, and local populations have risen to the forefront as the tourism industry around the world has experienced extraordinary growth in recent years. To ensure that tourism activities do not jeopardize the destination's integrity and resilience, both for the present generation and for generations to come, sustainable destinations place a high priority on the long-term health of the elements that make up the destination. We will delve into the relevance of sustainable destinations, the primary principles that direct them, and the most effective techniques for achieving sustainability in the tourism industry as part of this in-depth research.

The Importance of Environmentally Friendly Vacation Spots

Protection of Natural Ecosystems: Sustainable vacation locations are an essential component in the protection of natural ecosystems, including vulnerable ecosystems, hotspots for biodiversity, and sensitive habitats. These destinations limit the negative affects of tourism activities, such as deforestation, habitat degradation, and pollution, by applying sustainable practices, which in turn ensures the protection of natural resources for future generations.

Preservation of Cultural history A great number of vacation spots have a plethora of rich cultural history, which may include historic sites, traditional practices, and indigenous communities. These cultural assets are the focus of efforts to maintain and develop sustainable tourism initiatives, with the overarching goal of fostering respect for local traditions, lifestyles, and customs. Destinations are able to preserve their distinct cultural identities, prevent the exploitation of their cultural traditions, and enhance cultural interchange and understanding when they engage in behaviors that promote sustainability.

Empowerment of Local Communities Sustainable vacation spots place a high priority on the health and independence of their surrounding communities. Destinations have the potential to generate chances for socioeconomic development, job creation, and capacity building if they involve members of the local community in the planning and decision-making processes pertaining to tourism. In addition, sustainable tourism practices work to ensure that the advantages of tourism are shared among local stakeholders in a manner that is more equitable. This helps to reduce socioeconomic disparities and strengthens the community as a whole.

Environmental Education and Awareness: Sustainable destinations serve as platforms for environmental education and awareness, both for vacationers and for the populations that call those locations home. Destinations have the ability to build a culture of environmental stewardship and consciousness by supporting environmentally friendly practices and promoting environmentally responsible travel behaviors. Education programs can include anything from informative nature trails and visitor centers to workshops on sustainable living and conservation activities; the overarching goal of these programs is to instill a feeling of environmental responsibility in all parties involved.

Overtourism is a phenomenon that can lead to overcrowding, environmental degradation, and cultural commodification. Sustainable tourism practices assist alleviate the negative impacts of overtourism, which is a phenomenon that can lead to overpopulation and environmental deterioration. Destinations are able to guarantee that tourism activities do not overrun local infrastructure, ruin natural attractions, or disrupt citizens' day-to-day lives by employing carrying capacity evaluations, visitor management measures, and seasonal tourism planning.

Principles Essential to the Creation of Sustainable Destinations

The protection of the environment is a top priority for sustainable vacation spots, as are the

preservation of natural resources, ecosystems, and biological diversity. This principle calls for the preservation of natural ecosystems, the encouragement of environmentally responsible methods of land use, as well as the development of efficient procedures for the management of waste and the prevention of contamination.

Cultural Preservation: Sustainable vacation spots recognize the significance of their own cultural histories, customs, and identities, and work to conserve them. This concept places an emphasis on the preservation of historic sites, the encouragement of cultural events and activities, and the provision of opportunities for local communities to take an active role in the process of cultural preservation.

Participation of Local Communities in Tourism Development and Decision-Making Processes: A Priority for Sustainable Destinations Community involvement and participation of local communities in tourism development and decision making processes is a priority for sustainable destinations. This principle calls for the development of job prospects in the local area, as well as the promotion of locally owned enterprises and artisanal endeavors, and the facilitation of tourism endeavors that are driven by the local community.

Education of Visitors: Sustainable travel destinations make it a priority to educate and raise the knowledge of its visitors on the environmental, cultural, and social impacts of tourism.

This concept places an emphasis on the sharing of information on environmentally responsible travel practices, the encouraging of responsible behavior among visitors, and the promotion of cultural interchange and understanding.

Economic Viability Sustainable destinations work to secure the continued economic health and success of the communities in which they are located over the long term. This principle calls for the encouragement of tourism businesses that are environmentally responsible, the diversification of the community's economy, and the fair sharing of tourism income among the various community stakeholders.

Enhancement of Residents' Quality of Life: A top priority for environmentally responsible vacation spots is the improvement of the residents' quality of life. This principle calls for the strengthening of the community's physical infrastructure, the delivery of essential services and conveniences, and the development of an atmosphere that is welcoming and accepting of both permanent inhabitants and temporary guests.

How to Achieve Sustainable Destinations Through the Use of Best Practices

Destination Management Planning (DMP): Create all-encompassing destination management plans that incorporate strategies for stakeholder participation, sustainable tourism best practices, and long-term development objectives. To ensure that destination management is approached in a manner that is both comprehensive and welcoming, DMPs should solicit the cooperation of local communities, businesses, governmental institutions, and environmental organizations.

The Construction of Eco-Friendly Infrastructure Make the construction of eco-friendly infrastructure, which includes energy-efficient buildings, waste management facilities, and sustainable transportation networks, a top priority in the construction of new infrastructure. To reduce the negative impact that tourism has on the surrounding environment, it is important to adopt green building practices, promote the use of renewable energy sources, and improve public transit.

Implementing Programs for the Conservation of Biodiversity and Ecotourism: These programs should promote the natural beauty and biological value of the destination in order to encourage ecotourism and biodiversity conservation. Protected areas, wildlife reserves, and other nature-based tourism activities should be established so as to encourage the preservation of the natural environment while also providing educational and recreational possibilities for tourists.

The protection of cultural heritage should include the development of cultural preservation programs as well as heritage tourism initiatives that highlight the distinctive cultural traditions, arts, and history of the area. Fostering cultural interchange, promoting cultural awareness, and empowering local communities to preserve their cultural identities are all important goals that can be accomplished through supporting local craftspeople, cultural events, and community-based tourism programs.

Implementing Responsible tourist Promotion techniques It is important to put into practice responsible tourist promotion techniques that highlight environmentally conscious consumer behavior, responsible travel habits, and ethical shopping. Collaborate with tour operators, travel agencies, and businesses in the hospitality industry to promote responsible tourism packages, environmentally friendly accommodations, and community-based tourist experiences that stress sustainability and responsible travel.

Foster Collaboration and Capacity Building Among Local Stakeholders Encourage collaboration and capacity building among local stakeholders, such as community members, companies, non-governmental organizations (NGOs), and government agencies. Fostering a sense of ownership and responsibility for the destination's long-term growth through the creation of partnerships and educational programs that give local people the ability to actively participate in tourism planning, management, and decision-making processes is an important step in this direction.

Certification and Accreditation for Sustainable Tourism It is recommended that certification and accreditation for sustainable tourism be sought from internationally recognized organizations and certifying authorities. Adhere to global sustainable tourism standards, guidelines, and best practices to demonstrate a dedication to environmental protection, cultural preservation, and community engagement. This will enhance the legitimacy of the destination and make it more appealing to eco-conscious travelers and responsible vacationers.

Education and Awareness Programs for Visitors: Initiate education and awareness programs for visitors that encourage environmentally responsible tourist practices, cultural sensitivity, and responsible stewardship of the environment. It is important to provide tourists with instructional materials, interpretive signage, and interactive displays that educate them about the natural and cultural legacy of the destination. This will encourage visitors to make choices that are both informed and responsible while they are experiencing the destination.

Considerations for the Future in Light of Obstacles Facing Sustainable Destinations

Despite the many advantages and examples of sustainable destinations that have been implemented successfully, there are a number of obstacles and factors to take into account that need to be addressed in order to assure the continuous development and efficiency of this strategy.

Sustainable destinations face the challenge of creating economic growth and prosperity for local communities while conserving environmental and cultural integrity. Striking a balance between economic growth and sustainability is essential to attaining sustainability. It is vital to strike a balance between economic development and sustainability in order to guarantee that locations will continue to be desirable and profitable over the long run.

Climate Change and Resilience: In order for destinations to be considered sustainable, they need to confront the problems that are brought by climate change. Some of these challenges include increasing sea levels, extreme weather events, and altering tourism seasons. In order to safeguard the location from the hazards that are caused by climate change, it is absolutely necessary to develop adaptation and resilience methods.

Sustainable Transportation: Traveling is a major source of carbon emissions, and one of the biggest contributors to this is the transportation sector. To lessen the toll that tourism takes on the environment, sustainable locations need to prioritize the creation of environmentally friendly modes of transportation. Some examples are electric buses, bicycle-sharing programs, and public transportation systems that run smoothly.

Empowering Local populations It is still a problem in many destinations to ensure that local populations benefit from sustainable tourism operations. In order to achieve true sustainability, it is essential to give local populations the power to play an active role in the management and decision-making processes pertaining to tourism.

Overtourism is still a problem in many attractive areas, and the resulting congestion can have a harmful influence not just on the environment but also on society and culture. In order to spread the negative effects of tourism more fairly, sustainable destinations need to use visitor management measures such as booking limits, defined visitation dates, and the promotion of lesser-known attractions.

Effective Marketing and Education: One of the main issues in the tourism industry is promoting environmentally conscious destinations and teaching passengers about responsible tourism practices.

It is necessary to have effective marketing strategies as well as educational initiatives if one wishes to ensure that travelers are aware of sustainable travel practices and participate in them.

The tourism industry is undergoing a significant paradigm shift, and sustainable destinations are at the forefront of this movement. These locations place a high priority on issues such as environmental protection, cultural preservation, community engagement, and responsible travel practices. This helps to ensure that the positive aspects of tourism are enjoyed by all parties involved while the negative aspects are mitigated to the greatest extent possible. Sustainable destinations have the potential to play a major role in the development of a tourism industry that is more responsible, equitable, and in tune with its natural surroundings. This may be accomplished by adopting best practices, adhering to the basic principles of sustainability, and tackling current issues. Our collaborative commitment to making tourism more sustainable and responsible is essential to ensuring the long-term health of travel destinations, as well as the well-being of the populations that reside there and the planet itself.

4.1 The Role of Destination Management Organizations

The tourist industry is constantly undergoing change, and in order for a location to flourish and distinguish itself from other destinations in today's cutthroat environment, it is essential to have Destination Management Organizations (DMOs). Destination management organizations (DMOs) play the role of orchestrators and facilitators, working quietly in the background to promote the smooth and sustainable growth of destinations. In this in-depth research, we will investigate the many facets of DMOs' roles, including their significance in the development of outstanding tourism and the strategies they employ to address the difficulties facing the tourism sector today.

Before we begin:

Destination management organizations, or DMOs, are organizations that are responsible for the strategic management and promotion of a destination. Whether it be a city, region, or country, destination marketing organizations (DMOs) play an essential part in the process of establishing and improving the attractiveness and competitiveness of the destination they serve. They serve as the industry's fulcrum, bringing together a wide variety of stakeholders, forming strategies, marketing the destination, and assuring the industry's continued viability.

DMOs and the Role They Play

Planning and development of a strategic strategy:

Destination Marketing Organizations (DMOs) are responsible for engaging in extensive strategic planning for their particular destinations. They seek to determine the distinctive selling points of the location, as well as establish objectives for the destination's continued growth.

These goals might include making improvements to the infrastructure, providing a better experience for tourists, and promoting economic expansion. DMOs play an essential part in the development of a destination's tourism quality by laying out a plan for the destination's future development.

Coordination Among Stakeholders:

DMOs serve as a hub for all of the various stakeholders in the tourist industry that are located inside a location. These stakeholders can consist of local government entities, businesses, hotels, attractions, and travel operators, among other types of establishments. DMOs serve as a facilitator for communication between these many parties to ensure that a coherent strategy for destination development is implemented. Through the promotion of communication and cooperation, they contribute to the development of a tourism experience that is streamlined and well-coordinated for guests.

Advertising and public relations:

Destination marketing is one of the most prominent functions performed by DMOs. They advertise the location using a variety of methods, such as trade exhibitions, digital marketing, and traditional forms of advertising. DMOs are able to attract tourists, conferences, and events, all of which contribute to economic growth, by cultivating an image of their brand that is attractive and consistent.

Services for Visitors:

DMOs typically offer a variety of visitor services, including visitor information centers, websites, and mobile applications, in order to improve the overall experience for tourists. They make available information and advice to tourists, allowing such individuals to make the most of their time spent in the area. It is essential that this function be played in enhancing visitor satisfaction and encouraging repeat visits.

Research on the Market and Analyses of Data:

DMOs are responsible for collecting and analyzing data on a variety of topics, including market trends, visitor demographics, and economic impacts. This knowledge is crucial for making well-informed decisions and adjusting business strategies to meet the ever-evolving requirements of the tourism industry. DMOs also keep track of the feedback provided by visitors and modify their services based on the information gained.

Management of the environment and consideration of future generations:

The tourism industry is becoming increasingly concerned about environmentally responsible practices. DMOs are becoming more involved in efforts to reduce the negative effects that tourism has on the surrounding environment.

This involves the preservation of natural resources and the protection of delicate ecosystems, as well as the promotion of eco-friendly practices among the various stakeholders in the tourist industry, such as hotels and tour operators.

The Management of Events:

Events inside the destination are frequently organized by or supported by DMOs. This can include things like cultural celebrations and sporting events, as well as meetings and seminars. DMOs provide a contribution to the thriving economy of a place by luring and administering various events of this nature.

The Development of Products:

DMOs play a role in product development by detecting gaps in the offerings of the destination and providing assistance to local businesses and entrepreneurs in the creation of new products and services that are appealing to customers. This can mean developing novel itineraries, adrenaline-pumping activities, or unique dining experiences.

Management of Emergencies:

When there is an emergency, such a natural disaster or a health emergency like the COVID-19 epidemic, the function that DMOs play becomes extremely important. They offer assistance, information, and resources to both tourists and businesses within the tourism industry, which enables the destination to better manage and lessen the effects of any crises that may occur there.

The Importance of DMOs in the Production of Outstanding Tourism

The ability to compete and differentiate oneself:

In order to stand out in a competitive global market, locations need to find ways to differentiate themselves. Destination management organizations (DMOs) play an important part in the process of formulating and conveying a destination's distinctive selling propositions. This might refer to aspects such as the culture, heritage, natural beauty, or noteworthy events of the location. DMOs increase the competitiveness of a destination by building a powerful brand image for the location.

Growth of the Economy:

In many locations, tourism is an important factor that contributes to overall economic growth.

DMOs work toward the goal of increasing both the number of visitors and the amount of money spent by efficiently marketing the destination and developing tourism offers that are both appealing and diversified. This, in turn, helps local businesses and contributes to the creation of new jobs.

The Development of Infrastructure:

DMOs provide assistance in prioritizing and advocating for the development of infrastructure inside the destination. This covers modes of transportation, places of lodging, areas open to the public, and points of interest. DMOs ensure that a destination can accommodate an increasing number of visitors and give those guests with an experience that is both comfortable and convenient by investing in and improving the destination's physical infrastructure.

Preserving the Environment While Maintaining Sustainability:

DMOs have a responsibility to play a part in the promotion of sustainable tourism practices in this age of climate change and increased environmental awareness. DMOs provide a contribution to the long-term environmental health of a destination by backing ecologically responsible projects, as well as educating both tourists and local stakeholders about the importance of protecting the local ecosystem.

Empowerment of the Community:

Local communities are given more agency when they are included in the planning and management of tourism through DMOs. This not only helps to instill a sense of ownership but also guarantees that the advantages of tourism are distributed evenly across the entire community. Additionally, it contributes to the maintenance of cultural traditions and history.

Managing Emergencies and Building Resilience:

In times of crisis, disaster management organizations (DMOs) are crucial because they provide leadership, assistance, and a coordinated response. The reputation of the destination as well as its opportunities for the future are both protected when DMOs efficiently manage crises.

The Obstacles That DMOs Must Overcome

Regarding financial support, DMOs frequently rely on a mix of public and private financing sources. Maintaining one's funding can be difficult at times, particularly during economic downturns or periods of fluctuating public backing.

Overtourism is a problem that can arise in certain locations, and it occurs when the sheer volume of tourists starts to make the location difficult to enjoy for its intended purpose.

DMOs have a responsibility to address this issue by putting in place strategies for sustainable tourism and methods for visitor management.

Changing Visitor Preferences and Expectations Over time, the preferences and expectations of visitors change. DMOs are required to adjust to shifting demographics and preferences by creating novel and engaging experiences in order to keep up with the ever-increasing demand.

Environmental and Social Sustainability: Accomplishing one's desired level of sustainability can be a difficult and unending struggle. It is imperative that DMOs find a middle ground between economic expansion and preservation of the environment and society.

Support from Politicians and the Community The ability of DMOs to effectively implement their objectives can be impacted by alterations in both the political climate and the feeling of the local community. It is essential for their success that they have strong support from both the governmental system and the community.

Developments in DMO Technology

Digital Marketing: Destination Management Organizations (DMOs) have recognized the potential of digital marketing as a potent instrument for communicating with a worldwide audience. The use of social media, marketing through influencers, and data analytics are now fundamental components of their marketing strategy.

Certification for Sustainable Tourism: Many destinations marketing organizations (DMOs) are working toward obtaining sustainability certifications and standards in order to demonstrate their dedication to responsible tourism and attract tourists who are environmentally sensitive.

Collaborative Tourism Platforms Destination management organizations (DMOs) are increasingly partnering with peer destinations and sharing resources and ideas to address common concerns such as overtourism and sustainability through the use of collaborative tourism platforms.

Smart Tourism Technologies Destination management organizations are utilizing smart technologies such as data analytics, artificial intelligence, and the Internet of Things to enhance guest experiences, optimize resource management, and increase safety.

Tourism that is More Inclusive: Destination marketing organizations (DMOs) are aiming to make tourism more inclusive, with the goal of ensuring that all people of the community benefit from activities associated with tourism. This includes programs that encourage accessible tourism and provide support for enterprises that are owned by members of minority groups.

The success of tourism destinations all over the world is largely attributable to the efforts of Destination Management Organizations (DMOs). They are responsible for a wide variety of tasks, including strategic planning, stakeholder coordination, marketing, and the promotion of sustainable practices. The Destination Marketing Organization (DMO) is an essential component in the process of sculpting tourism excellence because it ensures that destinations are competitive, sustainable, and economically vibrant.

DMOs are required to make adjustments in order to keep up with the constantly shifting needs and difficulties posed by the tourist sector as it continues to develop. DMOs have the potential to continue playing an important part in shaping the future of tourism and ensuring that destinations will continue to be appealing, dynamic, and sustainable for many generations to come if they embrace innovation, sustainability, and community empowerment.

4.2 Sustainable Destination Certification Programs

The idea of "sustainable tourism" is becoming more prevalent as people all over the world become more conscious of the negative effects that tourism may have on the environment, society, and the economy. Sustainable Destination Certification Programs are at the center of this movement. The goal of these programs is to recognize and incentivize destinations that have made a commitment to responsible and sustainable tourism practices. In the following in-depth investigation, we will delve into the realm of sustainable destination certification programs, investigating their significance, guiding principles, important players, and the impact they have on both the travel industry and the earth as a whole.

Before we begin:

The tourism industry is a major contributor to the gross domestic product (GDP) and employment in a great number of countries throughout the world. Despite this, the rapid growth of the sector has resulted in a number of problems, such as the pollution of the environment, the erosion of cultural traditions, and economic imbalances. As a response to these issues, the idea of sustainable tourism has surfaced as a potential solution to help alleviate some of these issues. Certification programs for sustainable destinations play a critical part in this transformation by evaluating, certifying, and promoting locations that comply to sustainability standards.

The Significance of Programs to Obtain Certification as a Sustainable Destination

Protection of the Environment: These programs urge vacation spots to reduce their negative effects on the surrounding environment by putting into practice environmentally friendly procedures, preserving natural resources, and guarding delicate ecosystems. Certification programs encourage locations to act in a more environmentally responsible manner by praising their efforts and providing them with benefits for doing so.

Preserving a Destination's Cultural Heritage is an Important Part of Sustainable Tourism Environmental stewardship is only one aspect of sustainable tourism; another is the protection of a location's rich cultural history. Certification programs acknowledge and support cultural preservation projects, such as the protection of traditional traditions and the emancipation of indigenous populations. These types of initiatives are also recognized and promoted by the programs.

The creation of new jobs, the encouragement of small and medium-sized businesses, and a more equitable distribution of the benefits of tourism all contribute to the expansion of the local economy when responsible tourism practices are implemented. Certification programs aim to incentivize travel destinations to place a higher priority on the economic health of the communities they serve.

Differentiation in the Market: Certification gives locations a competitive advantage in the marketplace. In today's competitive tourist industry, certified sustainable locations stand out from the pack, attracting eco-conscious vacationers who are looking for genuine, responsible experiences.

Satisfaction of Tourists: Efforts to increase sustainability typically result in greater infrastructure, expanded services, and heightened levels of satisfaction for tourists. Certification programs lead to greater levels of tourist satisfaction by promoting locations that have strong sustainability criteria.

The Fundamentals of Responsible Tourism Certification Programs for Destinations

Environmental Management: This program analyzes a location's commitment to the preservation and protection of the surrounding natural environment. This can include efforts pertaining to the reduction of waste, the conservation of water, the efficiency of energy use, and the preservation of animals.

Preservation of Cultural Heritage Certification programs evaluate a destination's efforts to preserve its cultural heritage and award points accordingly.

This encompasses the preservation of historic places and customs, as well as the facilitation of community development at the neighborhood level.

Participation of Local Communities in Tourism Planning and Development is one of the Factors That Are Evaluated By Programs That Measure Community Engagement. Certification is sometimes given as a reward to locations that foster the creation of local employment possibilities, encourage the growth of local enterprises, and make certain that the advantages of tourism are distributed widely.

Infrastructure development is examined with an emphasis placed on eco-friendly techniques in the context of sustainable infrastructure. Higher certification ratings can be achieved through the implementation of sustainable transportation practices, green building standards, and the protection of public places.

Marketing and Education: Certification programs may require destinations to educate both visitors and local stakeholders on responsible travel practices, environmental conservation, and cultural preservation. Certification programs may also require destinations to preserve cultural and natural resources.

Impact on the Economy: Locations are ranked according to their capacity to stimulate economic development, which is measured by a number of factors including the generation of new jobs and the distribution of revenues generated by tourism.

Those Most Important to the Certification of Sustainable Destinations

EarthCheck is a science-based certification program that assists locations, businesses, and communities in measuring and managing the environmental and social implications of their operations. They are primarily concerned with assisting locations in achieving positive and measurable results.

GSTC stands for the Global Sustainable Tourism Council. Global guidelines for environmentally responsible travel and tourism are provided by the GSTC. They set guidelines that destinations, hotels, tour operators, and other businesses involved in the tourism industry should adhere to. Their standards are acknowledged in the industry at large and utilized by a variety of certification schemes.

Green Destinations: Green Destinations is an organization that offers an evaluation and certification scheme aimed to evaluate the level of sustainability efforts made by a particular location. They evaluate a large number of characteristics, such as aspects of nature, the environment, culture, and the local community.

Blue Flag: The program that awards the Blue Flag serves as a certification for sustainable boating tourism providers, as well as beaches and marinas. The water quality, environmental management, safety, and accessibility of the facility are the primary priorities of the certification.

Biosphere is a nonprofit organization that promotes environmentally responsible travel and offers certificates to locations, hotels, and travel companies. Their accreditation requires them to meet criteria that address issues of environmental, social, and financial sustainability. In addition to this, they offer training and support for businesses that are working toward certification.

EarthCheck: EarthCheck is an organization that provides benchmarking and certification programs for environmentally responsible travel and tourism. They collaborate with various tourist locations and organizations in order to assess and manage the environmental and social repercussions of tourism.

The Effects That Sustainable Destination Certification Programs Have On Visitors and Businesses

Increased Accountability Certification schemes ensure that destinations are held accountable for the efforts they make to reduce their impact on the environment. When working toward attaining or keeping accreditation, destinations are more likely to take seriously the commitment they have made to sustainable and responsible tourist practices.

Education and Awareness: Through the use of these programs, both destinations and tourists are made more aware of the significance of preserving the environment. Through education of stakeholders as well as travelers, they are able to contribute to behavior change and the promotion of responsible travel practices.

Certification provides a distinct advantage in the market as it acts as a potent marketing tool. Certified locations have the potential to entice tourists who are environmentally sensitive, which can result in a rise in the number of visitors and revenue generated by tourism.

Growth in the economy is one of the potential outcomes of sustainable tourism, which is particularly relevant for local economies in areas where tourism accounts for a large portion of total revenue. Certification provides destinations with incentives to expand their employment prospects, strengthen their community's economy, and ensure that the advantages of tourism are shared equitably.

Certification programs encourage the protection of natural habitats as well as cultural assets in order to fulfill their mission statements. They urge locations to take care of their one-of-a-kind assets by praising and rewarding those who make similar efforts.

The Difficulties Incurred By Sustainable Destination Certification Programs And Their Detractors

Obtaining and retaining accreditation can be a difficult and expensive procedure, especially for less well-known locations or companies. This is especially true for smaller establishments. It can be challenging to find the necessary resources to complete paperwork, assessments, and audits.

Overreliance on Certification: Some people believe that certification programs can lead to an overreliance on the certification process itself. This can occur when destinations or enterprises concentrate on meeting the standards for certification rather than actually adopting the ideals of sustainability.

Lack of consistency Because there is no consistency among the many certification programs, it is difficult for destinations and passengers to compare the significance of various certifications and determine whether or not they are legitimate.

Greenwashing: Certain locations and businesses have been accused of engaging in "greenwashing," which refers to the practice of marketing themselves as sustainable without actually adopting responsible practices. The legitimacy of certification programs and the trust of environmentally concerned visitors is harmed as a result of this.

Some detractors contend that the enforcement and monitoring of recognized locations and enterprises can be lacking in strength, and they point to this as evidence. A certification may not actually guarantee genuine sustainability if it does not include stringent follow-up and review.

Upcoming Developments and Breakthroughs in the Field of Sustainable Destination Certification Programs

Blockchain Technology: The use of blockchain technology is now being researched with the goal of improving the transparency and traceability of efforts to promote sustainability. Certification programs have the potential to deliver a higher level of authenticity and confidence by recording and validating sustainable business practices on a distributed ledger called a blockchain.

Certifications for the Entire Destination Some vacation spots are looking to become certified as
"destination-wide," which means that the entire region, city, or island will be evaluated and given the green light. These initiatives are all-encompassing, taking into account the efforts made toward sustainability not just by individual enterprises but by the entire destination as a whole.

The COVID-19 pandemic has hastened the transition to digital audits and remote assessments. This is partially due to the fact that the pandemic boosted their acceptance. The use of these tools enables certification programs to evaluate locations and businesses without conducting in-person inspections, which streamlines the certification process and reduces its associated costs.

Certification for Online Travel Platforms Certification programs are beginning to broaden their purview to include online travel platforms and booking websites. By highlighting sustainable locations and businesses, these platforms have the potential to contribute to the promotion of sustainable tourism.

Incentives for Certification: Certain areas are investigating the possibility of offering financial incentives to locations and companies that have achieved certification. These incentives may take the form of tax breaks, assistance with marketing, or financial backing for programs that promote environmental responsibility.

The promotion of responsible tourism through the recognition of destinations that place a priority on environmental protection, cultural preservation, community engagement, and economic growth is made possible through the implementation of certification systems for sustainable destinations. Certification programs encourage locations to engage in responsible activities by imposing requirements and evaluating the extent to which sustainability efforts are being made.

Despite the fact that there are obstacles and criticisms, certification programs are continuously improving, innovating, and adjusting to meet the ever-evolving requirements of the tourism business.

Certification will play an increasingly important part in determining the trajectory of sustainable tourism in the years to come as a growing number of tourists are becoming more aware of the impact their travels have. Travelers who are concerned about their impact on the environment will be able to make more educated decisions, which will contribute to the creation of a tourism industry that is more environmentally friendly, responsible, and pleasurable for everyone.

Chapter 5

The Role of Technology in Sustainable Tourism

In this day and age of lightning-fast technical innovation, the combination of technology and eco-friendliness has the potential to completely rework the travel and tourist sector. It is now an absolute necessity on a worldwide scale to practice sustainable tourism, which is an approach to vacationing that works to reduce the adverse effects of travel on both the environment and society. When it comes to developing the concepts of sustainability in the tourism industry, technology is a potent weapon that has the potential to play a vital role. Within the scope of this in-depth investigation, we will investigate the myriad ways in which technology plays a part in eco-friendly tourism by investigating the ways in which it exerts an impact on numerous facets of the business, including traveler behavior, destination management, and modes of transportation and lodging.

Before we begin:

In a lot of different countries, tourism is a big economic driver, meaning it adds a large amount to the GDP and helps create jobs. On the other hand, the environmental, social, and cultural implications of tourism, in addition to the difficulties of overtourism, climate change, and resource depletion, have led to an increasing focus on sustainability in the tourism industry.

Technology has emerged as a transformative force in the field of sustainable tourism, bringing novel solutions to reduce the negative impacts of travel while simultaneously improving the quality of the trip experience. It provides an opportunity for destinations, businesses, and travelers to make decisions that are better for the environment. In the following discussion, we will investigate the ways in which technology is being utilized across a variety of aspects of environmentally responsible tourism.

Transportation and Efficient and Environmentally Sound Mobility

Electric Vehicles (EVs) and Hybrid Cars: The development of electric vehicles (EVs) and hybrid cars has resulted in an environmentally beneficial alternative to conventional gasoline-powered automobiles. Ride-sharing services and firms that rent out cars are gradually expanding their fleets to include hybrid and electric vehicle alternatives. In addition, the infrastructure for electric vehicle charging is growing, which makes it simpler for tourists to travel with electric vehicles.

Applications for Public Transportation The availability of mobile applications for public transportation has fundamentally changed the way in which individuals navigate cities. Travelers can be encouraged to use public transit by providing real-time information, route planning, and the ability to purchase tickets online. This will result in a reduction in the number of private vehicles on the road.

Services of Ride-Sharing: Ride-sharing platforms such as Uber and Lyft offer options for shared transportation, which can help reduce the number of cars on the road. Some platforms also provide shared rides to major transportation hubs like airports and rail stations, which encourages environmentally conscious modes of transportation.

E-Scooters and Bike-Sharing Programs: Sharing programs for bicycles and electric scooters have recently been implemented in a number of places. These solutions are favorable to the environment and give handy methods to explore urban areas while also lowering traffic and pollution.

Hyperloop and High-Speed Rail: Up-and-coming technologies such as the hyperloop and high-speed rail are working toward the goal of revolutionizing long-distance travel by providing options for transportation that are quicker, more efficient, and more environmentally friendly.

Carbon Offset Platforms: Some airlines and travel firms provide carbon offset programs, which enable travelers to compensate for the carbon emissions they cause by investing in environmental projects. These programs are offered by some airlines and travel companies. Travelers can assess their carbon footprint with the use of online calculators, and then they can decide whether or not to buy carbon offsets as part of the booking process.

Solutions for Smart Mobility Smart cities are putting into place technology such as intelligent traffic management systems, which optimize traffic flow in order to reduce both congestion and pollution. In addition, intelligent parking solutions can assist passengers in locating available parking spaces in a more expedient manner, hence decreasing the need for additional driving.

Ecologically Sound Lodging and Environmentally Friendly Technologies

Buildings that Are Efficient in Their Use of Energy Green building practices and environmentally conscious architecture are becoming increasingly prevalent in the hospitality industry. Solar panels, passive heating and cooling, and energy-efficient appliances are some of the elements that may be found in energy-efficient buildings. These buildings are designed to use as little energy as possible.

Smart room technologies allow visitors to access information and services using mobile apps or voice-activated systems. In-room technologies also allow guests to adjust the lighting, heating, and cooling in their respective rooms. This may result in reduced energy consumption as well as enhanced comfort for guests.

Waste Reduction: These days, hotels are turning to technology more and more to cut down on their trash. This includes the utilization of automated systems for the tracking and management of trash, as well as the utilization of intelligent thermostats and lighting systems that preserve energy when rooms are not occupied.

Water Conservation: Efforts to conserve water can benefit from the application of technology. For instance, some hotels have installed smart sensors to monitor water usage and look for signs of leakage. The installation of low-flow faucets, showerheads, and toilets are also helpful in cutting down on water usage.

Certifications for Environmental Stewardship A growing number of lodging establishments are looking into obtaining environmental certifications from groups such as LEED (Leadership in Energy and Environmental Design) or Green Key. These certificates are frequently exhibited in an effort to entice travelers with a concern for the environment and to demonstrate a dedication to sustainability.

Amenities That Are Better for the Environment Technology is making it possible to employ environmentally friendly amenities such as biodegradable toiletries and bulk dispensers in an effort to reduce the amount of waste produced by single-use plastic items.

Management of Destinations and Environmentally Friendly Tourism

Sustainable Destination Management Systems (SDMS): These systems make use of technology to gather, manage, and analyze data pertaining to the number of visitors, the use of resources, and the impact on the environment. Destinations are given the ability to make decisions based on data and to execute sustainable plans thanks to SDMS.

Signage and Interpretation in Digital Format Digital signage and interpretation tools provide information to visitors about the history, culture, and natural elements of a site. These solutions assist reduce the amount of paper waste by taking the place of traditional paper brochures and placards.

Augmented Reality (AR) and Virtual Reality (VR): The technology behind AR and VR can be used to provide virtual tours, interactive exhibitions, and immersive cultural experiences, all of which can make for a more enjoyable visit for guests. These technologies also have the potential to lessen the damage that traditional tourism practices cause to the environment.

Apps built for Sustainable Tourism Mobile apps that are built for sustainable tourism give travelers with information on environmentally conscious enterprises, cultural activities that are unique to their destination, and responsible tourism practices. Using these apps, travelers are able to make decisions that are better for the environment while they are away.

Monitoring the Environment Both current attempts to monitor the environment and conserve it can benefit from the application of technology. The tracking of wildlife, the identification of invasive species, and the monitoring of changes in ecosystems are all done with the use of drones and remote sensors.

Data on the Destination's Sustainability Is Crowdsourced Some places collaborate with visitors

and locals to collect data on the destination's sustainability via crowdsourcing platforms and apps. The use of this data in the development of policies and strategies can help improve sustainability.

Marketing and Promotion of Sustainable Destinations Sustainable destinations can leverage technology for marketing and promotion, targeting eco-conscious travelers and emphasizing their sustainability initiatives in digital campaigns. This allows sustainable destinations to reach a wider audience.

Alterations in both Sustainable Practices and Behaviors

Additionally, technology has an effect on tourist behavior and encourages environmentally responsible habits.

Booking and Making Payments Online Travelers can save time and money by using online booking services to make reservations for their lodging, transportation, and activities. This eliminates the need for paper paperwork and printed tickets.

Electronic Tickets and Boarding cards The usage of electronic tickets and boarding cards, which can be accessed via mobile apps, helps to reduce the amount of paper that is used and the amount of trash that is produced.

Carbon Footprint Calculators: Travelers can use internet tools to assess their own carbon footprint, which raises awareness of the negative influence their trips have on the environment.

Mobile Payments: Mobile payment systems provide tourists with the ease of conducting cashless purchases, hence decreasing the need for conventional forms of currency such as cash and coins.

Information on Sustainable Travel Websites and mobile apps geared toward travelers frequently feature sections on sustainable travel practices, responsible vacationing, and environmentally conscious lodgings and activities.

Travel Reviews and input Travel review websites like as TripAdvisor and Yelp give tourists the opportunity to share their experiences and provide input on the environmental policies and procedures of businesses and locations.

New technologies are having a significant impact on ecotourism.

Artificial Intelligence (AI): AI can assist in the prediction of tourism trends, the optimization of travel itineraries, and the provision of tailored travel suggestions that place an emphasis on environmentally responsible options.

Blockchain: The technology behind blockchain has the potential to improve the travel industry's level of transparency and traceability. It can be put to use for ensuring the safety and openness of carbon offset schemes, validating sustainable practices, and tracing the origins of environmentally friendly items.

Internet of Things (IoT): Devices connected to the IoT can be put to use for the administration and monitoring of resources and the environment. The use of less resources can be made possible by the installation of sensor-equipped public transit, energy-efficient lighting, and smart waste bins.

5G Connectivity: High-speed 5G networks can enable real-time data gathering and analysis, which can improve the effectiveness of systems for managing visitors, as well as transportation and lodging.

Robotics and Automation Robotics and automation can assist with duties such as the sorting of waste, cleaning, and the handling of luggage in hotels and airports, thereby lessening the negative impact these services have on the surrounding environment.

Biometric Technology: The implementation of biometric technology at border crossings and airports can help to streamline travel procedures, hence lowering the amount of time spent waiting in line and alleviating congestion at these locations.

Technology Based on Distributed Ledgers Technology based on distributed ledgers, which is analogous to blockchain, can be utilized for the purpose of securing and transparently allocating resources and managing locations.

Concerns and Things to Take Into Account

The "digital divide" refers to the unequal distribution of access to technology around the world; as a result, this disparity might prevent underprivileged populations from taking part in initiatives to promote sustainable tourism.

Concerns Raise Themselves Regarding Individuals' Right To Privacy And Security When Personal Information Is Collected And Used Both Of These Areas Come Into Question. It is imperative that travelers have the peace of mind of knowing that their personal information is in safe hands.

E-Waste: The swift progress of technology is one factor that contributes to electronic waste, often known as e-waste, which creates problems for the environment. Important are environmentally responsible procedures for the disposal and recycling of electronic gadgets.

Dependence on Technology: Placing an excessive amount of reliance on technology can result in overdependence as well as a lack of personal touch in one's trip experience. It is necessary to strike a balance between human engagement and technological advancement.

unforeseen implications The application of technology can have unforeseen implications, such as the digital disruption of local economies, which can have a negative impact on society. To lessen the severity of these effects, thorough planning and attention are necessities.

Technology's Long-Term Prospects It is a concern that the technology industry itself will not be around for very much longer. Both the manufacturing and disposal of electronic devices have an impact not only on the environment but also on society.

The Prospects for the Development of Eco-Friendly Tourism Technology

Individualized Itineraries Focused on Sustainability: Algorithms powered by artificial intelligence will make it possible to create individualized travel itineraries that place an emphasis on sustainable practices and experiences.

Experiences of Travel in Virtual Reality VR will provide passengers with immersive travel opportunities that are favorable to the environment and allow them to virtually explore destinations and participate in cultural events.

Sustainable Mobility Solutions: The widespread implementation of electric and autonomous vehicles, as well as the development of hyperloop technology, will completely transform the transportation industry, making it both more environmentally friendly and more productive.

AI will help optimize resource allocation, including water and energy management in hotels as well as transportation and waste reduction in cities. AI will also play a role in improving supply chain management.

Blockchain for Sustainable Supply Chains: The technology behind blockchain will be used to track the origin of sustainable products in the tourism sector, such as locally manufactured souvenirs and eco-friendly hotel amenities. This will be possible because to blockchain's ability to provide immutable records.

Data-Driven Destination Management: Destination management systems will leverage big data analytics to make decisions for tourism planning and development that are driven by the data.

Platforms for Community Engagement Digital platforms will give local communities the ability to participate in tourist management and benefit from money related to tourism as a result of their involvement.

The tourist industry is undergoing a transformation as a result of the combination of technology and sustainable practices, which is offering novel ways to address environmental and social concerns.

Technology is a key factor in sustainable tourism on several fronts, including destination management, traveler behavior, and the sustainability of various modes of transportation and accommodations.

Despite the fact that there are obstacles and things to think about, the potential for a good impact is enormous. Technology that supports sustainable tourism has the potential to contribute to a lower environmental footprint, improved tourist experiences, and economic benefits for the communities in which it is implemented. By embracing and advancing technology-driven sustainability, the travel industry can create a tourism experience that is more responsible, less harmful to the environment, and more pleasurable for everyone.

5.1 Advancements in Green Technology

The development of environmentally friendly technology is more important than it has ever been in the 21st century, as the globe struggles to cope with the effects of climate change and the deterioration of the natural environment. The term "green technology," which also goes by the names "clean technology" and "eco-friendly technology," refers to an expansive spectrum of advances with the goal of mitigating the harmful effects that human activities have on the natural environment. These innovations in environmentally friendly technology are radically altering the way in which people live, work, and interact with the globe in which we find ourselves. This includes anything from sustainable agriculture and waste reduction strategies to renewable energy sources.

Green technology is not only a passing fad; it is an absolute necessity for the survival of our planet. In this piece, we will discuss the incredible strides that have been made in environmentally friendly technologies, as well as the potential they have to contribute to a more sustainable future.

Resources d'énergie renouvelables :

In the realm of environmentally friendly technology, the development of renewable energy sources has been one of the most important steps forward. In recent years, renewable sources of energy such as solar power, wind power, hydropower, and geothermal energy have gained popularity as clean alternatives to traditional fossil fuels. Solar panels, for instance, have undergone significant advancements in terms of both their efficiency and their cost, which has made them an affordable and accessible source of renewable energy for both home and commercial applications.

Wind turbines have also gotten more successful at harnessing the power of the wind to generate electricity on a big scale, and they have become more efficient in doing so.

Another essential component of the movement toward cleaner forms of energy is the research and development of new energy storage methods, such as improved battery technology. These technological advancements make it possible to store and distribute renewable energy, which guarantees a steady supply of power even when the wind and sun aren't blowing and the temperatures aren't warm enough. As a direct consequence of this, renewable forms of power are exhibiting an increasing degree of dependability and are gradually supplanting fossil fuels in the terrain of the world's energy landscape.

Vehicles Powered by Electricity

Because of recent developments in environmentally friendly technologies, the automotive industry is in the midst of a major transition. Due to the fact that they are better for the environment, electric cars (EVs) are gaining more and more consumers' attention. Electric vehicles don't emit any emissions at the tailpipe, which means they're better for the environment and less dependent on fossil fuels. Electric cars have seen improvements in both their driving range and their level of convenience as a result of technological advancements, which has led to an increase in the number of people who are considering purchasing one.

In addition to electric vehicles, the development of hydrogen fuel cell vehicles is another potentially fruitful area of research. These automobiles produce solely water vapor as a byproduct of the electricity generation process, which is accomplished through the use of hydrogen gas. This technology has a lot of promise for a more environmentally friendly transportation future, despite the fact that the infrastructure for hydrogen fuel cell vehicles is still being developed.

Smart grids and the efficient use of energy:

The improvements brought about by green technology are not limited to the generation and utilization of energy. The implementation of intelligent power grids is causing a sea change in the administration and distribution of energy. The flow of electricity is monitored and controlled by smart grids using digital technology, which maximizes the efficiency of energy use and minimizes waste. This not only improves energy efficiency but also makes it easier to incorporate renewable energy sources like solar and wind into the system.

In addition, the use of energy-saving devices is becoming increasingly widespread in both private residences and commercial establishments. LED lighting, energy-efficient appliances, and smart thermostats are just a few examples of ways to reduce one's energy consumption. These solutions not only lower energy usage but also result in cost savings for end users, which is a major benefit.

Agriculture that is Environmentally Sound:

Agriculture is a significant contributor to a number of environmental problems, including deforestation, contamination of water sources, and emissions of greenhouse gases. However, developments in environmentally friendly technology are making it easier to cope with these challenges. The negative effects that food production has on the surrounding environment are being mitigated by sustainable agricultural technologies such as vertical farming and precision farming.

The use of data and technology in agriculture is known as precision farming, and it aims to maximize agricultural yields while reducing the amount of resources consumed. It features tractors equipped with GPS navigation, drones, and soil sensors that provide farmers with the ability to make educated choices regarding planting, irrigation, and the application of fertilizer. The practice of vertical farming, on the other hand, entails cultivating plants indoors in stacked layers, while utilizing as little space and water as possible. Not only can these techniques boost overall food production, but they also lessen the requirement for potentially hazardous pesticides and herbicides.

Reduce Your Waste and Recycle What You Can:

Recycling and waste prevention are two further areas in which great progress can be made thanks to green technology. The amount of waste that is being sent to landfills is being cut down with the help of innovative recycling methods such as chemical recycling and technology that convert waste into electricity. Chemical recycling, for instance, can transform discarded plastic into its constituent parts, so enabling the material to be repurposed for use in the production of brand-new goods. The environmental impact of landfills can be mitigated through the use of waste-to-energy technologies such as incineration and gasification, which transform garbage into usable forms of energy.

In addition, the development of materials that are biodegradable and packaging that is sustainable is helping to reduce the environmental imprint that consumer items have. These materials decompose through natural processes, hence lowering the total amount of waste in the environment that is not biodegradable.

Technologies for the Purification of Water:

It is a fundamental human right to have access to water that is both clean and safe to drink.

The problems of water pollution and dearth are being alleviated by advances in environmentally friendly technology. These issues are being met by developments in areas such as sophisticated water filtration systems and desalination technology, which are giving solutions.

The removal of contaminants from water sources can be accomplished by more sophisticated filtering systems by a combination of physical, chemical, and biological processes. This technique is essential for the purification of drinking water as well as the treatment of wastewater. The process of desalination, on the other hand, involves removing salt and other contaminants from seawater in order to render it fit for human consumption and irrigation use. These technologies are especially useful in areas that are arid and have a limited supply of freshwater supplies.

Building with less impact on the environment and sustainable architecture:

The construction industry is increasingly adopting green building and sustainable architecture principles in an effort to lessen the negative impact that buildings have on the surrounding environment. These practices put an emphasis on reducing waste, conserving resources, and using energy in an efficient manner. Materials that are better for the environment, such as those that can be recycled or maintained indefinitely, are increasingly being used in the construction of eco-friendly buildings.

Buildings are also beginning to incorporate passive design features, such as natural lighting and ventilation, in an effort to reduce the amount of artificial heating and cooling that is required. Insulation is enhanced and urban heat island effects are mitigated by the use of green roofs and walls, both of which are covered in plant. In addition, the idea of "net-zero energy buildings," which are structures that create the same amount of energy as they consume, is becoming more practical as a result of the incorporation of renewable energy sources and designs that are more energy efficient.

Transportation That Is Kind to the Environment:

Electric automobiles and vehicles powered by hydrogen fuel cells are just two examples of green technology. Other environmentally friendly innovations, such as environmentally responsible public transit systems and bike-sharing programs, are currently making their way into the transportation industry. Several municipalities have begun investing in electric buses and trams, which will result in less emissions and lower levels of noise pollution. Bike sharing programs encourage people to cycle as a form of transportation because it is good for their health and the environment.

Additionally, the research and development of environmentally friendly aviation technologies is gaining momentum.

Investigations are being conducted into the development of hybrid and electric aircraft, and the aviation industry is looking into alternative fuels that generate fewer pollutants.

Monitoring of the Environment and Analyses of the Data:

The accumulation and examination of environmental data are intrinsically linked to the development of environmentally friendly technologies. Monitoring the effects of climate change, deforestation, changes in the quality of air and water, and the attempts to conserve animals all make use of remote sensing technologies, satellite imagery, and sensors. These methods, which are driven by data, offer insightful information that might be useful to scholars, politicians, and environmentalists.

In order to evaluate and comprehend the huge volumes of environmental data that are being collected, researchers are turning to data analysis, artificial intelligence, and machine learning techniques. This makes it possible for more precise predictions and decisions to be made, which is helpful in the management of natural disasters, the preservation of natural resources, and the reduction of the effects of climate change.

Policy on the Environment and Environmental Advocacy:

The advancement of environmentally friendly technology is having an impact not just on environmental policy but also on environmental advocacy initiatives. Governments and international organizations are creating legislation and incentives to promote the adoption of environmentally friendly technology as the benefits of these technologies become increasingly apparent along with their viability. A few examples of policy measures include financial incentives for the use of renewable energy sources, systems for trading emissions, and increased rigor in environmental regulation.

In addition, advocacy groups and grassroots movements are gaining ground in their efforts to promote environmentally friendly behaviors and technologies. The growth of teenage climate activism, led by figures such as Greta Thunberg, has brought global attention to the urgency of tackling environmental challenges and embracing green technology. This attention has brought about a shift in attitudes and policies around the world.

Concerns and Things to Take Into Account:

The cost of developing and implementing green technology can be high, which can be a barrier to their use, particularly in economically depressed areas of the world.

Infrastructure: The shift toward environmentally friendly technologies frequently necessitates considerable infrastructure renovations and modifications, which can be logistically challenging and time-consuming to implement.

Availability of Resources: Certain environmentally friendly technology, such as lithium-ion batteries, are reliant on uncommon elements. In order to maintain a constant supply, it is necessary to find recycling methods and sustainable sources of supply.

Barriers Caused by Technology Despite the constant progress made in environmentally friendly technology, researchers and engineers continue to run into technological obstacles that need to be conquered.

Behavioural Modification: The widespread adoption of environmentally friendly technologies frequently necessitates that people and communities make modifications to their routines and practices, which might be greeted with opposition.

The world we live in is undergoing a profound transformation as a result of developments in environmentally friendly technology, which raises the possibility of a future that is both more sustainable and more environmentally conscientious. These advancements can be found in a variety of fields, including agriculture, transportation, energy, and waste management, to name a few. The international society is currently confronted with the urgent difficulties of climate change, the depletion of resources, and the destruction of the environment; yet, green technology offers a way ahead.

To realize the full potential of green technology, however, not only does additional research and development need to be conducted, but also widespread adoption of the technology and a commitment to it on the part of individuals as well as institutions. It is imperative that governments, businesses, and individuals work together to put into action policies, investments, and behaviors that put the long-term health of our planet and its inhabitants first.

It is crucial that we continue to be diligent and proactive in our efforts to safeguard the environment, especially as we continue to watch the emergence of environmentally friendly technology. The developments that are discussed in this article show that we now possess the resources and the knowledge necessary to make the planet a more sustainable place. The question that has to be answered is whether or not we have the willpower to make effective use of them and secure a better and more sustainable future for future generations.

5.2 Digital Platforms for Sustainable Travel Planning

In an era in which the effects of travel on the environment are becoming a growing source of worry, digital platforms have arisen as a ray of hope for the planning of environmentally responsible travel. These platforms offer travelers the information, tools, and resources they need to make decisions that are environmentally responsible while they are adventuring across the world. These digital solutions are at the forefront of changing the way people plan their journeys and the way they experience those journeys in light of the ever-increasing focus placed on environmentally friendly practices.

Travelers may minimize their environmental footprint, support local communities, and develop a greater appreciation for the world's different cultures and ecosystems with the assistance of digital platforms that facilitate the planning of sustainable vacations. These platforms are really helpful tools. The following is a more in-depth examination of the function and relevance of these platforms:

Information on the location, as well as environmentally responsible alternatives:

These platforms' principal purpose is to supply tourists with detailed information on their destinations, which is one of their primary functions. This comprises information regarding the social, cultural, and environmental elements of a particular location. Travelers have access to information on a variety of topics, including well-known tourist destinations, hotels that are friendly to the environment, regional food, and more.

In addition to this, these platforms frequently include alternatives that encourage environmentally responsible travel choices. For example, they may recommend going to places that are less crowded and friendlier to the environment, which will help alleviate the strain that is placed on sites that already receive an excessive amount of tourism. These tips educate tourists so that they can make decisions that are better for the environment and the communities they visit.

Calculators of One's Carbon Footprint:

Carbon footprint calculators are commonly included on digital platforms that promote sustainable travel. These calculators give tourists the ability to assess the emissions that are related with their trips. These tools take into account a variety of factors, including modes of transportation, types of accommodations, and types of activities. When passengers are aware of their carbon footprint, they are better equipped to make decisions that reduce their impact on the environment, such as selecting travel options with a lower carbon footprint.

Booking Information for Eco-Friendly Lodging:

There are many online portals that provide booking services for eco-friendly hotels and other accommodations. These include eco-lodges, sustainable hotels, and vacation rentals that have earned green certifications from various organizations. The vacation rental options available to guests now include those that prioritize conservation of natural resources and the proper management of water and energy resources. Tourists can provide direct support to businesses that are devoted to sustainability simply by selecting these alternatives.

Alternatives for Transportation:

Platforms for environmentally responsible travel offer a plethora of information on various modes of transportation. They may suggest environmentally friendly modes of transportation, such as electric buses or trains, and offer advice on how individuals can minimize their individual carbon footprints by carpooling or taking public transportation more frequently. When it is necessary to use one's own private transportation, these individuals frequently recommend either carpooling or renting electric or hybrid vehicles.

Exchanges of cultures and involvement in local communities:

Travel isn't only about going to different locations; it's also about being involved with the communities and cultures of the areas you visit. Platforms that promote sustainable travel frequently place an emphasis on responsible tourism and offer insights into the traditions, customs, and etiquette of local communities. They encourage travelers to interact with local communities in a manner that is courteous and meaningful, so helping local economy while simultaneously fostering cultural interchange.

Activities That Are Kind to the Environment

The scope of digital platforms dedicated to sustainable travel extends far beyond the simple act of recommending locations and hotels. They also offer information on activities that are sustainable and kind to the environment, such as going trekking in protected regions, participating in wildlife conservation experiences, or finding opportunities to volunteer. It is possible for tourists to select vacation activities that are congruent with their beliefs and make a good contribution to the preservation of the local environment.

Responsible Tourism in Wildlife Areas:

The problem of unethical wildlife tourism needs to be addressed, as it is one of the most important aspects of sustainable vacation planning. Many online resources are now teaching tourists about the potential dangers of engaging with wild animals that are kept in confinement and promoting alternatives that are more morally sound, such as watching wild animals in their natural habitats.

Responsible Decisions Regarding Food:

Platforms that promote sustainable travel frequently emphasize how important it is to patronize local food sources that are also sustainable. They might suggest farm-to-table restaurants, food vendors on the street, or cooking workshops that teach tourists about the regional cuisine and the ingredients used in it. Not only does this help the local farmers and food producers, but it also helps minimize the carbon footprint that is involved with the shipping of food.

Tourism that is based on local communities:

Digital platforms that promote sustainable travel encourage community-based tourism projects. These programs aim to empower local communities and assist them in benefiting from tourism in a manner that is responsible. There are chances for tourists to stay with local families, take part in cultural exchanges, and contribute to community development projects all over the world.

Blogging about sustainable travel and creating content generated by users:

On these sites, you'll frequently find user-generated material, like blogs and vlogs from sustainable travel enthusiasts. People who travel share their experiences of traveling in a way that is good for the environment, as well as their ideas and advice, in the hopes of motivating other people to travel more responsibly.

5.3 The Influence of Artificial Intelligence and Big Data

Both Artificial Intelligence (AI) and Big Data have emerged as two revolutionary forces in the world of technology, as well as in the world of business and society in general. The convergence of these two fields has resulted in breakthroughs and discoveries on a scale that has never been seen before, fundamentally altering the ways in which we work, live, and make choices. The impact of artificial intelligence and big data is significant, and it can be seen in almost every facet of our everyday life.

Industries That Are Revolutionizing the World:

The change of a variety of different businesses is one of the most obvious effects that artificial intelligence and big data have had. There has been a fundamental change in the way that businesses in the healthcare, financial, transportation, and industrial industries carry out their operations and provide their services. For instance, in the medical field, AI-driven diagnostics and predictive analytics make use of enormous databases to enhance patient outcomes while simultaneously lowering associated expenses. In the world of finance, artificial intelligence algorithms are employed for a variety of purposes, including the identification of fraudulent activity, trading, and the provision of individualized financial advice.

Individualization of content and the user experience:

The way in which businesses communicate with their customers has been fundamentally transformed by AI and Big Data. Companies have the ability to create highly tailored experiences by utilizing insights produced by data. Online merchants utilize recommendation algorithms to make product suggestions for customers based on their purchase history, browsing behavior, and demographic information. These algorithms take into account the user's browsing history as well. Artificial intelligence is used by streaming companies like Netflix to make recommendations of movies and episodes to users based on their viewing history. Not only does this customisation make the user experience better, but it also increases consumer engagement and loyalty.

Improved Capacity for Making Decisions:

Decision-making has been enhanced across all sectors as a result of Big Data and AI. By analyzing massive datasets, businesses are able to get useful insights about the patterns of the market, the behavior of consumers, and the effectiveness of their operations. This translates to better strategic planning, risk assessment, and resource allocation in the world of business. In addition, predictive analytics backed by AI can anticipate future occurrences with an impressive degree of accuracy, enabling businesses to take preventative measures.

Improvements Made in Healthcare:

The convergence of artificial intelligence and large amounts of data has brought about a revolution in the medical industry in ways that were previously unimaginable. A more accurate diagnosis can be made by medical professionals, disease outbreaks can be predicted, and even individualized treatment regimens can be developed based on a patient's genetic profile thanks to the ability to analyze enormous databases. In the field of drug development, machine learning algorithms have been deployed, which has substantially sped up the process of identifying molecules that may have therapeutic applications. Wearable health trackers are one example of an AI-powered medical technology that can monitor patient health in real time and provide users with the information they need to make more educated decisions about their medical care.

Sustainability in Relation to the Environment:

Artificial intelligence and large amounts of data are also playing an important part in the effort to solve environmental problems. Insights driven by data are beneficial to initiatives relating to the management of resources, climate change, and conservation. For instance, climate modeling is dependent on enormous datasets and artificial intelligence algorithms in order to forecast weather patterns and evaluate the long-term influence that human activities has on the ecosystem. AI is also utilized in precision agriculture, where it helps to maximize agricultural yields while simultaneously minimizing resource usage and waste.

Cities and infrastructure that are smart:

The idea of smart cities makes use of artificial intelligence (AI) and large amounts of data to produce urban environments that are more productive, sustainable, and livable. IoT sensors are able to collect data in real time regarding the flow of traffic, the consumption of energy, and the conditions of the environment. This information is processed by AI in order to improve public transit, lessen the impact of congestion, and cut energy use. The implementation of smart city initiatives improves the planning and maintenance of urban infrastructure, which in turn contributes to the general well-being of urban inhabitants.

Instruction and Distance Learning:

The landscape of education has been altered by AI and Big Data, making it possible to have more personalized and adaptive learning experiences. AI is being implemented into educational systems so that it can assess data on student performance, pinpoint areas in which individuals require assistance, and deliver individualized learning materials. This strategy gives students the freedom to learn at their own pace while also ensuring they get the support they require, which ultimately leads to better educational outcomes.

Employment and the Working Population:

The workforce is not immune to the effects of artificial intelligence and big data. Even though there is anxiety that automation would cause jobs to be lost, the reality is that these technologies will also provide new work opportunities. Vacancies abound in the fields of artificial intelligence (AI) development, data analysis, and cybersecurity. In addition, technologies that are driven by AI can expedite processes, freeing workers to concentrate on more complex and creative work. The benefits of higher production and cost-efficiency are realized by organizations.

Considerations Regarding Ethical Conduct and Personal Privacy:

The influence of AI and Big Data brings with it a host of difficulties in terms of ethics and privacy. Concerns regarding privacy and safety are raised when large amounts of personally identifiable information are gathered and used. There is also the possibility of algorithmic bias, which occurs when AI systems unintentionally discriminate against particular groups due to the use of biased training data. It is a continuing process, but these concerns need to be addressed and ethical norms need to be established for AI and big data.

Possibilities for the Future:

The impact of these technologies is likely to increase even more as the algorithms underlying AI get more complex and as big data continues to amass more and more information. The emergence of artificial intelligence (AI) in creative domains, such as art and music, has the potential to disrupt and alter established human-centric businesses.

Both the transportation industry and the manufacturing sector are on the cusp of being revolutionized by autonomous vehicles and robots powered by artificial intelligence. It is possible that the future could bring about breakthroughs in natural language processing, which will make the connection between humans and machines more fluid and natural.

Chapter 6

Community Engagement and Empowerment

Participation in community life and individual empowerment are critical elements in achieving sustainable development, maintaining social cohesion, and enhancing the well-being of society as a whole. These ideas revolve around the active participation of individuals and groups in the process of decision-making, the resolution of problems, and the growth of their own communities. In the course of this in-depth investigation, we will delve into the complexities of community engagement and empowerment, including their relevance, methods, problems, and case studies that highlight their potential for bringing about positive change.

A Better Understanding of Community Participation and Empowerment
How to Define Participation in the Community

The term "community engagement" refers to the process of involving members of a community in the design, implementation, and assessment of initiatives, projects, or policies that have a direct impact on their lives. It includes a wide variety of actions, including consultation and collaboration, partnership and shared leadership, and more. Participation in community activities is done with the intention of ensuring that the viewpoints and requirements of the community are recognized and incorporated into the decision-making processes.

The Meaning of the Term "Community Empowerment"

On the other side, community empowerment refers to the process of providing individuals and communities with the information, resources, and self-confidence necessary for them to reclaim control of their lives, make decisions based on accurate information, and bring about positive change. Empowerment is more than just participation; it also encourages a sense of ownership and self-determination among members of the community, giving them the ability to direct their own destinies and futures.

The Importance of Involvement in, and Empowerment of, Local Communities
Increasing Cohesion Within the Community

Participation in community life and the empowerment of its members are both necessary components in the construction of communities that are robust and resilient. These techniques generate a sense of belonging and shared responsibility among participants by giving them a voice in the decision-making process. Because of this, social cohesion is increased, which in turn leads to a reduction in crime, improved health outcomes, and an overall improvement in the well-being of the community.

Meeting the Demands of the Community

To guarantee that decisions are in line with the actual requirements of a community, engagement and empowerment are both essential. This individualized approach assists in the effective distribution of available resources as well as the development of solutions that are adapted to the specific circumstances. When trying to find solutions to problems ranging from education and healthcare to housing and infrastructure, having knowledge and perspectives from the local community can be extremely helpful.

Promoting an Attitude of Inclusivity

Engagement in the community and empowerment of its members both promote inclusion by ensuring that underrepresented or underprivileged groups are afforded a voice and a place at the table. By incorporating a wide variety of points of view, we may produce solutions that are both more thorough and successful. When it comes to tackling issues of equity and social justice, the importance of this inclusivity cannot be overstated.

Fostering an Attitude Towards Long-Term Sustainability

The concept of sustainability is an essential part of a thriving community. Sustainable development is supported by community engagement and empowerment, which enables communities to make decisions that place a higher priority on the long-term environmental, economic, and social sustainability of their communities. The ability to make judgments based on accurate information can lead to improved resource management and less damage to the environment.

Fostering Health and Happiness in Both Individuals and Communities

Particularly important to the process of bettering the health of people as well as the general state of the community as a whole is the concept of empowerment. It encourages a sense of self-efficacy, which in turn leads to improved mental health and higher levels of self-esteem.

Empowered communities as a whole have a greater likelihood of cooperating with one another to overcome shared difficulties, which will ultimately result in improved living circumstances and possibilities.

Strategies for Participation in and Empowerment of the Community

Making decisions through group participation

In a process known as participatory decision-making, people of the community are invited to take part in debates and votes regarding various policies, projects, or programs. This approach may take the form of public hearings, consultations, citizen juries, or participatory budgeting, among other possible approaches. The goal is to inspire thoughtful consideration as well as to include the voices and perspectives of individuals whose lives will be impacted by the decision.

Increasing One's Capacity

The process of capacity building, which focuses on giving individuals and communities with the knowledge and skills necessary to make informed decisions and take action, is often the means by which empowerment can be attained. Training in leadership, problem-solving, financial literacy, and other essential skills may be included in this type of instruction. Building people's capacities enables them to participate more actively in the process of community development.

The ABCD model, which stands for asset-based community development

ABCD is a strategy for community engagement that focuses on locating and utilizing the existing resources and advantages that are present in a community as part of its overall mission. ABCD focuses on the good characteristics and resources that people of the community have, as opposed to merely addressing the community's deficiencies. Communities have the potential to work together to bring about positive change if they acknowledge and make use of the resources at their disposal.

Organizing in the Community

Community organizing is a method that draws individuals together so that they may jointly advocate for their interests and address problems that are shared by a group. It frequently includes activities such as community gatherings, grass-roots movements, and campaigns aiming at bringing about social or political change. Individuals can acquire the power to influence the policies and systems that are relevant to them by participation in community organizing.

Developing One's Social Capital

The social networks, the relationships, and the trust that exist within a community are all examples of social capital. Developing social capital in a community entails cultivating ties and trust among its people, which, when done successfully, can boost the efficiency of engagement and empowerment initiatives aimed at the community. Gatherings in the neighborhood, membership in organizations and associations, and other activities can all help to build social capital.

Obstacles & Obstacles along the Way

Inadequate Access to Resources

There may be obstacles in the way of successful involvement and empowerment for communities who have little resources. Building the capabilities of community members and making it easier for them to participate in decision-making processes often requires providing them with access to educational opportunities, technological resources, and financial resources.

Inequalities as well as Marginalization are Present

The marginalization of particular groups within a community can be the result of inequalities such as those linked to race, gender, or financial status. In order for community involvement and empowerment initiatives to be successful, one of the most important challenges that must be overcome is that of guaranteeing equitable participation.

Opposition to the Process of Change

It doesn't matter if it comes from individuals, institutions, or the power structures that are already in place; change resistance can stymie efforts to empower communities. People may be anxious about giving up control or fearful of the repercussions of upsetting the status quo. Both of these emotions are common.

Insufficient Trust

Building trust within a community is necessary in order to conduct successful engagement and empowerment activities. Trust can be damaged and future attempts can be hampered if there have been previous instances of betrayal, corruption, or poor endeavors.

Obstacles to Effective Communication

When engaging with a community, effective communication is absolutely necessary. It is possible for effective discourse and cooperation to be hampered by factors such as language difficulties, limited access to information, or poor communication methods.

Participation in community life and individual empowerment are two crucial aspects that must be addressed when constructing robust, durable, and resilient communities. These behaviors encourage inclusivity, cater to the requirements of the community, and help to strengthen social cohesion. People and communities can seize control of their destinies and become agents of positive change by employing strategies such as asset-based community development, participatory decision making, and capacity building. The transformative potential of community participation and empowerment is demonstrated by successful case studies from around the world, despite the constraints relating to resources, inequities, and resistance to change. It is possible for us to pave the way for communities that are more inclusive, egalitarian, and powerful if we acknowledge the value of these practices and strive toward overcoming the problems that are associated with them.

6.1 Community-Based Tourism Initiatives

Community-based tourism (CBT) initiatives have developed as a potent means of supporting sustainable development, protecting cultural heritage, and strengthening local communities. These goals can all be accomplished simultaneously. These projects place a strong emphasis on the active participation of community residents in the tourist industry. This enables community members to display their culture, traditions, and natural resources while simultaneously creating chances for economic growth. During this in-depth investigation, we will delve into the complexities of community-based tourism, including its relevance, benefits, and problems, as well as successful case studies from around the world.

A Better Understanding of Tourism Based on Communities

Community-based tourism is a form of sustainable tourism that incorporates local communities
in the planning, development, and management of tourism activities. Community-based tourism is also known as "sustainable tourism with a local focus." Fostering cultural interchange, environmental protection, and socio-economic development are some of the key objectives of CBT, which aims to achieve its fundamental objective of creating a good exchange between tourists and the host community. CBT places a higher priority on the well-being of the community as well as the preservation of its natural and cultural legacy, in contrast to conventional tourism, which frequently results in the exploitation of local resources and the commercialization of cultural practices.

The Importance of Tourism Programs that Focus on Local Communities
The Safekeeping of Our Cultural Traditions

CBT projects are critically important to conserving the cultural heritage of the communities in which they are implemented. These types of programs assist local communities in preserving and reviving their distinct cultural identities by drawing tourists' attention to long-standing customs, artistic and artisanal expressions, and cultural celebrations.

This preservation not only encourages a sense of pride and belonging among residents of the town, but it also contributes to the cultural enrichment experienced by visitors to the area.

Development of the Economy That Is Not Only Sustainable

CBT projects act as engines of sustainable economic growth in areas that would likely have limited prospects in the absence of these initiatives. Community members have the ability to diversify their sources of income and minimize their reliance on a single industry by participating in tourism-related activities. Some examples of these activities include homestays, local guiding, the manufacturing of handicrafts, and cultural performances. The community's overall resilience is improved as a result of the diversification of its economic base.

Protection of the Natural Environment

Ecosystems and natural resources can both benefit from community-based tourism's advocacy for their protection. Local communities are given incentives to maintain and responsibly manage their natural environments since it is recognized how important the natural surroundings are to the overall quality of the tourism experience. This typically results in the establishment of responsible tourist practices that aim to reduce the adverse effects that tourism can have on the ecosystem of the surrounding area.

Empowerment of Neighborhood and Community Groups

Community-based tourism (CBT) initiatives provide local communities more authority by instilling in them a sense of ownership and control over the tourism resources in their area. Members of the community can improve their self-assurance, leadership abilities, and ability to advocate for their own interests if they take an active role in the decision-making processes that take place inside the community and reap the economic benefits of tourism. As a result of this empowerment, there is an improvement in social cohesion within the community, as well as a stronger collective voice.

Encouragement of Mutual Compatibility Between Cultures

The development of an awareness and appreciation of other cultures is facilitated by community-based tourism. Local community members and tourists have the opportunity to exchange knowledge, beliefs, and customs with visitors from other backgrounds when they engage in conversation with tourists. This helps to build mutual respect and an awareness of other cultures. Not only does this cultural interchange make the vacation experience more meaningful, but it also contributes to the maintenance of international peace and tolerance.

Examples of Exemplary Practices in Community-Based Tourism Projects

Building People's Capabilities and Providing Training

The provision of capacity-building programs and training opportunities to community members should be the primary emphasis of CBT projects. Workshops on topics such as customer service, sustainable tourist practices, language skills, and hospitality are potential components of these programs. CBT projects make it possible for community members to actively participate in the tourism sector and to create high-quality experiences for tourists by providing them with the information and skills that are necessary for doing so.

Respect and Sensitivity Towards Other Cultures

CBT projects must always be sensitive to and respectful of different cultures in order to be successful. Visitors should be given information on local customs, traditions, and proper etiquette so that they can interact with the local community in a manner that is courteous and sensitive to the community's culture. In a similar vein, individuals of the community ought to be incentivized to share their cultural history with pride while simultaneously preserving the authenticity of their customs.

Working Together and Forming Partnerships

For community-based tourism (CBT) initiatives to be successfully implemented, collaboration and partnership among community people, local authorities, and tourism stakeholders are very necessary. A more comprehensive and inclusive approach to community-based tourism can be fostered through the cultivation of discussion, the sharing of responsibilities, and the forging of relationships that are beneficial to both parties. These collaborations may also make it easier to design tourism regulations and practices that are more environmentally friendly.

Management of Resources in a Sustainable Manner

For CBT projects to be successful over the long run, sustainable resource management is an absolutely necessary component. It is important for residents of a community to take an active role in the protection and administration of its natural and cultural resources. It is possible to contribute to the preservation of the environment and assure the continued viability of the tourism industry by putting sustainable practices into action. These activities include the management of waste, the conservation of energy, and the protection of biodiversity.

A Fair and Balanced Sharing of the Benefits

CBT programs ought to make certain that members of the community share economically beneficial outcomes in an equal manner. A more equal distribution of earnings generated by tourism can be accomplished with the help of transparent financial mechanisms, pricing techniques that are fair, and decision-making procedures that are led by the community. Through the use of this strategy, social inclusion is encouraged, and the potential for economic imbalances within the community is lessened.

Initiatives for community-based tourism face a number of challenges and have a number of limitations

There are limits on our capacity

It's possible that many communities are limited in their capacity in terms of their infrastructure,

their skills, and their resources, which can make it difficult for them to participate in tourism activities efficiently. The successful implementation of CBT efforts may face substantial hurdles as a result of limited access to training programs, technology developments, and marketing resources.

Variations in accordance with the seasons and heightened market volatility

Communities that rely significantly on tourism as a source of revenue may face difficulties as a result of the cyclical nature of tourism as well as the volatility of the market. Community-based tourism efforts can be greatly impacted in terms of their stability and sustainability if the number of tourists visiting the area fluctuates, the economy experiences a downturn, or a worldwide crisis occurs, such as a pandemic or a natural disaster.

Striking a Balance Between Commercialization and Tradition

In community-based tourism, it can be a challenging challenge to strike a healthy balance between the protection of cultural traditions and the satisfaction of commercial demands. It is possible that the pressure to modify cultural traditions in order to satisfy the preferences of tourists and the current trends in the market would result in the commercialization of culture and the watering down of truly authentic experiences offered by locals.

The Negative Effects of Overtourism on the Environment

The threat of overtourism and the environmental damage it causes is becoming an increasingly pressing issue for many communities that depend on tourism for their livelihood. It is imperative to control the amount of tourists who visit an area, reduce the ecological impact of tourism as much as possible, and put in place tourism policies and practices that are sustainable in order to lessen the detrimental effects that overtourism has on the surrounding ecosystems and communities.

It is possible for community-based tourism efforts to have a beneficial and long-lasting impact not just on the communities that are visited, but also on the tourists that come to such places.

These programs not only help to protect cultural heritage, but they also create economic opportunities, encourage the conservation of natural resources, and give local people the ability to take charge of their own futures. We can cultivate a future in which community-based tourism thrives by embracing best practices, tackling problems, and learning from successful case studies. In doing so, we can contribute to the overall well-being of communities and further the cause of fostering cross-cultural understanding and appreciation on a global scale.

6.2 The Importance of Local Engagement

The term "local engagement" refers to the active participation of individuals, organizations, and communities in the decision-making processes, activities, and development efforts that directly influence their immediate surrounds. Local engagement can also refer to the involvement of a community in the decision-making processes of larger-scale projects. It is an essential component of both efficient government and social cohesiveness, as well as environmentally sustainable growth. In the course of this investigation, we will investigate the relevance of local participation, its numerous advantages, and the ways in which it may lead to positive change at the level of the community, the region, and even the world.

Comprehension of the Role of Local Engagement

Participating in neighborhood associations and going to town hall meetings are two examples of the wide range of activities that fall under the umbrella term "local engagement." Other examples include volunteering for local initiatives and campaigning for the improvement of the community. It is founded on the principle that people and organizations need to have a say in the making of decisions that have an effect on their day-to-day lives as well as the prosperity of their communities. This idea acknowledges that those who reside in a certain location are frequently the most knowledgeable individuals regarding the requirements, challenges, and possibilities that are specific to that location.

The Importance of Participating in Community Activities

Advancing the Cause of Inclusivity

Participation at the community level is essential to inclusiveness. It guarantees that the opinions and perspectives of all members of the community, especially those who have historically been marginalized or underrepresented, are heard and included in the processes that lead to decisions being made about the community. This inclusiveness helps to establish a sense of belonging and shared responsibility, both of which are crucial for the development of communities that are both robust and diverse.

Making decisions in a productive manner

Participation at the local level leads to decision-making that is both more informed and more effective. It is more probable that decisions will be well-informed and reflective of the actual needs and goals of the community when citizens participate in defining policies and programs that directly touch their lives. This results in a more effective and focused use of resources, improved outcomes, and an increased level of satisfaction among the general population.

Facilitation of Community Empowerment

Participation at the community level gives individuals and groups the ability to shape their own futures. Members of a community can foster feelings of ownership and self-determination in themselves by taking an active role in the planning, development, and governance of their community. People are encouraged to advocate for their own interests, invest in the development of their local communities, and work together to find solutions to problems as a result of this empowerment.

Development That Is Sustainable

Participation at the neighborhood level is essential to ensuring sustainable development. We can ensure that the efforts we put into development are in line with our long-term goals of sustainability if we involve the communities where we work in the decisions that affect the environment, the economy, and society. This strategy helps communities become more resilient, lessens the influence that growth has on the environment, and minimizes the gaps that exist between different social groups.

Strengthening the Bonds of Community

Participation in meaningful activities in the community is a primary factor in social cohesion. It promotes people to engage with one another in a variety of ways, including through neighborhood associations, volunteer work, and participation in local activities. These connections help to cultivate a sense of trust and belonging, both of which are essential for lowering the incidence of criminal behavior, enhancing mental health, and bolstering the social fabric of communities.

Accountability as well as openness to information

Participation at the local level can improve both accountability and openness in governance. When communities take an active role in the decision-making process, governments and institutions are forced to answer for the consequences of their actions. The public's ability to access information, monitor progress, and examine the acts of authorities is made possible when processes and decisions are transparent. This helps to reduce the likelihood that resources will be misused and that there will be instances of corruption.

Advantages of Participating in Your Community

Informed Decision-Making Local participation results in better informed decision-making processes because it provides first-hand knowledge and insights into the needs and objectives of communities.

Community Resilience: Communities that are empowered have a greater capacity to solve difficulties and adapt to change, which fosters community resilience.

Solutions at the Grassroots: The encouragement of local interaction leads to the development of grassroots solutions that are adapted to the specific conditions that exist within a community.

Trust and Cooperation: Participation in community activities helps to foster trust and cooperation among members of the community, which in turn makes it easier for members to work together and find solutions to problems.

Economic Development: Towns and cities that have robust local participation tend to be more appealing to businesses and investors, which in turn leads to more economic activity and new employment prospects.

The degree of well-being in a community tends to be greater, crime rates are lower, and mental health outcomes are improved when the community as a whole is more engaged.

Approaches to Community Involvement

Making decisions through group participation

In the process of participatory decision-making, members of the community are invited to participate in the deliberations and choices that are made on local policies, projects, or initiatives. This can take place in the form of community discussions, town hall meetings, focus groups, or public hearings. Residents are given the opportunity to voice their thoughts and desires, which ultimately leads to decisions that are more inclusive and well-informed.

Organizing in the Community

People are brought together in the process of community organizing so that they can collectively advocate for their interests and address concerns that are common.

It frequently manifests itself as grass-roots movements, local associations, and campaigns aiming at bringing about social or political change. People have the ability to exert influence over the policies and systems that are relevant to their lives through participation in community organizing.

Volunteering in the Community

Individuals can practically engage with the communities in which they live by giving their time to volunteer work on a local level. Individuals have the ability to make a positive impact on the health of the community as well as cultivate personal ties with other people by volunteering their time and expertise to support initiatives at the community level.

Governance on a Local Scale

Participation of community members in the decision-making processes and institutions of their own communities is an essential component of local governance. Participating in local councils, boards, or committees, which have the power to influence policies and initiatives that have a direct impact on the community, may fall under this category.

Initiatives at the Local Level

Grassroots initiatives are projects and activities that are led by the community and are designed to address local concerns or achieve particular goals. These activities, which can range from programs aimed at environmental conservation to cultural events and initiatives aimed at economic development, frequently rely on the initiative and originality displayed by members of the community.

Obstacles to Overcome and Restrictions

Inadequate Access to Resources

It's possible that the required resources, including money, infrastructure, or technology, are lacking in many communities, making it difficult to support successful local engagement. For communities that are interested in actively participating in decision-making processes, having access to resources might be a big barrier to overcome.

Unevennesses and Disparities

Disparities in local engagement can be caused by inequalities connected to factors such as racial background, level of income, level of education, and geographic location. It can be difficult to establish truly inclusive decision-making since vulnerable and marginalized groups frequently experience larger impediments to participation than other groups.

Opposition to the Process of Change

Efforts to involve local communities might be hampered by people's unwillingness to change, whether they come from individuals, institutions, or the existing power structures. People may be anxious about giving up control or fearful of the repercussions of upsetting the status quo. Both of these emotions are common.

Problems With Trust

Building and sustaining trust within a community is one of the most important steps toward achieving successful local participation. The erosion of trust and the impediment it places in the way of future involvement efforts might be caused by previous experiences of betrayal, corruption, or failed activities.

Obstacles to Effective Communication

In order to be successful in local engagement, effective communication is essential. It is possible for effective discourse and cooperation to be hampered by factors such as language difficulties, limited access to information, or poor communication methods.

Participation at the local level is essential to efficient governance, as well as to ecologically sound and socially cohesive growth. It encourages diversity, it gives communities more power, and it leads to more informed and better decision-making. We can cultivate a future in which local participation thrives by embracing best practices, tackling problems, and learning from successful case studies. This will allow us to contribute to the overall well-being of communities and provide individuals the ability to take charge of their own destinies. When it comes down to it, the significance of local engagement in the process of constructing communities that are more robust, more inclusive, and more resilient at the local, regional, and global levels cannot be understated.

6.3 Economic Empowerment Through Sustainable Tourism

Recent years have seen a rise in interest in sustainable tourism as a potent instrument for economic empowerment, the promotion of responsible travel, the preservation of natural resources, and the enhancement of community development. The goal of this approach to tourism is to provide economic benefits while also protecting the environment and preserving the culture of the local area. It is a comprehensive strategy. We will look into the relevance of economic empowerment through sustainable tourism, as well as its many benefits, obstacles, and successful case studies that highlight its transformative potential during this investigation.

Gaining an Understanding of the Role of Sustainable Tourism in Economic Empowerment

Economic empowerment through sustainable tourism is the process of using tourism as a driver for local economic growth and empowerment while also limiting the negative affects on the environment and protecting cultural heritage. This process is referred to as "economic empowerment through sustainable tourism." It places an emphasis on responsible and ethical travel activities, which are actions that generate economic opportunities for local people and support the long-term sustainability of destinations. The fundamental concept is to encourage economic prosperity while simultaneously developing environmental and social responsibility.

The Importance of Economic Empowerment through Environmentally Responsible Tourism

Expanding of the Area's Economy

Economic empowerment can be achieved through the practice of sustainable tourism, which results in major economic advantages for the communities that are visited. It not only helps local small and medium-sized businesses (SMEs), but it also produces money for those firms and provides employment opportunities. This rise in economic activity may result in higher wages, improved livelihoods, and a reduction in poverty in the villages that are the final destinations for tourists.

Multiple Streams of Revenue Diversification

Tourism that is environmentally responsible helps local communities diversify their economic sources. Communities become less reliant on a small number of sectors when chances are presented to residents to participate in a variety of tourism-related activities. These activities can include giving tours, producing handicrafts, and hosting visitors in their homes. The increased resilience that results from this diversification can be seen in the face of adverse environmental or economic conditions.

The protection of our earth's natural resources

Tourism practices that are sustainable emphasize the proper use of natural resources and the preservation of such resources. These methods have the goals of preserving ecosystems, reducing the environmental impact of tourism, and ensuring the continued viability of tourist sites over the long term. Economic empowerment through environmentally responsible tourism helps to preserve the natural resources that are attractive to tourists in the first place. This is accomplished by protecting the environment.

Protecting Our Cultural Heritage

The protection of cultural heritage is a necessary prerequisite for achieving economic empowerment through environmentally responsible tourism.

It respects the local rituals, customs, and cultural expressions and works to prevent tourism from commercializing or watering down certain aspects of the culture. Instead, it gives communities the opportunity to exhibit their culture in a way that is genuine and respectful, so conserving the culture's singularity.

Improved Capacity of Both Infrastructure and Services

The economic benefits that are generated from ecotourism can lead to improvements in infrastructure and public services in the towns that are host to this type of tourism. It is possible that as a result of an increase in the number of tourists who visit a certain area, the local governments and authorities will invest more money in various forms of infrastructure, such as roads, healthcare facilities, and educational institutions. This will result in an improvement in the citizens' quality of life.

Empowerment of Neighborhood and Community Groups

Local communities achieve economic empowerment through sustainable tourism because it

gives them a sense of ownership and control over their tourism resources, which in turn gives them the authority to make decisions about those resources. Individuals and communities are granted the opportunity to take an active role in the decision-making processes that affect them, to advocate for their interests, and to have a say in the development of their community.

Exchange Between Different Cultures

Tourism that does not harm the environment encourages communication and understanding between different cultures. Local community members and tourists have the opportunity to exchange knowledge, beliefs, and customs with visitors from other backgrounds when they engage in conversation with tourists. This helps to build mutual respect and an awareness of other cultures. Not only does this cultural interchange make the vacation experience more meaningful, but it also contributes to the maintenance of international peace and tolerance.

Advantages of Financial Independence through Ecologically Responsible Tourism

Work Creation: Sustainable tourism creates work opportunities, particularly for persons and communities that are underserved and for those who have a limited amount of formal education.

improved Incomes and Economic Empowerment As a result of its support for local companies, craftspeople, and service providers, it results in improved incomes for those involved.

Sustainable tourism promotes responsible resource management as well as cultural preservation, which helps to protect the distinctive qualities that make a destination so appealing to visitors.

Increased Investment in Infrastructure and Public Services: Economic growth brought about by tourism frequently results in increased investment in infrastructure and public services, which in turn improves the citizens' general quality of life.

Increase in Economic Resilience Resulting from Reduced Dependence on a Single Industry Tourism helps increase economic resilience by diversifying sources of revenue and reducing reliance on a single industry.

Intercultural Communication: Tourism acts as a catalyst for intercultural communication and mutual understanding, which in turn contributes to increased global harmony and heightened cultural awareness.

The Role of Ecotourism in the Promotion of Methods of Economic Empowerment

Tourism that is Based on Communities

Community-based tourism is a form of tourism that encourages active participation from local communities and provides benefits to such areas. This strategy involves staying at community members' homes, attending cultural performances, and going on guided excursions conducted by locals. Local communities can develop economic opportunities and preserve their cultural legacy at the same time by cultivating direct relationships with tourists.

Ecotourism

Ecotourism is a form of responsible tourism that has a primary emphasis on preserving natural habitats and wild animal populations. It invites people to experience and enjoy the natural world while simultaneously reducing the harm that tourists have on the ecosystem. The profits made from ecotourism are frequently invested in projects that serve to maintain and preserve natural areas and provide financial assistance to the communities that are located there.

Ecologically Sound Lodging Options

Eco-lodges and green hotels are two examples of types of sustainable lodging that adhere to ecologically friendly business practices and frequently purchase their supplies and services from local businesses. These accommodations contribute to economic empowerment and environmental conservation by providing employment opportunities, by supporting local suppliers, and by implementing environmentally friendly measures.

The Tourism of Culture

Cultural tourism is a type of tourism that focuses on highlighting the historical, artistic, historical, and heritage characteristics of a particular location. Visitors who participate in regional traditions, such as those involving art, music, and cuisine, help preserve cultural heritage while also creating economic advantages for regional craftspeople, cultural performers, and local businesses.

Agricultural Tourism

Agritourism is when agricultural pursuits are combined with tourist activities. Farming, harvesting, and other agricultural experiences are available for visitors to participate in, so providing support for local farmers and rural economies. Farm tours, cooking lessons, and the selling of locally produced commodities are common components of agritourism enterprises.

Obstacles to Overcome and Restrictions

Excessive tourism

If the expansion of tourism is not properly controlled, it may result in overtourism, which can lead to traffic congestion, the destruction of natural areas, and adverse effects on the communities that are directly affected.

The Commercialization of Culture

There is a possibility of cultural commercialization, which occurs when local customs are turned into nothing more than tourist attractions, so watering down their genuineness and relevance.

Influence on the Environment

If it is not carefully managed, tourism can have a negative effect on the environment, which can have repercussions for ecosystems, wildlife, and natural resources. Sustainable tourism is not exempt from this possibility.

Losses to the Economy

A significant obstacle is economic leakage, which describes the situation in which the wealth generated by tourism does not trickle down to assist the local communities but instead mostly benefits huge firms or foreign groups.

Variations Caused by the Seasons

There are many vacation spots that experience seasonal shifts in the number of visitors, which can result in income insecurity for the surrounding communities.

Economic empowerment through environmentally responsible tourism has a huge potential to bring about positive change in the communities it serves while also helping to protect the natural and cultural resources of the places it visits. Sustainable tourism may both provide economic benefits and contribute to the long-term well-being of communities if it prioritizes the preservation of cultural heritage, the protection of natural environments, and the support of behaviors that are environmentally sustainable. The transformative force of economic empowerment through sustainable tourism is obvious in numerous case studies from throughout the world. Challenges such as overtourism and cultural commodification need to be addressed, but the power of economic empowerment through sustainable tourism is clear. We can create a future in which local communities flourish, natural resources are conserved, and cultural diversity is cherished through the practice of sustainable tourism if we continue to push for responsible travel and embrace it as a core value.

Chapter 7

Challenges and Barriers to Sustainability

In recent years, sustainability has emerged as a popular buzzword, which reflects a growing worldwide awareness of the environmental, social, and economic difficulties that humanity is currently facing. The idea of sustainability covers a far wider range of topics than only protecting the environment for future generations, despite the fact that this is one of its most common associations. The concept of sustainability refers to the peaceful coexistence of humans, the planet, and financial gain. Obtaining sustainability is not an easy task because there are a great deal of obstacles and problems that stand in the way of growth. This essay dives into the myriad difficulties and roadblocks that stand in the way of achieving sustainability. It provides a thorough examination of these hurdles and makes some recommendations for how these issues might be overcome.

Consumption of Resources

The exhaustion of natural resources is one of the most significant obstacles standing in the way of sustainability. The way that we now consume is putting a pressure on the few resources that our planet has to provide, such as its fossil fuels, minerals, and freshwater. An excessive reliance on nonrenewable resources depletes those resources at a rate that is greater than the rate at which they can naturally regenerate, which makes it unsustainable over the long term.

Reduce dependency on fossil fuels by making the switch to renewable energy sources such as solar, wind, and hydroelectric power. The solution is to make this transition. Reducing resource depletion can also be accomplished by putting into practice more effective resource management methods, such as recycling and reusing materials.

Changes in Climate

The emission of greenhouse gases into the atmosphere is the primary driver of climate change, which has become an urgent issue of concern. Temperatures around the world are on the rise, which, along with extreme weather and rising sea levels, poses a huge threat to ecosystems and human culture. Changes in climate make many of the challenges to sustainable living even more difficult and also create their own obstacles.

The solution is to cut greenhouse gas emissions by embracing clean energy technology, instituting carbon pricing, and increasing the availability of environmentally responsible modes of transportation. For the purpose of mitigating the effects of climate change, adaptation methods, such as the construction of infrastructure that is resilient, are absolutely necessary.

Too many people

The rate at which the global population is expanding places a burden on the world's natural resources, accelerates the degradation of the environment, and makes it more difficult to ensure that people have equal access to opportunities and resources. The availability of food, water, and energy are all put under significant stress due to the world's growing population.

The solution is to encourage education and family planning, particularly for women, as previous research has shown that educated women have a tendency to have fewer children than uneducated women. It may be possible to reduce the negative impacts of overpopulation by promoting sustainable urban design and resolving existing disparities.

It's a Pollution

Pollution in the air, water, and soil poses significant dangers to the health of ecosystems as well as to people. Pollutants are released into the environment as a result of industrial activities, transportation, and agricultural practices; these pollutants contribute to climate change and have a negative impact on biodiversity.

The solution is to impose stringent environmental laws and standards in order to cut down on emissions and discharges. To cut down on pollution, it is important to encourage the development of cleaner technology and sustainable agricultural practices.

Loss of Biological Diversity

The instability of ecosystems and the welfare of humans are both put in jeopardy by the loss of biodiversity. The loss of biodiversity is caused by the destruction of habitat, pollution, overexploitation, and the introduction of exotic species. This loss has enormous repercussions for agricultural practices, medical practices, and the overall health of ecosystems.

To maintain and restore biodiversity, the solution is to create and expand protected areas, strictly enforce laws against poaching and illegal wildlife trading, and encourage sustainable land use practices.

Inadequate Facilities and Equipment

In many areas, the infrastructure that would be required to support sustainable development is lacking. This includes having access to potable water, adequate sanitation, and dependable sources of energy. A lack of adequate infrastructure can contribute to the perpetuation of poverty and inequality.

The solution is to make investments in the development of infrastructure, particularly in places that are neglected and undeveloped. Inaccessible locations may benefit from the expansion of services made possible by novel approaches such as decentralized renewable energy systems.

Inequality on a Socioeconomic Scale

A fundamental obstacle to sustainability is seen in the existence of socioeconomic disparity. It makes poverty worse, makes it more difficult to get an education and healthcare, and reduces the number of options for professional and financial progress. A more fair division of available resources and opportunities is necessary in order to address the issue of sustainability.

The solution is to put into effect laws and programs that are geared on leveling out income and wealth disparities. Help underserved communities have access to educational opportunities and medical treatment so that they can improve their standard of living and encourage more environmentally responsible behavior.

Concerns on Both the Political and Economic Fronts

Often, powerful political and economic interests place a higher priority on short-term advantages than on the long-term sustainability of their operations. Lobbying, the influence of corporations, and political divisiveness are all factors that might work against the creation and implementation of sustainable policies.

The solution is to push for policies that place a higher priority on long-term sustainability than they do on short-term profits, encourage openness in corporate operations and politics, and place restrictions on the role of money in political processes.

A lack of consciousness as well as education

There are a lot of people that either do not understand the significance of sustainability or do not have the information or skills necessary to make sustainable decisions. Education and awareness are absolutely necessary components in the process of developing a culture of sustainability.

The solution is to encourage teaching about sustainable practices in institutions of higher learning as well as through public awareness campaigns. Encourage learning that continues throughout one's life and create rewards for making environmentally responsible decisions.

Barriers of a Cultural and Behavioral Nature

The individual behaviors of people and the cultural norms that they uphold can be substantial obstacles to sustainability. Many times, efforts to lessen environmental impacts are hampered by things like consumerism, decisions that are driven by convenience, and opposition to change.

The solution is to foster cultural shifts that place a priority on sustainable living and to stimulate behavior change through the use of incentives, such as tax incentives for green technologies and sustainable products. Make sustainable options more readily available and more reasonably priced.

Vacancies in Technology and Innovative Capabilities

The availability of environmentally friendly technology and breakthroughs may be restricted in some areas, which slows the spread of these developments. Inequalities in access to clean energy, clean water, and healthcare can be made worse by discrepancies in technological capability.

The solution is to encourage innovation by investing in research and development, to offer financial incentives for the creation of environmentally friendly technologies, and to provide support for the transfer of knowledge to developing regions.

Global Supply Chains That Are Complicated

Because of their global character, supply chains can make it difficult to track the environmental and social implications of the goods and services they produce. The complexity of supply networks can play a role in the development of practices that are not sustainable.

The solution is to increase customer knowledge, implement certification systems, and comply with legislation in order to increase supply chain transparency. In order to promote sustainable sourcing and production techniques among businesses, encourage their adoption.

Inconsistencies in the Policy

Confusion and inefficiency in sustainability initiatives can be caused by policies that are inconsistent on all levels, including the local, national, and international levels.

Progress can be slowed down when there is a lack of coordination and when there are regulations that contradict one another.

The solution is to encourage more policy alignment and coordination at all of the different levels of government. Through the use of agreements and treaties, promote international collaboration on issues pertaining to global sustainability.

Opposition to the Process of Change

Whether it comes from individuals, businesses, or governments, resistance to change is a common occurrence in all three settings. The dread of undergoing sustainable adjustments can be stymied by worries about the economy, their jobs, and their cultural ties.

Solution: Include stakeholders in the planning and decision-making processes, as well as discussions on the benefits of sustainability, and engage stakeholders in these conversations. Create transition strategies that take into account both the economy and society's concerns.

A failure to plan for the long term.

Thinking in the short term, whether it be motivated by political cycles, commercial profit objectives, or individual goals, can be detrimental to the planning and implementation of long-term sustainability.

The solution is to incentivize the creation of long-term sustainability goals and plans that go beyond the present political or economic cycles. Establish objectives that are crystal clear and measurable, and evaluate your progress frequently.

Problems Associated with Financing

The requirement of significant investments, which is common in sustainability programs, can be a hurdle for governments, organizations, and individuals alike. The implementation of environmentally responsible policies and procedures may be hampered by limited access to available finance choices.

The solution is to develop financial structures in order to support sustainability projects. Some examples of these mechanisms include green bonds, sustainable investment funds, and public-private partnerships. Make environmentally responsible investments more attractive by offering financial incentives, such as tax exemptions and subsidies.

Regulatory Obstacles

Laws and regulations that are out of date or overly restrictive might be a barrier to sustainability efforts. In other situations, they may even act as an incentive for actions that are destructive to the environment.

To solve this problem, advocates should work to change laws and regulations that stand in the way of sustainability. Encourage national governments to match the legal systems of their countries with the aims of sustainable development.

Multiple, competing interests

It can be difficult to strike a balance between the competing interests of many parties, such as those of industry representatives and environmentalists. It is possible for competing interests to cause a standstill in the process of developing and implementing policy.

The approach is to encourage collaboration and communication among various stakeholders in order to locate areas of agreement and come up with ideas that benefit all parties involved. In the process of decision-making, it is important to encourage the participation of all relevant stakeholders.

Capabilities of the Institutions Are Restricted

It is difficult for many governments and organizations to effectively implement sustainable practices and policies because they lack the capacity to do so. The lack of enough financial and human resources can be a barrier to advancement.

The solution is to make investments in capacity building and training in order to provide organizations and governments with the knowledge and abilities necessary to drive sustainability activities. The best practices will be shared, and technical assistance will be provided as required.

Insufficient International Coordination

The problems that arise with sustainability are frequently of a global nature, and the only way to solve them is through international cooperation. The failure of nations to come together and work together to address concerns such as the loss of biodiversity and climate change can be a barrier to those efforts.

The solution is to foster international cooperation by means of forums, agreements, and organizations whose primary focus is on resolving issues relating to global sustainability. Encourage the use of diplomacy as a technique of locating common ground and finding solutions.

Threat Posed by New Technologies

Sometimes, positive innovations with the intention of advancing sustainability wind up having unanticipated and undesirable effects. The use of technologies that have not been thoroughly tested can put people's health and the environment at danger.

The solution is to establish stringent guidelines and testing procedures for newly developed technologies. Encourage the use of a cautious approach when implementing new technologies, particularly in areas where there is the potential for major harm.

The appropriation of cultures as well as their displacement

Some activities aimed at sustainability unintentionally result in the appropriation of indigenous cultures or the uprooting of indigenous tribes from their traditional grounds. This might be a roadblock in the way of effective solutions for sustainability.

The solution is to make the participation and consultation of indigenous groups a priority in all sustainability projects that may have an effect on the traditional practices or lands of these communities. The cultural history of indigenous peoples should be respected and carefully preserved.

Psychological Health and Overall Well-Being

The urgency of sustainability concerns, such as climate change, can have a significant influence on both mental health and well-being if the stress and anxiety associated with these challenges is not managed well. This can make it more difficult for individuals and communities to participate in initiatives to promote sustainability.

The solution is to increase awareness of mental health issues and support services, particularly for those individuals who are working on sustainability projects. Encourage self-care and the development of coping techniques as a means of managing the emotional toll that the challenges of sustainability can take.

Deficiencies in Data and Information

The development of and the monitoring of sustainability efforts might be hampered by data that is either inaccurate or insufficient. The absence of some types of information can make it difficult to evaluate how beneficial various programs and projects are.

Investing in the gathering, analysis, and reporting of data is the solution. Encourage transparency and the sharing of information in order to close any data gaps and make it possible for decisions to be based on evidence.

A Dearth of Motivating Factors

Individuals and corporations frequently lack the incentives necessary to adopt environmentally friendly activities. It's possible that financial incentives like tax rebates and subsidies won't be offered or that there won't be enough of them.

The solution is to institute financial incentives for environmentally responsible actions, such as the production of renewable energy or the implementation of technology that are energy efficient. In order to stimulate adoption, you should promote the economic benefits of sustainability.

To achieve sustainability, which is a complex and multi-dimensional notion, it is necessary to handle a wide variety of obstacles and challenges along the way. The challenges to sustainability are manifold and multifaceted, ranging from depletion of resources and climate change to resistance from cultural groups and discrepancies in legislation. However, a significant number of these problems are intertwined, and resolving even one of them can have positive repercussions across the full range of sustainability issues.

Changes in public policy, advances in relevant technologies, adjustments in individuals' patterns of behavior, and increased international collaboration are required to address these difficulties. There is no one-size-fits-all answer to the problem of sustainability; rather, it calls for a wide variety of initiatives that are adapted to the particular requirements and conditions of each community, region, and country.

7.1 Economic and Commercial Challenges

Because of the interconnected nature of the world, the economic and commercial issues that arise are constantly changing. These changes are brought about by a variety of sources, ranging from advances in technology to tensions in international politics. There are a variety of challenges that must be overcome by companies, entire industries, and entire economies in order to achieve growth, innovation, and long-term sustainability. For the sake of creating economic stability and preserving the prosperity of commercial enterprises, it is essential to have an understanding of these issues and work to address them. This essay explores the complexities of economic and commercial difficulties, providing insights into the diverse nature of these challenges and recommending solutions to efficiently traverse them.

Uncertainties Regarding Global Trade

Businesses that operate in a globalized market face considerable obstacles as a result of the numerous uncertainties surrounding global trade. These include trade wars, protectionist laws, and evolving international trade agreements. Tariffs and other trade obstacles can cause disruptions in supply chains, drive up costs, and impede market access, all of which contribute to an environment that is turbulent and uncertain for doing business.

The solution is to diversify supply chains so that less dependence is placed on particular countries or areas. Take an active role in lobbying and diplomatic efforts to advance trade policies that are just and inclusive. In order to reduce the negative effects of the uncertainty surrounding global trade, regional cooperation and trade agreements should be strengthened.

Altering Rates of Exchange for Different Currencies

Businesses that participate in international trade may see a large reduction in their profits if there is a lot of volatility in the currency exchange rates. A sudden shift in the exchange rate can have an effect on the cost of importing and exporting goods, which can lead to an increase in the financial risks that firms face, particularly those that operate with narrow margins of profit.

To reduce the negative effects that currency fluctuations can have, the solution is to put in place efficient risk management measures such as hedging. Gain a thorough understanding of the foreign exchange markets and keep a close eye on the major economic indicators in order to arrive at decisions on currency exposure that are well-informed.

Inflation and Unpredictability of Prices

The combined effects of inflation and price volatility can have a negative impact on consumers'

purchasing power, as well as on businesses' production costs and profit margins. Increasing rates of inflation can result in higher manufacturing costs, which may be difficult or impossible to pass on to customers, particularly in areas with strong levels of competition.

To lessen the effect that inflation has on production costs, the solution is to put effective cost management measures into action, such as stricter control of inventories and improved optimization of supply chains. Utilize pricing tactics that take into account shifts in production costs so that you can maintain your position as a competitive player in the market.

The Disruption Caused by Technology

Rapid technology breakthroughs and digital disruptions are altering industries and business structures, bringing both difficulties and possibilities in the process.

Businesses who are unable to adjust to the advances in technology run the risk of becoming irrelevant, whereas companies that are open to innovation have a better chance of gaining a competitive advantage.

Investing in research and development is the solution for staying ahead of the latest technical breakthroughs and trends in the market. Develop a culture of innovation inside your organization to foster lifelong learning and flexibility. Embrace digital transformation to simplify processes and improve the quality of experiences provided to customers.

Burdens Related to Regulation and Compliance

For organizations, particularly those operating in more than one country, the presence of regulatory frameworks that are both difficult to understand and always subject to change can impose considerable compliance challenges. Keeping up with the ever-changing legal standards may be time-consuming and expensive, particularly for smaller and medium-sized businesses that have fewer resources at their disposal.

Create robust compliance initiatives that place an emphasis on organizational transparency and accountability as the primary goals of the company. Invest in the experience of legal and regulatory professionals to ensure complete conformity with all applicable national and international legislation. Advocate for regulatory improvements that will simplify things for businesses and make the rules more transparent.

Availability of Capital and Financial Resources

It is absolutely necessary for a company's growth and expansion to have access to capital and funding. However, many firms, particularly small and medium-sized enterprises, struggle to obtain sufficient finance due to stringent lending criteria, high interest rates, and a lack of available collateral. This is an issue that many businesses encounter.

The solution is to investigate many alternative forms of fundraising, such as crowdfunding, angel investing, and venture capital, in order to diversify the sources of funding. Establish credible connections with investors and financial institutions to expand your access to financing and boost your business's legitimacy. Make a case for policies that encourage the expansion of small and medium-sized businesses by making affordable and easily accessible finance available to them.

Concerns Over a Lack of Available Talent and Available Skills

It can be difficult for businesses to expand and innovate when there is a lack of available talent and skilled workers.

Rapid technological improvements call for a highly qualified labor force, but it can be challenging for organizations to locate candidates who possess the essential skills and competencies.

The solution is to make financial investments in workforce development and training programs in order to fill skill gaps that exist within the firm. Develop collaborations with educational institutions in order to encourage the acquisition of skill sets that are now in demand. It is important to be able to recruit and keep top people, therefore be sure to offer competitive wage packages and employee benefits.

Saturation of the Market and Increasingly Fierce Competition

Businesses that are trying to differentiate themselves and gain market share face obstacles brought on by the saturation of the market as well as the intensification of competition. In order to win new consumers and keep the ones they have, organizations operating in oversaturated marketplaces have to be constantly innovative and offer distinct value propositions.

The solution is to carry out market research in order to discover customer requirements and potential for niche markets. Create a competitive advantage for your goods and services by innovating them, enhancing their quality, and providing outstanding service to your customers. Create powerful marketing strategies in order to effectively communicate one-of-a-kind value propositions to the people you are targeting.

Instability and Dangers in International Politics

Businesses who are active in regions that are experiencing geopolitical instability are exposed
to a number of severe hazards, some of which include political conflicts, trade disputes, and sanctions. Unanticipated geopolitical events have the potential to wreak havoc on supply chains, obstruct market access, and heighten operational risks.

To predict and reduce the impact of geopolitical risks, the solution is to carry out exhaustive risk assessments and scenario planning. Increase your presence in a variety of markets to lower your vulnerability to particular geopolitical threats. Keep the lines of communication open and work together with interested parties to keep track of geopolitical changes and the potential consequences they could have.

Environmental Sustainability and the Responsibility of Businesses Towards Society

Businesses face a variety of difficulties and opportunities as a result of the growing emphasis on environmentally sustainable practices and on the social responsibility of corporations.

As a result of the movement in consumer preferences toward environmentally friendly and socially responsible goods and services, businesses are being forced to realign their operations in accordance with sustainable and ethical standards.

The solution is to adopt environmentally responsible and ethical corporate practices that place a priority on the conservation of natural resources and social responsibility. Include sustainability in your company's business plans and day-to-day operations to lessen your impact on the environment and make a beneficial contribution to society. Maintain open lines of communication with customers regarding sustainable projects and activities related to corporate social responsibility.

Dangers posed by Cyberspace

The proliferation of cyber threats, which includes data breaches, ransomware attacks, and phishing schemes, creates major dangers for businesses, which can result in financial losses, damage to reputation, and legal liability. Because of the growing digital nature of today's corporate world, ensuring data security has emerged as a top priority for all companies.

Implementing robust cybersecurity measures, like as firewalls, encryption, and frequent security
audits, is the solution to protecting sensitive data and systems from cyber threats. These methods may be found in the solution. Employees should be made aware of best practices in cybersecurity, and a culture of attention and accountability should be encouraged. Make an investment in cybersecurity insurance to reduce the financial risks that are related with the possibility of data breaches.

Alterations in the Preferences and Behaviors of Customers

Businesses that are trying to keep up with increasing market needs face a number of obstacles as a result of shifting consumer tastes and behaviors, which are influenced by evolving social trends and cultural transformations. To maintain their relevance in the market and their ability to compete, businesses need to maintain a constant awareness of the shifting tastes of their customers.

The solution is to conduct consistent market research and customer satisfaction polls in order to understand the shifting tendencies and preferences of consumers. Adjust your product offerings and marketing methods so that they are in line with the shifting behaviors of consumers. Encourage active participation and input from customers to help develop solid relationships and strengthen brand loyalty.

The economic and commercial difficulties we confront are ever-evolving and complex, taking form as a result of the myriad of internal and external factors that have an impact on the operations of businesses and the economies of the world. In order to manage these problems strategically and adopt ways that are both adaptable and proactive, businesses are required to do so in order to secure their resilience and long-term viability. Businesses are able to overcome economic and commercial challenges and prosper in a dynamic and competitive global marketplace if they embrace innovation, promote a culture of adaptability, and prioritize stakeholder involvement. In addition, for the purpose of addressing systemic difficulties and promoting equitable and sustainable economic growth on a global scale, coordination between national governments, private companies, and international organizations is essential.

7.2 Policy and Regulatory Hurdles

In a world that is becoming ever more interconnected and globalized, the role that laws and regulations play in sculpting the economic, social, and environmental landscape is of the utmost importance. If they are poorly conceived, excessively burdensome, or out of touch with the fast changing reality of society, badly planned policies and regulations can become significant barriers to economic progress and public welfare. On the other hand, well-crafted policies and regulations can enhance public welfare and drive economic growth. This essay investigates the intricate and numerous issues that are provided by policy and regulatory impediments. It delves into the influence that these challenges have on individuals, corporations, and governments and provides insights into effective solutions for overcoming them.

Excessive regulation

One of the most significant challenges posed by policy and regulation is over-regulation, which occurs when there are restrictions that are both excessive in number and excessive in complexity. This stunts economic growth and innovation. Businesses, particularly small and medium-sized enterprises, might be overburdened by the requirements for compliance, which may lead to a reduction in productivity and hamper their capacity to compete in the market. Small and medium-sized enterprises are particularly susceptible to this problem.

The solution is to rationalize and streamline regulations in order to lessen the administrative burdens imposed on businesses while at the same time addressing real concerns. Establish a process for the regular assessment and analysis of regulations, with the goal of locating and removing provisions that are either obsolete or unnecessary. In order to minimize duplication of effort and inconsistent laws, regulatory organizations should work toward improving their ability to coordinate with one another and communicate effectively.

Lack of Clarity in Regulatory Procedures

Regulations that are ambiguous or lack clarity can present substantial issues for both enterprises and individuals.

It is possible for legal conflicts, increased costs associated with complying with regulations, and reluctance to invest in new business endeavors to arise when it is unclear how a legislation should be construed or applied.

The solution is to draft regulations that are lucid and without ambiguity, with terminology that is well defined and implementation procedures that are detailed. Participation from relevant parties in the rule-making process, such as corporations, individuals with expertise in the law, and members of civil society, is essential for achieving both clarity and unanimity.

The Costs of Compliance

Businesses typically incur significant additional expenses in order to be in full compliance with all applicable requirements. These costs may include administrative expenditures, legal fees, and the financial strain of complying with particular laws. Particularly burdensome in terms of cost may compliance requirements be for newly founded companies and small firms.

Create cost-benefit studies for any new regulations in order to evaluate the potential impact these restrictions could have on firms. Implement mechanisms for decreasing compliance costs, such as streamlining reporting requirements and giving businesses with assistance on how to more efficiently satisfy regulatory criteria.

Capture of the Regulatory System

The phenomenon known as regulatory capture takes place when regulatory agencies, which are supposed to serve the public interest, become unduly influenced by the industries that they are supposed to supervise. This leads to the creation of laws and regulations that prioritize the interests of a small number of powerful stakeholders, typically at the expense of the welfare of the general population.

The solution is to adopt open appointment processes for top positions within regulatory agencies in order to strengthen regulatory independence and accountability. Increase the level of transparency by requiring that all meetings and other interactions between regulators and industry representatives be disclosed to the public. It is important to encourage civil society organizations and consumer advocacy groups to actively monitor regulatory decision-making and provide input wherever possible.

Accelerating Rates of Technological Progress

In many cases, the rate of technological progress is faster than the ability of regulators to keep up with it.

Artificial intelligence, blockchain, and biotechnology are three examples of emerging technologies that create unique difficulties that may not be fully addressed by the policies that are now in place. This gap has the potential to cause confusion for both consumers and businesses.

The solution is to put in place flexible regulatory frameworks that are able to accommodate developing technologies. Engage with subject matter experts and key players in the sector to gain a deeper understanding of the consequences of emerging technologies and to establish policies that encourage innovation while also addressing possible dangers. Foster international collaboration on the development of global regulatory standards applicable to emerging technology.

Unsuitable Levels of Enforcement

If they are not sufficiently implemented, even carefully written policies and regulations run the

risk of becoming ineffectual. A culture in which non-compliance is permitted can be fostered when there is insufficient enforcement, which can damage the public's faith in the regulatory system.

Investing in enforcement capability, which includes employing and training officers, as well as providing resources for monitoring and oversight, is the recommended solution. It is necessary to implement penalties and consequences for non-compliance that are sufficiently deterrent if one is to achieve the desired result of obtaining compliance from both organizations and individuals. In order to increase public confidence, transparent enforcement actions should be encouraged.

Regulations that are both consistent and inconsistent with one another

Businesses that operate in numerous jurisdictions may face considerable obstacles as a result of regulations that are in conflict with one another or that are inconsistent with one another at the municipal, national, or international levels. These inconsistencies have the potential to result in compliance problems as well as additional expenditures.

The solution is to encourage coordination and cooperation among different regulatory agencies in order to harmonize the regulations that are in place in various jurisdictions. In order to guarantee coherence in the manner in which cross-border issues are addressed, it is necessary to develop international standards and agreements. Encourage the use of technology-based solutions, such as regulatory sandboxes, for the purpose of testing innovations and rules in controlled conditions prior to their more widespread application.

Political Uncertainty as well as Constant Regulatory Reform

It is possible for there to be frequent modifications in policies and regulations when there is political instability and frequent leadership turnover in the government. This kind of unpredictability can make it difficult for companies and investors to engage in long-term planning, which in turn contributes to an atmosphere of uncertainty.

The solution is to decrease the occurrence of sudden shifts in policy by fostering stability through the establishment of democratic institutions, the rule of law, and the separation of powers. Participate in stakeholder engagements and regulatory impact assessments to guarantee that choices about regulatory matters are made on the basis of sound evidence and analysis rather than political motivations.

Innovation Restriction Caused by Regulations

An excessive amount of laws can impede innovation since they might result in high barriers to entry for new enterprises and startups. These obstacles have the potential to dissuade entrepreneurs from exploring fresh ideas, which in turn would slow economic progress.

The solution is to develop "regulatory sandboxes" and "innovation hubs" that make it possible
for start-ups and established firms to test out novel concepts and forms of technology inside the confines of a strictly regulated setting. In order to create methods that will both support and promote technology advancements, regulatory bodies should be encouraged to engage closely with innovators.

Processes of Consultation That Are Not Very Effective

When it comes to the creation of successful rules, consultation with various stakeholders, such as corporations, consumers, and members of civil society, is absolutely necessary. When consultation methods are inefficient or superficial, the regulations that arise may not meet the interests and concerns of people who are impacted in a sufficient manner.

The solution is to put in place comprehensive consultation procedures that involve a diverse group of interested parties at every stage of the rule-making process. Encourage openness in the process of gathering feedback from various stakeholders and using that information. Make genuine opportunities for public input available in order to guarantee that regulations are shaped by a wide variety of perspectives and areas of expertise.

Observance of terms outlined in international agreements

There are additional difficulties with regulation that arise in the context of international accords and treaties.

When nations join international agreements, they take on international commitments and are obligated to align their domestic legislation with those obligations. This may be a difficult and time-consuming process for nations.

The solution is to make sure that domestic regulatory bodies and the organizations responsible for ensuring international treaty compliance coordinate with one another. Helping countries meet their international responsibilities by providing them with technical support and capacity-building opportunities. Foster multilateral cooperation to facilitate the development of internationally standardized practices.

Policy and regulatory obstacles are difficult issues that can influence individuals, corporations, and even nations. In order to effectively address these challenges, it is vital to find a balance between preserving public interests, stimulating economic growth, and promoting innovation. Only in this way can we hope to be successful. It is essential to have a regulatory environment that is malleable and adaptable, taking into account the continuously shifting landscape of both technology and society. Transparency, accountability, and productive involvement on the part of stakeholders are essential components for overcoming these roadblocks and ensuring that regulations are working toward the greater good. In today's globalized world, when problems can arise anywhere, it is more important than ever for states to work together and achieve greater regulatory consistency at the international level. We will have a much easier time navigating the complex landscape of governance and regulation in our fast changing world if we put these solutions into action and cultivate a culture of regulatory responsiveness and effectiveness.

7.3 Social and Cultural Complexities

The social and cultural intricacies that exist in our globalized and interdependent society each contribute a unique thread to the tapestry of human experiences, beliefs, and identities. These intricacies are intricately entwined with both individual and collective identities, and as a result, they shape our thoughts, behaviors, and interactions. To construct communities that are peaceful and welcoming to all members of society, it is necessary to first have an understanding of the complex social and cultural difficulties and then work to find solutions to those challenges. This essay examines the complicated terrain of social and cultural complexity, diving into how such complexities have an effect on the society we live in today and providing some useful insights on how to successfully navigate those complexities.

The Value of Inclusivity and Diversity

The term "diversity" refers to distinctions in a number of categories, including but not limited to: race, ethnicity, gender, sexual orientation, religion, and socioeconomic status. When we talk about inclusion, we mean making sure that people who come from all kinds of different backgrounds are accepted, appreciated, and given equal chances in every facet of society.

The challenges that result from institutional discrimination, unconscious bias, and societal inequities frequently contribute to the complexity of diversity and inclusion efforts.

The solution is to promote policies and practices that are inclusive, which celebrate diversity and create equitable opportunities for groups that have been excluded. Create educational initiatives to increase awareness of discrimination and bias, both conscious and unconscious, in order to cultivate a more welcoming atmosphere in both the workplace and the community.

Senses of Self and Belonging

Our sense of community and our sense of belonging are inextricably linked to our individual and collective identities, regardless of whether such identities are based on our nationality, our race, or our religion. However, when many identities collide with one another, conflicts and tensions frequently emerge, which can then lead to disagreements, discrimination, and social exclusion.

The solution is to foster open communication and cultural interchange across different cultures in order to develop a sense of shared understanding. Create programs that honor multiculturalism and encourage cultural interaction in order to cultivate a deeper awareness for the myriad ways in which people can express themselves.

The Taking of Ideas From Other Cultures

The practice of cultural appropriation refers to when someone adopts or imitates aspects of a culture that is not their own, most of the time without comprehending or recognizing the cultural value of those aspects. This technique has the potential to result in the erasing of cultural identities as well as the exploitation of cultures that are marginalized.

The solution is to educate folks about the cultural meaning of various symbols, customs, and articles of clothing in order to promote cultural awareness and respect. In order to ensure that cultural exchange is respectful and useful to all parties, it is important to encourage communication between representatives of different cultures.

The Practice of Prejudice and Stereotyping

It is possible for prejudice and stereotyping to result in prejudiced judgments and discrimination based on factors such as a person's ethnicity, gender, or religious affiliation. These prejudices contribute to the maintenance of existing social and cultural differences and interfere with efforts to foster social harmony.

The solution is to initiate extensive educational initiatives that begin at a young age to combat stereotypical thinking and prejudice. Encourage empathy and comprehension by exchanging personal narratives and experiences that challenge preconceived notions and facilitate the formation of links between various populations.

Obstacles in the Way of Language and Communication

Language is one of the most essential aspects of culture; nonetheless, language limitations can make it difficult to communicate effectively, restrict individuals' access to opportunities, and cause communities and individuals to feel isolated.

The solution is to increase linguistic variety and financial investment in language education programs in order to break down barriers caused by language. Create information and technologies that can be used in multiple languages in order to make it easier for people from different linguistic backgrounds to communicate and access services.

Conflicts between Cultures

When people from various cultures have interactions with one another, this can result in cultural clashes, which can then lead to misunderstandings and disputes. These conflicts are capable of manifesting themselves on a variety of sizes, ranging from interpersonal exchanges to international relations.

The solution is to encourage intercultural competence by equipping individuals with the information and skills necessary to manage cultural differences in a manner that is both courteous and successful. Encourage intercultural communication and the use of techniques for conflict resolution in order to resolve cultural differences and locate areas of agreement.

Equal treatment of men and women in society's norms

Traditional societal conventions frequently contribute to the perpetuation of gender disparities and stereotypes. As a result, opportunities are restricted and the power dynamic between the sexes is exacerbated.

The solution is to fight for gender equality by challenging traditional gender roles through awareness campaigns and educational programming. Adopt and put into effect policies that encourage women to take on positions of leadership and to pursue economic possibilities. In the fight for gender equality, it is important to enlist men and boys as allies.

Movements of People and Forced Relocations

The migration of people across international borders, whether for economic, political, or environmental reasons, offers complicated social and cultural issues. These challenges are exacerbated by the interconnected nature of these factors. Ongoing challenges exist in the areas of integration, social cohesion, and the protection of the rights of migrants and refugees.

The solution is to develop comprehensive integration initiatives that will assist migrants and refugees in becoming socially and economically included in their new communities. Encourage the adoption of laws that safeguard the legal rights of people who have been displaced and give them the means to start over in new environments.

Indigenous Peoples' Rights and the Maintenance of Culture

Indigenous groups frequently struggle with issues involving the protection of their cultural history, the assertion of their rights to land, and the acknowledgement of their distinct identities. Ongoing problems include the theft of cultural practices, the expropriation of land, and insufficient political representation.

The solution is to uphold the rights of indigenous groups to their territory, culture, and the ability to decide for themselves. Work together with leaders of indigenous communities to devise policies and programs that will help to preserve and publicize the cultural traditions of those communities.

Hate Crimes and Other Forms of Discrimination

In many different countries, discrimination, hate crimes, and other forms of social injustice continue to exist. Those on the margins of society are frequently the targets of harassment and violence, which undermines social cohesion and causes both physical and mental suffering.

The solution is to enact stringent anti-discrimination laws and regulations that shield marginalized groups from harm. Through public awareness campaigns and education, foster an environment of tolerance, acceptance, and unity; at the same time, hold individuals and institutions accountable for hate crimes and discrimination.

Freedom of Expression and Tolerance of Religion

Many people view their religious beliefs as an essential component of their culture. Conflicts involving religious views and practices can often rise to intolerance and discrimination against others with different faiths.

The solution is to uphold the values of religious freedom and tolerance by safeguarding the rights of individuals to practice their faith without being subjected to harassment or hostility. Build bridges of collaboration across different religious communities by emphasizing the importance of interfaith communication and understanding.

Disparities in Socioeconomic Status
Disparities in socioeconomic status frequently overlap with cultural and social variables, which can result in unequal access to resources, education, and healthcare as well as economic prospects.

The solution is to enact policies that target socioeconomic disparities and create possibilities for people to move up the social ladder. It is important to work toward providing all members of society, regardless of their ethnic or social origins, with inexpensive access to high-quality education and medical care.

The social and cultural intricacies that exist in our diverse and interconnected world are essential components of these features. Understanding the nuances of one's identity, beliefs, and practices is necessary in order to successfully navigate these complexities. We need to encourage discourse, celebrate diversity, and promote inclusion if we are going to be successful in addressing these difficulties. It is also our responsibility to strive toward eliminating the stereotypes and barriers that contribute to the maintenance of social and cultural gaps. By accepting these answers, we may cultivate a society that is more welcoming, respectful, and peaceful. This will create an environment in which people from a variety of backgrounds are able to flourish and contribute to the depth of our common humanity.

7.4 The Global Context: Climate Change and Its Impacts
The effects of climate change are one of the most urgent problems that our world must deal with in the current global setting. The scientific community is in agreement that human actions, most notably the burning of fossil fuels, the destruction of forests, and the operation of industrial processes, have contributed to a rise in the concentration of greenhouse gases in the atmosphere, which has resulted in an increase in the average temperature throughout the globe. The effects of climate change are quite widespread and will have an effect on ecosystems, communities, and economies all around the world.

Temperatures have been continuously climbing over the world, which has led to the occurrence of heatwaves that are both more common and more severe. This results in potential health hazards, difficulties for agricultural production, and increased energy requirements for air conditioning.

Glaciers and polar ice caps are melting at an accelerated rate due to the warming environment, which is also contributing to rising sea levels. As a direct consequence of this, sea levels are climbing, which poses a threat to low-lying areas and coastal populations.

Extreme Weather Events The rate of occurrence of extreme weather events, such as hurricanes, droughts, and wildfires, has been shown to rise as a direct result of climate change. These calamities have a devasting impact on the areas they affect, leading people to be displaced, destroying property, and taking lives.

Acidification of the Oceans Acidification of the oceans occurs when they take in an excessive amount of carbon dioxide from the atmosphere. This causes disruption in marine ecosystems, which in turn harms coral reefs, fisheries, and affects the availability of food.

Loss of biodiversity is caused by climate change, which wreaks havoc on ecosystems and habitats, causing alterations in the distribution of species and putting a great number of plant and animal species in jeopardy. This decline in biodiversity has significant repercussions for the integrity of ecosystems and the way people make their living.

Scarcity of Water: In many parts of the world, the lack of available water is caused by shifting weather patterns and rising evaporation rates. Agriculture, the availability of drinking water, and sanitation all suffer as a result of this.

The effects of climate change on crop yields and food production can lead to higher food costs and increased food insecurity for vulnerable populations. Agricultural challenges include these effects.

Risks to Public Health: Climate change adds to the spread of diseases and heat-related ailments, putting a strain on healthcare systems and disproportionately harming communities that are already susceptible.

Economic Consequences There will be significant costs involved with disaster recovery, property loss, and infrastructure restoration as a direct result of climate change, which will have substantial repercussions on the economy. A decrease in labor productivity and disruptions in the supply chain are examples of indirect costs.

Social Disparities: Existing social disparities are made worse by climate change, which disproportionately affects underprivileged populations who have fewer resources to adapt and recover from the effects of climate change.

To effectively combat climate change, a concerted effort on a global scale is required. The Paris Agreement, which was ratified in 2015, represents a huge step forward in international collaboration, with the goal of limiting global warming to well below 2 degrees Celsius over pre-industrial levels. This goal was established with the intention of combating climate change. To adapt to the unavoidable effects of climate change and alleviate the effects of climate change, however, higher commitments and more aggressive initiatives are required.

It is absolutely necessary for nations to make the transition to cleaner energy sources, implement sustainable land-use practices, and support conservation and resilience initiatives in the context of the global setting. Reducing carbon emissions and campaigning for climate action also requires significant contributions from individuals, as well as the public and corporate sectors and civil society.

The problem of climate change is a complicated one that transcends national boundaries. It emphasizes the interconnection of the global community and urges for a concerted effort to protect our planet and ensure the well-being of future generations.

Chapter 8

Success Stories from Around the World

Grameen Bank, located in Bangladesh :
Grameen Bank was established in the 1970s by the economist Muhammad Yunus with the intention of providing microloans to persons in Bangladesh who were living in poverty, particularly women. This innovative approach to microfinance enabled millions of people to launch small enterprises, allowing them to lift themselves out of poverty and create sustainable lifestyles for themselves. Yunus was awarded the Nobel Peace Prize in 2006 in recognition of his work, which brought attention to the role that microfinance plays in the fight against worldwide poverty.

The Extraordinary Progress Made by Rwanda - Rwanda:
After the tragic genocide that took place in Rwanda in 1994, the country immediately began an extraordinary journey of recovery and prosperity. The nation made maintaining peace, expanding the economy, and reducing tensions among society some of its highest priorities when President Paul Kagame was in office. Since then, Rwanda has made major strides forward in the fields of healthcare, education, and technology, presenting itself as a model for the growth and governance of other African nations.

Transition to Renewable Energy Sources in Denmark:
In its pursuit to shift to renewable energy sources, Denmark has achieved great gains in recent
years. The nation has committed to becoming carbon-neutral by the year 2050, one of its lofty goals, and it has already accomplished a number of noteworthy milestones in the production of wind energy. The success of Denmark's measures to transition to renewable energy sources has established the country as a frontrunner in environmentally friendly technologies and serves as a global example for the transition to more sustainable energy sources.

Bhutan: the Green Revolution Bhutan:

The dedication of Bhutan's government and people to the preservation of natural resources and the promotion of sustainable practices has garnered international attention. The nation has put into action a one-of-a-kind model of holistic development based on the concept of Gross National Happiness (GNH), which places a high priority on the preservation of environmental resources, cultural traditions, and sustainable economic expansion.

The unwavering commitment of Bhutan's government to the protection of the country's natural landscapes, including the nation's lofty objective to remain carbon-negative, serves as an illuminating model for environmental stewardship on a worldwide scale.

The American region known as Silicon Valley:
Silicon Valley, which is located in the San Francisco Bay Area, has become a center of innovation and technological development on a global scale. It has been instrumental in the development of a great number of new businesses, including Apple, Google, and Facebook, as well as a great many startups. The success story of Silicon Valley shows the strength of an entrepreneurial spirit, the involvement of venture capital, and an ecosystem that is supportive of innovation and risk-taking in the quest of technological advancement.

Women's Emancipation in the State of Kerala, India:
The Indian state of Kerala has advanced significantly in terms of women's empowerment and gender equality in recent years. Kerala is located in southern India. Kerala has enabled women to actively participate in both the economic operations and the decision-making processes of the state through programs such as Kudumbashree, which focuses on the formation of women's self-help groups and the general improvement of communities. The accomplishment of these projects has resulted in enhanced social indices and a more equitable distribution of wealth across the state.

Agriculture that is Friendly to the Environment in the Netherlands - Netherlands:
Through the use of forward-thinking agricultural practices like precision farming, vertical farming, and greenhouse growing, the Netherlands has established itself as a leader in the field of environmentally friendly agriculture. Because of these techniques, the nation has been able to maximize food production while simultaneously decreasing resource use and the impact on the environment. The Dutch agricultural model serves as a blueprint for sustainable farming techniques around the world, particularly in densely populated countries that face issues connected to land and water scarcity. In particular, the Netherlands is a prime example of how sustainable farming can be done.

The Economic Revolution in South Korea - South Korea:
The quick economic transformation of South Korea, often known as the "Miracle on the Han River," highlights the country's astonishing progress from a war-torn nation to a global economic powerhouse. This change is sometimes referred to as

the "Miracle on the Han River." South Korea has achieved unprecedented levels of industrialization and modernization as a result of smart investments in education, technology, and infrastructure. As a result, the country has become a world leader in a number of industries, including technology, automotive production, and consumer electronics.

The Status of Women's Political Rights and Participation in New Zealand:

In recent years, New Zealand has made tremendous progress toward its goal of achieving gender equality and increasing the political engagement of women. The nation is extremely proud of its history of strong female leadership, especially the fact that in 1893 it was the first country in the world to give women the right to vote. Because it has a significant number of women serving in critical leadership roles, New Zealand is a shining example of gender-inclusive governance and a model for the advancement of women's rights on a worldwide scale.

Planning for a Sustainable and Livable City in Singapore:

Singapore has emerged as a world leader in the planning and development of environmentally friendly cities. The city-state has been able to attain a high quality of life despite having a limited geographical area thanks to its holistic approach to urban design. This strategy includes the incorporation of green spaces, efficient public transportation, and sustainable infrastructure. Other fast rising cities that are confronted with issues associated with urbanization can benefit greatly from learning from Singapore's achievements in the area of urban sustainability.

Healthcare Provided by the Community in Cuba:

The community-based healthcare system in Cuba, which places an emphasis on preventative medicine and public health, has garnered praise from people all over the world for its efficiency and ease of use. Cuba has accomplished a great deal in the field of healthcare despite its limited resources, as seen by the country's high life expectancy and low infant mortality rates. The system of healthcare that is used in Cuba highlights the significance of giving top priority to community health initiatives and methods of illness prevention.

Recent Developments in Microchip Technology in Taiwan:

Taiwan has firmly established itself as a world leader in both the manufacturing of semiconductors and the technologies associated with microchips. The country's semiconductor industry, which is powered in large part by enterprises such as TSMC (Taiwan Semiconductor Manufacturing Company), has been a driving force behind the expansion of the worldwide electronics industry. Because of Taiwan's pioneering contributions to the microchip industry, the country now has a preeminent place in the worldwide supply chain for technology.

These examples of triumph from different parts of the world illustrate how people, groups, and even entire nations can work together to achieve extraordinary results in a variety of arenas. They serve as sources of inspiration and useful lessons for addressing urgent global concerns, inspiring innovation, and promoting positive change in our globally interconnected world.

8.1 Lessons Learned and Best Practices

In the course of traveling through life and engaging in its myriad activities, one amasses a priceless treasure trove of wisdom through the accumulation of useful lessons learnt and tried-and-true methods. Individuals, companies, and communities are able to better handle problems, stimulate growth, and improve decision-making when they embrace best practices and learn from both their successes and failures. This essay examines a wide variety of life lessons and best practices in a variety of fields, such as business, leadership, education, personal development, healthcare, and environmental stewardship, among others, encompassing these topics and more.

1. **Some Life and Business Lessons I've Picked Up Along the Way**
   Capacity for Adaptation in the Face of Alteration:
   When it comes to being successful in business, one of the most important factors is an organization's capacity to adjust when faced with new challenges. The COVID-19 pandemic instilled in us the value of adaptability and quickness of movement. As a result of the need of adaptability, many companies have implemented practices such as remote work, redesigned supply chains, and begun to engage in online shopping.
   Approach that Is Focused on the Customer:
   The key to commercial success lies in fully appreciating and satisfying the requirements of one's clientele. The most successful businesses place a high priority on the customer experience, consistently solicit input from their clients, and make extensive use of data analytics to improve their goods and services.
   Risk Management and the Capacity to Adapt:
   The economic crisis that began in 2008 brought to light the significance of effective risk management. Lessons that are helpful for businesses to learn include diversifying their investments, managing their liquidity, and stress testing their financial plans.
   Invention and Creative Problem Solving:
   Businesses that encourage creative thinking and new ideas are more likely to succeed. Companies such as Apple and Tesla are great examples of the importance of pushing the limits of what is possible, introducing innovative technologies, and developing consumer solutions that are one of a kind.
   Accepting and Embracing Defeat:
   The journey to success frequently begins with an encounter with failure. Icons of entrepreneurship such as Elon Musk and Richard Branson stress the significance of gaining wisdom from mistakes and remaining resilient in the face of adversity.
   Practices That Are Sustainable:

At this point, sustainability can no longer be considered a choice but rather a need. Environmental, social, and governance (ESG) principles are progressively being incorporated into business plans by a growing number of companies. These companies are also increasing their adoption of sustainable business practices.

2. **Life Experiences That Have Helped Me Become a Better Leader and Manager**

   Setting a Good Example to Follow:
   Leaders that are effective teach their teams by setting an example for others to follow by emulating the beliefs and actions they want to see from their followers. This behavior cultivates trust and encourages others to behave in a similar manner.

   Putting Teams in Charge:
   Increased engagement and productivity are the direct results of giving teams more autonomy through the delegation of authority and the promotion of a sense of ownership. A defining characteristic of effective leadership is the ability to delegate decision-making authority to subordinates.

   Transparency in Communication:
   Leadership requires strong communication skills in order to succeed. Stronger connections and more productive work environments are the direct result of leaders who communicate well, actively listen, and offer criticism that is constructive.

   Capacity for Adaptation and Resilience:
   The COVID-19 epidemic highlighted the need for leaders who can adjust to changing circumstances. In times of uncertainty, successful leaders demonstrated resilience, provided support for their teams, and made quick decisions based on accurate information.

   Learning That Never Stops:
   Leaders that continue to educate themselves are more effective. They actively seek out new information, experiences, and feedback in an effort to develop their leadership abilities and remain flexible in the face of shifting conditions.

   The importance of diversity and inclusion:
   In addition to improving the overall performance of the team, embracing diversity and working to create an inclusive environment in the workplace is consistent with contemporary ethical standards and the expectations of society.

3. **Life Experiences and Education That Have Influenced My Development as a Person**

   Having a Growth Mindset :
   The psychologist Carol Dweck is credited with popularizing the idea of a growth mindset, which focuses on the assumption that one's abilities and intelligence can be increased through the application of devotion and hard work.

The development of a growth mindset encourages resiliency as well as a passion for furthering one's education.

The Importance of Mentors and Role Models:
The wisdom and experience gained from having mentors and role models is priceless. Their support and direction can be both a road map and a source of motivation for one's own personal and professional growth.

Reflection on Oneself and Attention to the Present:
Individuals can better manage stress, improve their mental health, and make more considered decisions when they engage in techniques that cultivate self-awareness and mindfulness, such as meditation.

Establishing Objectives and Ranking Concerns:
The process of developing oneself begins with the formulation of specific, attainable objectives and the organization of responsibilities according to priority. The framework for defining goals known as SMART, which stands for Specific, Measurable, Achievable, Relevant, and Time-bound, is frequently utilized to improve effectiveness.

Resistance to stress and an ability to change:
Unanticipated difficulties are frequently to be found in life. It is essential to have resiliency and flexibility in order to successfully navigate uncertainty, learn from experiences, and develop as unique individuals.

Competence in global affairs and sensitivity to other cultures:
In a world that is becoming more interconnected, having a global competence and being able to understand other cultures are skills that are becoming increasingly important. They encourage empathy, cooperation, and effective communication in a variety of settings and situations.

4. **Important Things I've Learned About Health and Wellness**

    Care that is Preventive:
    Treatment is not always more effective or cost-efficient than prevention. Prevention can be. Exams and vaccinations at regular intervals, as well as making decisions in one's lifestyle that support one's health, are essential components of healthcare.

    Becoming Aware of Mental Health:
    The state of one's mental health is an essential component of one's total well-being. Lessons in healthcare that are vital to learn include decreasing the stigma that surrounds mental health concerns and seeking help and treatment as soon as possible.

    Care Focused on the Patient:
    Listening to patients, including them in decision-making processes, and treating them with empathy and respect are all components of patient-centered care, which is becoming an increasingly prominent focus among providers of medical services.

Care that is centered on patient values:
The transition from fee-for-service models to value-based care models places more of an emphasis on the quality of care offered to patients as opposed to merely the amount of services rendered. This strategy contributes to improved overall patient experiences as well as more effective delivery of healthcare.

Telemedicine and Patient Monitoring from a Distance:
The COVID-19 epidemic pushed the healthcare industry to move more quickly toward adopting telehealth and remote monitoring technologies.
These technologies make it simpler to gain access to healthcare services, lessen the strain placed on physical institutions, and provide patients with greater convenience.

Collaborative Efforts Made Across Disciplines:
Interdisciplinary collaboration is becoming more and more accepted in the healthcare industry, as indicated by the shift toward a team-based approach to dealing with difficult medical problems. Collaborative care among specialists in the healthcare industry results in patient-focused and comprehensive approaches to treatment.

5. **Environmental Stewardship and the Lessons It Has Taught Us**
Reduced carbon emissions and the use of renewable energy:
Lessons in environmental stewardship that are crucially important include lowering carbon emissions and making the switch to renewable energy sources. Due to the critical nature of the climate change problem, numerous pledges have been made to work toward the goal of reaching net-zero emissions and to accelerate the adoption of renewable energy technology.

Preservation of Nature and the Variety of Life:
It is absolutely necessary, for the sake of the health of the earth, to take measures to preserve natural ecosystems and biodiversity. These teachings can be seen in action through projects like reforestation, wildlife preservation, and marine protection, among others.

Sustainable Business Practices and the Circular Economy:
The idea of a circular economy, which seeks to reduce waste while maximizing the utilization of
available resources, has recently gained popularity. Recycling, cutting down on single-use plastics, and reusing materials are all examples of behaviors that contribute to sustainability.

Cooperation on a Global Scale:
To effectively address the issues facing the environment, international collaboration is required. The significance of multilateral cooperation in environmental protection is highlighted by recent agreements such as the one reached in Paris regarding climate change.

Education and Support of Causes:

Environmental stewardship involves many different activities, but two of the most important ones are educating communities and advocating for environmentally acceptable actions.

Earth Day and other events that raise environmental awareness and promote environmental education serve as an inspiration for individuals and groups to take environmental protection into their own hands.

Creativity and technological advancement:

In order to lessen our effects on the environment and slow the progression of climate change, technological advancements such as renewable energy solutions, carbon capture devices, and environmentally responsible agricultural methods are essential.

6. **Insights Gained Regarding the Growth of Communities and Societies**
   Resilience of the Community:

   Developing communities that can withstand adverse conditions is an essential step in both preventing and responding to emergencies. It is critical to have robust social networks, adequate preparation for emergencies, and community support systems.

   The promotion of inclusivity and empowerment:

   For the purpose of establishing social fairness, it is essential to promote inclusivity and the empowerment of underrepresented communities. These teachings may be seen in action through organizations that are working toward racial justice, LGBTQ+ rights, and gender equality.

   Giving to charitable causes and being responsible members of society:

   When it comes to finding solutions to social problems, everyone from individuals to businesses to charitable groups all play a vital part. Philanthropy and social responsibility are exemplified by the ways in which they have contributed to worthy causes, projects with a positive social impact, and initiatives that promote sustainable development.

   Resolution of Conflicts and the Building of Peace:

   The resolution of crises by peaceful means, such as mediation, diplomacy, and talks, is absolutely necessary for the upkeep and preservation of global peace and stability. Conflicts can be avoided and peace can be promoted thanks to the efforts of organizations such as the United Nations.

   Literacy and Educational Opportunities:

   It is critical to increase access to education as well as literacy rates in order to overcome cycles of poverty and inequality. Initiatives such as the Global Partnership for Education (GPE) are centered on the goal of enhancing educational opportunities in areas that are underserved.

   Inclusion in the Digital Age and Connectivity:

   It is essential to ensure that all persons have access to information, opportunities, and services in today's increasingly digital environment, and digital inclusion

is the key to achieving this goal. Connectivity is being emphasized as a fundamental component of global growth by many initiatives that aim to close the digital gap.
7. **Insights Gained Into the Workings of Governance and the Public Sector**

Accountability and Openness to the Public:
Trust and confidence in government are increased when there is transparency and accountability. In democratic countries, open government programs and systems that hold leaders and institutions responsible for their actions are absolutely necessary.

Independence of the Judiciary and the Rule of Law:
A society that is just and equitable must place a high priority on preserving the separation of powers in the judicial system as well as the rule of law. A robust legal infrastructure and an impartial judicial system are necessary for protecting individual rights and preserving order.

Preparedness of the Public Health System:
The COVID-19 pandemic drove home the significance of having a ready reaction and adequate preparation for public health emergencies. For the most effective management of public health emergencies, teamwork on a national and international level and investments in healthcare infrastructure are required.

Protections for the Socially Vulnerable and Welfare:
During times of economic strain, social safety nets and welfare programs are absolutely necessary for providing support to communities that are particularly vulnerable. They provide a vital support system for people and families that are struggling to make ends meet.

Diplomacy on a global scale and efforts to resolve conflicts:
For the purpose of settling international disputes, promoting peace, and tackling transnational concerns such as nuclear disarmament, human rights, and trade agreements, diplomacy and international cooperation are of the utmost importance.

Electronic Administration and Online Services:
Accessibility, efficiency, and openness are all improved when it comes to public administration thanks to digital government services. E-government programs broaden citizens' access to government information and resources, particularly vital services.

Individuals, groups, and entire societies can use these best practices and lessons learned as guiding principles to direct their actions. They offer a road map to success, a basis for growth, and a framework for handling the difficulties of the modern era. Adopting these guiding principles gives us the ability to draw lessons from the past, arrive at well-informed judgments, and steadily progress toward a more affluent, just, and environmentally responsible future. In a world that is always evolving, the insight that has been distilled from these experiences and recommendations for best practices becomes an extremely valuable asset. It enables us to negotiate the difficulties of the here and now and to construct a better future.

8.2 Innovations and Collaborations Driving Change

Innovation and cooperation have emerged as important drivers of change in a world that is marked by rapid technical breakthroughs, interconnected global networks, and ever-evolving societal concerns. These forces are transforming our communities, economies, and surroundings in a variety of ways, from ground-breaking scientific discoveries to disruptive business models and alliances spanning multiple industries. The purpose of this essay is to investigate the ever-shifting landscape of innovations and collaborations that are driving good change in a variety of fields and to illustrate how these efforts are influencing the future.

1. **Breakthroughs in Scientific Research and Technological Development**
   Computing on the Quantum Level:
   Utilizing the fundamentals of quantum mechanics, quantum computing is ushering in a new era of information processing that is truly revolutionary. Companies such as IBM and Google are leading the charge in the development of quantum computers, which have the ability to tackle difficult problems significantly more quickly than conventional computers. Cryptography is just one of the many applications, along with drug discovery and optimization difficulties.
   Synonyms: artificial intelligence and machine learning.
   Automation, data analysis, and improved forecasting capacities are just some of the ways that artificial intelligence and machine learning are revolutionizing several business sectors. Applications have been developed in a variety of fields, including healthcare, banking, and autonomous vehicles, thanks to developments in natural language processing, computer vision, and neural networks.
   Recent Developments in Biotechnology:
   Recent advances in biotechnology have led to the development of gene-editing technologies such as CRISPR-Cas9. These tools have the potential to heal genetic illnesses, promote regenerative medicine, and generate genetically engineered species.
   Technologies that use renewable energy sources:
   The move to cleaner energy sources and the reduction of carbon emissions are being driven by innovations in the technology used to generate renewable energy. Some examples of these innovations are enhanced solar panels, wind turbines, and energy storage solutions.
   Printing in three dimensions (3D printing) and additive manufacturing:
   The use of 3D printing is bringing about a revolution in manufacturing processes, making it possible to create complex products in a manner that is both more efficient and more customizable. This technology is being adopted by a variety of industries, including the aerospace industry, healthcare, and the construction industry.

2. **Efforts Made in Collaboration With Others in the Fields of Healthcare and Medical Research**
   Initiatives for International Health:
   In order to solve global health emergencies, promote vaccination campaigns, and fight diseases like Ebola and COVID-19, organizations such as the World Health Organization (WHO) and Médecins Sans Frontières (Doctors Without Borders) work together.
   Collaborations between the public sector and the private sector:
   The discovery of new drugs is sped up and access to essential pharmaceuticals is broadened because to partnerships between pharmaceutical corporations, governments, and charitable organizations. An excellent illustration of an organization that is actively developing such relationships is the Access to Medicine Foundation.
   The Consortiums for Precision Medicine:
   Initiatives in the field of precision medicine involve collaboration between public and private institutions in order to personalize medical treatments based on patients' genetic profiles. These efforts improve the efficiency of the treatment while also reducing the unpleasant side effects.
   Research Consortiums in the Medical Field:
   The goal of consortiums like the Cancer Genome Atlas (TCGA) and the Human Cell Atlas (HCA) is to improve our understanding of diseases and human biology by bringing together researchers, institutions, and funding. The diagnosis and treatment methods can be improved as a result of this collaborative research.
   Collaborations in the Fields of Telemedicine and Health Technology:
   Collaborations between healthcare providers, tech businesses, and regulators are being driven by innovations in telemedicine and digital health technology. The goals of these collaborations are to increase patient access to healthcare, boost diagnoses, and remotely monitor chronic illnesses.
3. **Breakthroughs in Environmentally Responsible Agriculture and Food Systems**
   Combining Hydroponics and Vertical Farming:
   The advent of new techniques in hydroponics and vertical farming has made it possible to cultivate crops in urban areas throughout the entire year. This has two major benefits: it has lessened agriculture's impact on the environment and it has increased food security.
   Agriculture with a Focus on Precision:
   The use of data and advanced technology in agriculture allows for the optimization of farming operations, which in turn improves crop yields, resource efficiency, and environmental sustainability.
   Meat that is grown in a lab or is derived from plants:

The development of plant-based and lab-grown meat products has the potential to provide environmentally friendly alternatives to traditional animal agriculture by lowering emissions of greenhouse gases and cutting resource use.

The Role of Blockchain in the Supply Chain:
The application of blockchain technology in food supply chains helps to improve transparency and traceability, which in turn helps to reduce instances of food fraud and ensures that products are genuine and safe to use.

Agriculture that is Regenerative:
The methods of regenerative agriculture place an emphasis on the health of the soil and the restoration of ecosystems. As a result, these techniques encourage biodiversity and the capture of carbon while simultaneously improving the long-term sustainability of farming.

4. **Partnerships for the Protection of the Environment and the Fight Against Climate Change**

    Agreements on Climate Change at the International Level:
    Efforts on a global scale, such as the Paris Agreement, bring nations together in their fight against climate change by establishing goals for the reduction of emissions and fostering collaboration on a worldwide scale.

    Alliances That Cut Across Sectors:
    Collaborations between the public and corporate sectors, such as The Climate Group and RE100, aim to advance the use of renewable energy sources, achieve carbon neutrality, and encourage sustainable business practices.

    The acronym "NGOs" stands for "non-governmental organizations"
    Greenpeace and the World Wildlife Fund (WWF) are two examples of organizations that aim to safeguard ecosystems, increase environmental awareness, and fight for the conservation of natural resources and environmental sustainability.

    Community-Driven Efforts to Conserve Resources:
    Projects that are carried out in conjunction with local communities give those populations the ability to take an active role in biodiversity conservation, reforestation, and habitat restoration.

    Innovation in Environmentally Friendly Technology:
    The development of environmentally friendly technologies, such as electric vehicles, solar electricity, and building materials with high energy efficiency, is driving progress toward a more sustainable and low-carbon future.

5. **Educational Breakthroughs and Partnerships for Continuing Education and Improvement**

    Various Platforms for Online Education:
    Online learning systems such as Coursera, edX, and Khan Academy make it possible for people all over the world to have access to education of a high standard. These breakthroughs are made possible by collaboration between educational institutions and technology corporations.

OER stands for open educational resources.
OER efforts encourage the creation of educational content, textbooks, and resources as well as their distribution in order to reduce educational expenses and increase educational accessibility.

Partnerships Between the Public and Private Sectors in Education:
The outcomes of educational initiatives, the digital divide, and efforts to encourage employability in a labor market that is undergoing rapid change can all be improved by partnerships between governments, corporations, and non-profit organizations.

Continuing Education for Teachers and Professional Networks:
Educators engage together through networks and online communities to share successful pedagogical practices, resources, and instructional methods for the purpose of enhancing the learning experiences of their students.

Initiatives for a Lifetime of Learning:
Programs and initiatives that support individuals in their pursuit of lifelong learning, such as libraries, community colleges, and online courses, enable individuals to acquire new skills and knowledge at any point in their lives.

6. **New Approaches and Collaborative Projects in the Fields of Social Work and Philanthropy**

Investing with a Focus on Social Impact:
Impact investing brings together financial and social goals with the intention of allocating capital to projects that would have a beneficial effect on the environment and/or society as a whole. This trend is pushing the development of novel financial instruments and the distribution of funds to initiatives with these goals.

CSR stands for "corporate social responsibility"
Businesses, as well as charitable organizations and local communities, are working together to find solutions to societal and environmental problems. CSR programs, like Microsoft's various charitable activities, have the intention of giving something back to the community.

Entrepreneurship with a focus on society:
Social entrepreneurs are at the vanguard of resolving societal concerns such as poverty, access to clean water, and quality education via the use of business models. These entrepreneurs are at the forefront of the movement to solve social problems using business models.

Partnerships That Cut Across Multiple Sectors:
The strengths of each sector can be leveraged in order to accomplish social and economic goals through the formation of partnerships between the government, businesses, and members of civil society. These alliances have the potential to propel development in areas such as the fight against poverty and the improvement of public health.

Community-Driven Planning And Development:
Microfinance projects and village savings and loan associations are two examples of successful collaborative initiatives that empower local communities to drive their own development goals. These types of initiatives have been successful in reducing poverty and fostering social development.

7. **Business and Economic Models That Have Undergone Innovations Thanks to Collaborations**
Platforms for the Sharing Economy:
The models of the sharing economy, which are exemplified by companies such as Airbnb and Uber, make it possible for individuals to share resources with one another and redefine old industries.

The Blockchain and Its Cryptocurrency Applications:
Cryptocurrencies, such as Bitcoin, were made possible by blockchain technology. These cryptocurrencies present a challenge to conventional forms of financial management and offer decentralized and secure means of conducting transactions.

Practices of the Circular Economy:
By reusing, recycling, and refurbishing things, the circular economy model helps to reduce waste and the negative impact that it has on the environment. This in turn promotes resource efficiency and sustainability.

Models of Business That Are Hybrid:
Hybrid business models combine parts of for-profit and nonprofit enterprises in order to simultaneously solve societal and environmental concerns and ensure the continued viability of the enterprise financially.

Sourcing with an Impact:
Employing members of underserved communities enables these individuals to improve their
economic standing while also enabling impact sourcing businesses to provide superior products and services to their customers.

8. **Collaborative Efforts in the Practice of Diplomacy and International Relations**
Resolution of conflicts and maintenance of peace:
International organizations such as the United Nations work together to arbitrate conflicts, offer relief to those in need, and keep the peace and security in regions that are prone to instability.

Alliances of the Diplomatic Kind:
The promotion of economic cooperation, cultural interaction, and international safety can be accomplished through the development of diplomatic alliances and bilateral contacts between nations.

Initiatives for International Health:
Public health and international solidarity are both improved when countries

work together to combat global health problems, share medical expertise, and provide vaccines.

Trade Accords and Economic Groupings:
Trade agreements, both regional and international, help to develop economic cooperation and make it easier for countries to trade goods and services with one another.

Agreements Regarding the Environment:
Countries are encouraged to work together to find solutions to problems affecting the environment on a global scale via international environmental agreements such as the Kyoto Protocol and the Convention on Biological Diversity.

9. **New Approaches and Collaborative Projects in the Field of Urban Development and Smart Cities**

Initiatives for a Smarter City:
Projects that aim to create a smart city make use of data, technology, and innovation in order to enhance urban planning, infrastructure, and services, thereby improving the citizens' quality of life.

Innovation in the Transportation Sector:
Innovations in public transportation, electric automobiles, and autonomous vehicles are being driven by collaborations between private enterprises and government agencies, with the goal of reducing congestion and pollution caused by vehicles.

Agriculture in the city and environmentally friendly infrastructure:
Urban agricultural projects and sustainable infrastructure development work together to make cities more environmentally friendly and resilient, and to make living conditions in urban areas better.

The Internet of Things and Digital Connectivity:
The expansion of digital connection as well as the internet of things (IoT) can be facilitated by municipal partnerships with technology companies. This helps to produce urban environments that are more connected and efficient.

Accessibility and Inclusion in the Design:
The inclusive planning of cities should be a priority for collaborative efforts, since this will ensure that cities are accessible to persons with disabilities and people with a variety of requirements.

The modern world is shaped in large part by fundamental forces such as innovations and collaborative efforts. These dynamic and interrelated factors are driving beneficial change across a range of fields, including but not limited to science and technology, healthcare, environmental conservation, educational development, social development, and more.

Examples from this post illustrate how novel concepts and collaborative efforts have the ability to cross borders, encourage creative thinking, and find solutions to urgent problems on a global scale.

The problems that we face in this era, such as climate change, educational access, healthcare inequities, and social injustice, call for creative solutions and cross-sector partnerships. We can collectively create revolutionary change and construct a future that is more egalitarian, sustainable, and affluent if we embrace an attitude of creativity, cultivate inclusivity, and nurture a worldwide culture of collaboration. The inventions and collaborations of today will define the opportunities and challenges of tomorrow, and they will lead us toward a future that is characterized by progress, resilience, and shared prosperity.

Chapter 9

Policies and Regulations Promoting Sustainable Tourism

Tourism is a vital contributor to economic growth and a medium for the exchange of cultural traditions; nevertheless, it also has important negative effects on the natural world and on people's social and cultural lives. The idea behind sustainable tourism is that it is necessary to strike a balance between the positive aspects of tourism and the potential drawbacks that can arise from it. Policies and regulations pertaining to sustainable tourism play a critical part in directing the tourism industry in the direction of a course that is more responsible and ethical. During this in-depth investigation, we will delve into the realm of sustainable tourism, gaining an understanding of its guiding principles and analyzing a variety of policies and regulations from across the world that support an approach that is friendly to the environment and centered on the needs of local communities.

1. **Comprehending the Concept of Sustainable Tourism**
   The Idea Behind Tourism That Is Sustainable:
   The goal of sustainable tourism, which is also sometimes referred to as responsible tourism or ecotourism, is to find a way to maximize the economic benefits of tourism while also minimizing negative impacts on the local community and the natural environment. It contains a set of guiding principles that direct actions associated with tourism toward a future that is more sustainable and equitable.
   The Three Key Metrics to Consider:
   The "triple bottom line" idea, which evaluates the economic, environmental, and social aspects
   of anything, is frequently utilized in the process of evaluating sustainable tourism. The goal is to make sure that the positive effects of tourism are felt across all three dimensions, rather than just one of them, so that none of them suffers as a result.
   The following are the core tenets of sustainable tourism:

The goals of sustainable tourism are to have as little of an adverse effect on the environment as possible, to protect natural and cultural heritage, to offer concrete benefits to the people that are visited, and to ensure that tourists have a positive experience by providing them with memorable activities.

2. **Frameworks and Declarations at the International Level**
The Global Sustainable Tourism Council, or GSTC, is an organization that:
The Global Sustainable Tourism Council (GSTC) establishes a standard set of objectives and performance metrics for environmentally responsible tourism. These criteria are utilized on a global scale to advise destinations as well as enterprises in their own efforts to promote sustainability.

The Sustainable Development Goals (SDGs) of the United Nations are as follows:
Quite a few of the Sustainable Development Goals (SDGs) have a direct bearing on tourism, including Goal 8 (Decent Work and Economic Growth), Goal 12 (Responsible Consumption and Production), Goal 14 (Life Below Water), and Goal 15 (Life on Land). It is imperative that the rules and practices of the tourism industry are in line with these goals in order to achieve global sustainability.

The Earth Summit, which took place in Rio de Janeiro in the year 1992:
The Earth Summit was essential in the development of the concept of sustainable tourism by highlighting the necessity of striking a balance between the growth of tourism and the protection of the environment. The need of environmentally responsible vacationing was emphasized in the final document for the Agenda 21 summit.

3. **Policies and Regulations Fostering Environmentally Responsible Tourism**
The Ecotourism Model Used in Costa Rica:
The policies of Costa Rican ecotourism are well-known for their emphasis on the preservation of biological diversity and the reduction of adverse effects on the surrounding environment. The country's reputation as a destination for environmentally responsible tourism is helped along by the presence of national parks and wildlife reserves, as well as rigorous controls on land use and development.

Tourism's Contribution to Bhutan's Gross National Happiness (GNH)
The unique Gross National Happiness (GNH) tourism policy of Bhutan places a premium on the joy and health of the country's residents. The amount of visitors allowed into the country is capped, there is a mandated minimum daily spend, and the government utilizes the money collected to pay for essential public services. This policy safeguards the natural environment while also encouraging environmentally responsible and valuable tourism.

Great Barrier Reef in Australia Regulations regarding:
In order to prevent damage to the Great Barrier Reef, Australia has imposed rigorous limits on activities such as boating, fishing, and other pursuits.

Additionally, in order to ensure the reef's continued existence into the future, Australia's Reef 2050 Plan prioritizes the improvement of water quality, the mitigation of the effects of climate change, and conservation initiatives.

Community-Based Conservation Organizations in Kenya:
The form of conservancy that is used in Kenya emphasizes the participation of local populations in animal protection. By limiting the number of tourists and offering financial incentives to local communities, it encourages the development of tourism that does not harm the environment. This method not only helps to preserve natural resources but also gives economic agency to the surrounding community.

The Swedish Right to Roam, often known as the Allemansratten:
People in Sweden have the "Right to Roam," which is a regulation that gives them the ability to access and roam in the countryside without the permission of landowners. This freedom comes from the Allemansratten. This strategy encourages environmentally responsible tourism by enabling tourists to appreciate Sweden's natural beauty without causing any harm to the surrounding ecosystem.

4. **Encouraging the Long-Term Viability of the Environment**
   Labels and Certifications for Environmental Efficacy:
   Hotels, tour operators, and locations are awarded eco-labels like the Green Key, EarthCheck, and Blue Flag if they are found to be environmentally responsible and conform to stringent requirements. These certifications support responsible tourism and actions that are good for the environment.

   Regulations for the Protection of Wildlife:
   A great number of nations, including South Africa and India, have passed laws that protect their native species and the natural environments on their territories. Poaching, illegal trading, and the degradation of habitat are some of the problems that are addressed by these restrictions.

   Regulations Concerning Marine Conservation:
   The regulation of activities like marine tourism and conservation is absolutely necessary in order to ensure the survival of marine ecosystems. For example, the Galápagos Marine Reserve in Ecuador and the Great Barrier Reef Marine Park in Australia are both examples of places that have stringent rules in place to guarantee that tourism has a minimal impact on the environment.

   Strategies for the Mitigation of Climate Change:
   In an effort to slow the progression of climate change, a number of nations and tourist destinations are putting into place plans to cut the amount of carbon emissions generated by tourism. This includes the provision of lodgings that are low in energy use, the provision of environmentally responsible transportation options, and the promotion of low-carbon activities.

   Various Initiatives Regarding Waste Management and Recycling:

REDUCING CARBON FOOTPRINT

Tourism's negative effects on the natural world can be mitigated by the implementation of policies that encourage appropriate garbage disposal and recycling practices. Requirements for the separation of garbage and infrastructure for recycling are frequently included in regulations.

5. **Ensuring the Long-Term Viability of Socio-Cultural Systems**
   Safeguarding of the Cultural Heritage:
   The regulations that safeguard cultural heritage places and customs are an important part of keeping destinations unique and maintaining their identity. These laws are beneficial to UNESCO's World Heritage Sites, such as Machu Picchu in the country of Peru.
   Participation in the Local Community and the Distribution of Benefits:
   Communities will be able to more fully reap the benefits of tourism expansion if public policies are enacted to foster more community participation in tourism-related planning and revenue distribution. One example of a project that contributes to the empowerment of local communities is the Himba Community Campsite in Namibia.
   Initiatives Towards Gender Equality:
   Efforts to promote gender equality in the tourism industry, such as the "She Means Business" campaign, aim to address issues such as gender-based discrimination and violence, as well as to empower women currently working in the sector.
   Guidelines for the Regulation of Responsible Volunteer Tourism:
   The regulations that govern voluntourism, also known as volunteer tourism, have the goal of ensuring that volunteer activities are moral, beneficial, and in line with the requirements of the host community. These policies encourage responsible and meaningful participation in volunteer tourism.

6. **Ensuring the Long-Term Viability of the Economy**
   Distribution of Earnings from Tourism:
   To ensure the continued health of the economy, transparent policies regarding the distribution of
   profits from tourism are absolutely necessary. Certain locations provide a portion of their revenue generated from tourists to the improvement of local community facilities, infrastructure, and environmental protection.
   Regulations Regarding the Issuing of Licenses to Tour Operators:
   Licensing and regulation of tour operators ensures that these businesses adhere to particular standards and ethical criteria, which helps to build trust in the tourist industry and contributes to the sector's capacity to remain viable over the long term.
   Initiatives to Promote Fair Trade and Fair Tourism:
   Organizations that promote ethical and sustainable business practices, such as fair trade and fair tourism, aim to ensure that tourism is beneficial to the

communities and workers it visits.

Assistance with Microfinancing and Small Businesses:
It is possible to foster economic growth and encourage local community entrepreneurs by providing assistance to microfinance institutions and small businesses operating within the tourism industry.

7. **Obstacles to Overcome and Opportunities to Seize When Implementing Policies and Regulations Concerning Sustainable Tourism**

   Finding a Happy Medium Between Economic Development and Environmental Protection:
   Finding a happy medium between expanding the economy and protecting the natural world will continue to be a difficult task. Policies designed to be sustainable should have as their dual goals the promotion of responsible tourism and the guarantee of economic advantages for the destination.

   The Process of Monitoring and Enforcing:
   It is imperative to have efficient monitoring and enforcement of regulations in order for them to be successful. It is possible that policies will continue to be unsuccessful if enough resources and commitment are not provided.

   Excessive tourism:
   The problem of "overtourism," which happens when the number of tourists exceeds the capacity of the place, is an issue that some locations have to face. It is a difficult task to successfully implement rules that manage overtourism while still ensuring that local communities benefit.

   The principles of Inclusivity and Equity:
   It might be difficult to ensure that every person of the community is able to benefit from tourism and has a voice in the development of the industry. Inclusion and fairness ought to be given top priority in policymaking.

   Innovation and technological advancement:
   The tourist sector is undergoing a period of fast evolution, driven mostly by technological advancement and innovative thinking. Policies and regulations need to be revised to account for these shifts, taking into consideration concerns such as vacation rentals for a limited period of time, internet platforms, and intelligent tourism.

8. **The Importance of Stakeholders in the Tourism Industry for the Promotion of Sustainable Tourism**

   Authorities within Governments and Regulatory Organizations:
   When it comes to formulating tourist policy and regulations, governments are key players. They are required to give sustainable practices a high priority and allot resources to encourage those activities.

   Economy Based on Tourism:
   There is a responsibility on the part of enterprises involved in tourism, such as hotels, airlines, and tour operators, to adopt and promote environmentally

friendly practices. They have the ability to sway consumer decisions and work in collaboration with destinations.

Communities Close to Home:
Sustainable tourism relies heavily on the participation of local people as stakeholders. Their
participation and empowerment has the potential to result in tourist practices that are more inclusive and responsible.

Visitors, Vacationers, and Passengers:
Travelers have the ability to make decisions that are more environmentally friendly, such as picking eco-friendly hotels and showing respect for the cultures and surroundings of the places they visit.

The acronym "NGOs" stands for "non-governmental organizations"
Nongovernmental organizations (NGOs) play an extremely important part in promoting environmentally responsible tourist practices and providing assistance to local populations in target destinations.

9. **Emerging Patterns in Environmentally Responsible Tourism Policies and Regulations**

Technologies of the digital age and environmentally responsible tourism:
The future of sustainable tourism will be shaped by the incorporation of digital technologies, such as blockchain for creating transparent supply chains and artificial intelligence for creating individualized eco-friendly travel experiences.

The acronym "DMO" stands for "destination management organization"
The Destination Management Organizations (DMOs) will play a pivotal role in the promotion of destination-specific sustainability practices as well as the implementation of sustainable policies.

Tourism that is based on local communities:
It is expected that there will be an increased emphasis placed on community-based tourism, with more destinations working toward the goal of include local communities in decision-making and income sharing.

Resilience and Preparedness in the Face of Adversity:
To protect tourism assets from the effects of climate change and other risks, tourism policy will increasingly emphasize resilience and disaster preparedness.

Increase in Tourism That Includes Everyone:
Through the implementation of laws and regulations geared at fostering inclusiveness, the sector will work to guarantee that the expansion of tourism provides advantages to all parties involved.

Policies and regulations pertaining to sustainable tourism are absolutely necessary in order to adequately manage the worldwide difficulties faced by the tourism industry. These policies encourage responsible and ethical tourism by striking a balance between economic interests, concerns for the environment, and concerns for socio-cultural issues. In spite of the fact that problems such as overtourism and striking a balance between conflicting interests continue to be an issue, the achievements that have been made and the lessons that have been gained all over the world provide extremely helpful insights into how sustainable tourism might be attained.

Emerging technologies, shifting traveler preferences, and the growing need of preserving environmental and socio-cultural diversity will likely have a significant impact on the future of environmentally responsible tourism. However, the fundamental concepts of sustainability, which include economic, environmental, and social dimensions, will continue to be at the center of this business. This will ensure that it continues to make a good contribution to the world while also protecting the earth and the people who live on it.

9.1 Global and National Initiatives

It will take a concerted effort from everyone to overcome problems on a global scale such as poverty, climate change, and public health emergencies. At this point, both international and domestic initiatives enter the picture. These initiatives consist of strategic frameworks, programs, and collaborations that are aimed to solve critical concerns, generate changes that are sustainable, and foster global collaboration. In this article, we investigate the relevance of global and national initiatives by looking at specific examples of their impact in a variety of fields, such as the protection of the natural environment, the promotion of public health, the advancement of education, and the growth of social development.

1. **An Awareness of Both International and National Initiatives**
   What Do We Mean When We Talk About Global and National Initiatives?
   In order to solve issues that are prevalent all over the world, a number of nations, organizations on a global scale, and other interested parties have banded together to form global initiatives. On the other hand, national initiatives are programs and policies that are undertaken by particular nations to solve domestic challenges or to align with global efforts.
   How the Sustainable Development Goals (SDGs) Can Help:
   The Sustainable Development Goals (SDGs) established by the United Nations act as a global framework that serves to inspire and guide a wide variety of global and national efforts. The 17 Sustainable Development Goals (SDGs) cover a wide variety of topics, such as ending global poverty, protecting the environment, and achieving gender equality.
   Working Together and Engaging in Multilateralism:
   The necessity of working together and engaging in multilateralism is highlighted by global projects. They are aware that in order to effectively handle complex global concerns, it is often necessary for governments and organizations from all over the world to work together.

2. **International Efforts Towards the Protection of the Environment**
   The Agreement Reached in Paris:
   The historic worldwide initiative that tries to tackle climate change is known as the Paris Agreement, and it was adopted in the year 2015. It urges nations to cut their emissions of greenhouse gases, make the switch to cleaner forms of energy, and keep the increase in average world temperature to well below 2 degrees Celsius above pre-industrial levels.
   The Convention on Biological Diversity (often abbreviated as CBD):
   The Convention on Biological Diversity (also known as the CBD) is an international project with the goals of preserving biodiversity, ensuring the responsible use of natural resources, and encouraging the equitable distribution of benefits derived from genetic resources. Its goals are absolutely necessary for the long-term health of the environment.
   Initiative for a Sustainable Ocean under the auspices of the United Nations:
   The protection of seas and marine life across the globe is the objective of this program. It encourages environmentally responsible fishing practices, protects maritime ecosystems and biodiversity, and helps conserve marine resources.
   The Initiative for the Great Green Wall :
   The Great Green Wall is an initiative to address soil degradation and desertification in the Sahel region of Africa. This initiative is being led by the African Union. A mosaic of different trees and plants will be planted as part of this program, which will help repair degraded environments.
3. **International Efforts in the Field of Public Health**
   The Global Fund to Fight AIDS, Tuberculosis, and Malaria is comprised of the following
   organizations:
   This international effort brings together resources to battle the three most significant epidemics. It does this by providing funds for preventative measures, treatment options, and support programs in nations that are severely afflicted by these diseases.
   Plan d'action mondial pour la vaccination (GVAP):
   The Global Vaccination Action Plan (GVAP) is an international effort to increase the number of people who are vaccinated and to lower the number of diseases that can be prevented by vaccination. Its goal is to ensure that people in every community have access to immunizations that can save their lives.
   The Framework Convention on Tobacco Control, which was developed by the World Health Organization (WHO):
   This global initiative lays out measures to cut down on the use of tobacco and the negative effects it has on people's health. It incorporates safeguards to protect individuals from the negative effects of tobacco usage.
   The Global Initiative for the Eradication of Polio:

This program, which is a partnership between several nations, international organizations, and donors, aims to completely eradicate polio around the world. It entails carrying out large-scale immunization campaigns and monitoring initiatives.

4. **Educational Initiatives in the Global Community**
   Initiative for an Education That Is Available to All Students (EFA)
   The Education for All (EFA) initiative was started in the year 2000 with the intention of ensuring that every kid has access to a good education. It was a forerunner of the Sustainable Development Goal number 4, which aims to "ensure inclusive and equitable quality education and promote lifelong learning opportunities for all."
   The Global Partnership for Education (GPE) is comprised of the following:
   The Global Partnership for Education (GPE) is a global project that focuses on improving education in nations with low incomes. It does this by providing financial support as well as assistance of a technical nature to develop educational systems.
   Initiative for the Education of Girls Undertaken by the United Nations (UNGEI)
   The United Nations Gender Equality program (UNGEI) is a global program to promote gender equality in education. It campaigns for the education of girls, for changes in policy, and for the elimination of learning obstacles that are related to gender.
   The movement toward using open educational resources (OER)
   The Open Educational Resources (OER) movement is an international campaign that aims to make educational resources freely available to anybody who has access to the internet. This helps boost access to education and learning that can continue throughout one's life.

5. **Initiatives Internationales pour le Développement Social**
   The Sustainable Development Goals (SDGs) of the United Nations are as follows:
   The Sustainable Development Goals (SDGs) cover a wide variety of global projects with the
   objectives of eradicating poverty, lowering inequality, combating climate change, and advancing social justice and peace.
   Data from the Global Partnership for Sustainable Development
   This effort aims to improve data collection and utilization so that progress can be tracked on the Sustainable Development Goals (SDGs). For the purpose of establishing evidence-based policy and evaluating the impact of global and national initiatives, having data of a high quality is essential.
   An Agenda for Sustainable Development Based on the Year 2030:
   The 2030 Agenda for Sustainable Development is an international initiative

that offers a unified road map to achieve both peace and prosperity. It highlights the interconnected nature of global concerns as well as the necessity of taking an all-encompassing strategy.

The International Covenant on Civil and Political Rights:
The Universal Declaration of Human Rights is a statement of global commitment to the rights and dignity of all individuals, notwithstanding the fact that it was not a recent effort. It has served as the basis for a great deal of activity on a worldwide scale as well as at the national level in the field of human rights.

6. **National Initiatives That Are Driving Change That Is Sustainable**

   The Belt and Road Initiative (often abbreviated as BRI):
   The Belt and Road effort (BRI) is a national effort in China that will have global repercussions. It entails making improvements to existing infrastructure and forming economic alliances with nations located in Asia, Europe, and Africa.

   Swachh Bharat Abhiyan, often known as the Clean India Campaign in India:
   The improvement of sanitation and hygiene is the primary focus of this country-wide program, and its ultimate objective is to rid India of the practice of open defecation. It has had a huge impact on the health of the general population.

   Program of the Bolsa Famlia in Brazil:
   The Bolsa Famlia program is a nationwide project in Brazil that provides cash transfers to families with low incomes with the goal of lowering poverty levels and reducing inequality. It has helped millions of people rise above their poverty level.

   The Energiewende (sometimes spelled Energiewende) in Germany:
   The Energiewende is a nationwide program in Germany that aims to convert the country's energy sector to renewable sources and lower the country's emissions of greenhouse gases. Discussions over the world's energy policy have been impacted as a result.

7. **Obstacles to Overcome and Opportunities to Seize Within International and National Initiatives**

   Challenges Presented by Coordination and Implementation:
   The successful coordination and implementation of global and national activities is one of the most significant issues that must be overcome. It is necessary to have well-defined goals, resources that are specifically allocated, and collaboration among a wide variety of stakeholders.

   Finances and the Distribution of Resources:
   For initiatives to be successful, it is essential to have adequate financing and resources allocated to them. It might be difficult to ensure financial sustainability while also maintaining equity in the distribution of resources.

   Monitoring and Holding People Responsible:
   In order to measure progress and solve any deficiencies, having methods that are

both effective in monitoring and holding people accountable is vital. The process of establishing and continuing to maintain these systems might be difficult.

The principles of Inclusivity and Equity:

It is imperative that initiatives focus inclusivity and equity in order to guarantee that the benefits will trickle down to all groups, particularly those that are disadvantaged and vulnerable.

Capacity for Adaptation and Flexibility:

Initiatives on a global and national scale need to maintain their adaptability and flexibility in order to meet new and emerging concerns, such as those relating to public health or the environment.

8. **The Importance of Stakeholders to the Progress of International and Domestic Initiatives**

   Governments and Those Who Formulate Policy:

   Initiating, supporting, and carrying out the implementation of global and national projects are all primary responsibilities of governments. Policymakers are responsible for constructing the legal and regulatory frameworks that are the primary drivers of change.

   NGOs and the Civil Society:

   Organizations that are part of civil society and non-governmental organizations frequently play important roles in the success of projects, including those of champions, implementers, and watchdogs.

   Private Companies and the Industrial World:

   The private sector has the potential to be an invaluable partner in both international and domestic endeavors, making contributions of knowledge, resources, and creative answers.

   Institutions of Higher Education and Research:

   The evidence, information, and skills that are required to guide and drive activities in a variety of areas are provided by academia as well as research institutions.

   People on their Own and in Their Communities:

   Participation from individuals and the community at large is essential to the accomplishment of goals set by initiatives. Support from the general populace and engagement on the part of individuals are frequently required to accomplish aims.

9. **Upcoming Developments and the Changing Landscape of Initiatives**

   Innovation and technological advancement:

   The formulation and execution of initiatives will continue to be influenced by technological developments such as artificial intelligence, blockchain, and large amounts of data.

   Initiatives Regarding the Climate and Sustainability:

It is possible that the current worldwide emphasis on combating climate change and promoting sustainability will result in programs that are both more expansive and integrated.

Initiatives Regarding Health and the Prevention of Pandemics:
In light of the COVID-19 pandemic, the importance of global and national actions in health and pandemic preparedness has been brought into sharper focus. This will continue to be a primary area of focus in the future.

Initiatives to Promote Digital Inclusion:
The closing of the digital divide and the guaranteeing of digital inclusion for all people will become an increasingly significant goal of the various efforts that attempt to provide access to technology and online resources.

Initiatives Driven by Young People:
Initiatives and movements headed by young people will continue to have a big impact on both global and national agendas because they are propelled by the fervor and activism of young people.

Initiatives on a global and national scale show humanity's collective reaction to the intricately interwoven problems we confront. They function as road maps, leading us in the direction of a future that is more sustainable, equitable, and affluent. These programs, which encourage collaboration, innovation, and inclusivity, play a critical role in driving real change across a wide range of fields, from the protection of the natural environment and the promotion of public health to the advancement of education and social welfare. Individuals and communities' active participation is essential to the success of these projects, which are dependent not just on the cooperation of governments and organizations but also of individuals. Our ability to handle global and national concerns in a world that is becoming more globalized is dependent on our dedication to collective action and the quest of a better society for all of us. This commitment is essential if we are to survive in this interconnected and interdependent era.

9.2 Environmental Legislation and Agreements

The environmental problems that our planet is facing are more urgent than they have ever been. Both the health of ecosystems and people are at risk as a result of human activities such as pollution, habitat loss, climate change, and resource depletion. As a direct response to the problems posed by these issues, national governments and international organizations have adopted a plethora of environmental laws and accords. These legislative frameworks have as their goals the protection of the environment, the promotion of sustainability, and the resolution of urgent problems on a global scale. During this in-depth investigation, we will delve into the world of environmental legislation and agreements, gaining a grasp of their relevance, studying notable examples, and evaluating their influence on our efforts to create a future that is sustainable.

1. **The Importance of Laws and Treaties Concerning the Environment**
   The Importance of Having a Legal Structure:
   Legislation and agreements pertaining to the environment are crucial tools in the process of addressing environmental challenges. They are responsible for the establishment of standards, the provision of guidance, and the formation of enforcement procedures.
   Cooperation on the International Level:
   There are several environmental problems that affect the entire planet. Cooperation among nations is encouraged by international accords, which makes it possible for them to address global challenges like the loss of biodiversity and the conservation of ocean resources as a group.
   Goals for Sustainable Development (also known as the SDGs):
   The Sustainable Development Goals (SDGs) of the United Nations, in particular Goal 13 (Climate Action) and Goal 14 (Life Below Water), emphasize the significance of international collaboration and legal frameworks in order to solve environmental challenges.
2. **Major Environmental Treaties and Agreements at the International Level**
   In accordance with the Paris Agreement (2015):
   The historic global accord aiming at reducing the effects of climate change is called the Paris Agreement. It establishes a framework for countries to restrict global warming to far below 2 degrees Celsius above pre-industrial levels. This would be a significant achievement. Among the most important sections are those pertaining to nationally decided contributions and financial assistance for developing nations.
   The Convention on Biological Diversity (often abbreviated as CBD):
   The Convention on Biological variety is an international treaty that addresses the issues of conserving biological variety, making sustainable use of its components, and sharing the benefits in a fair and equitable manner. The Nagoya Protocol on access to genetic resources and benefit-sharing is included in this agreement.
   The United Nations Framework Convention on Climate Change, abbreviated as UNFCCC, is comprised of the following:
   The United Nations Framework Convention on Climate Change (UNFCCC), which was approved in 1992, is the cornerstone international convention addressing climate change. It ultimately resulted in the Paris Agreement after the Kyoto Protocol was established. The concentrations of greenhouse gases in the atmosphere are the target of this initiative.
   CITES is an acronym that stands for the Convention on International Trade in Endangered Species of Wild Fauna and Flora
   The Convention on International commerce in Endangered animals (CITES) is an international agreement that controls commerce in endangered animals. It

aids in the conservation of wildlife and discourages the illegal trade of plants and animals.

Convention of the United Nations on the Law of the Sea (abbreviated as UNCLOS)

The United Nations Convention on the Law of the Sea (UNCLOS) lays out the legal guidelines for the oceans and the resources found within them. It discusses topics such as the conservation and sustainable management of marine life as well as the biodiversity of marine ecosystems.

3. Legislation Concerning the Environment on the National Level

The Clean Air Act, which applies in the United States:

In the United States, the Clean Air Act is a comprehensive piece of environmental legislation that governs air quality standards and pollutants. It was passed in the 1970s. The protection of human health and the environment from the harmful effects of air pollution is the purpose of this act.

The European Union's Water Framework Directive entails the following:

The European Union has passed a law known as the Water Framework Directive with the intention of preserving and enhancing the quality of the water in Europe's rivers, lakes, and coastal waterways. It comprises strategies for the management of water and for the control of pollution.

The European Union's Environmental Impact Assessment Directive (often known as the EIA Directive):

The Environmental effect Assessment Directive (EIA Directive) requires all member states of the European Union to carry out environmental effect studies of specific public and private construction projects. It makes certain that environmental concerns are taken into account during the decision-making process.

The National Environmental Policy Act, which governs environmental policy in the United

States:

The National Environmental Policy Act (NEPA) is a statute in the United States that mandates environmental impact assessments to be conducted by federal agencies before certain actions can be taken. It places an emphasis on public engagement in decision-making as well as openness to information.

Act of India Relating to Forest Rights:

The Forest Rights Act in India acknowledges the rights of communities that live in or around forests and works toward the goal of protecting the traditional lands and resources of these communities. It is an essential piece of legislation for the protection of the environment and the rights of indigenous people.

Important Pieces of Environmental Legislation and Agreements, Categorized by Topic

Reduced Impacts of Climate Change

The Kyoto Protocol, which was signed in 1997: As an extension of the UN Framework Convention on Climate Change (UNFCCC), the Kyoto Protocol established legally binding targets for developed countries to cut emissions of greenhouse gases. Trading of emissions and the Clean Development Mechanism (CDM) were both initiated as a result.

The Regional Greenhouse Gas Initiative, or RGGI, consists of the following: The Regional Greenhouse Gas Initiative (RGGI) is a consortium of northeastern states in the United States working together to limit and cut carbon dioxide emissions from power plants. The reduction of emissions is accomplished through the employment of a market-based method.

The Protection of Biological Diversity

The United States of America's Endangered Species Act: This law makes provisions for the protection of endangered and threatened species in the United States, as well as the habitats in which they live. It has been extremely helpful in the preservation of a wide range of animal species.

The Wetlands Convention, often known as the Ramsar Convention: The Ramsar Convention is a global agreement that was made for the purpose of protecting wetlands and making their use more environmentally friendly. It designates some wetland areas as being of worldwide importance and promotes the protection of those wetland areas.

Oceans and the Conservation of Marine Life

The United States' Marine Mammal Protection Act mandates the following: This piece of law seeks to regulate activities that could be harmful to marine mammals like whales and dolphins in order to safeguard those animals through legislation. It involves methods to limit the amount of fish caught by accident.

The Port State Measures Agreement, or PSMA, entails the following: The Port State Measures Act (PSMA) is a multilateral agreement with the objective of preventing, discouraging, and ultimately eradicating illicit, unreported, and unregulated (IUU) fishing. It aids in the preservation of marine habitats as well as fish stocks.

Protection of Natural Areas and Habitats

Access to the Countryside and National Parks Act is a law in the United Kingdom that states: This act offers statutory protection and financial assistance to the UK's national parks and other areas of natural beauty that are designated as such. The protection and improvement of these landscapes are the primary aims of this initiative.

The Convention on the Conservation of Migratory Species of Wild Animals, also referred to as the CMS: The Convention on Migratory Species (CMS) is an international agreement with the purpose of preserving migratory species that are found on land, in water, and in the air. It contains action plans for a number of different species.

Governance of the Environment and Regulatory Compliance

The Aarhus Convention (UNECE): The Aarhus Convention offers the public certain rights on access to information, public involvement, and access to justice in matters pertaining to environmental concerns. It ensures both responsibility and openness to the public.

Act (Australia) for the Protection of the Environment and the Conservation of Biological Diversity: This regulation in Australia protects both the environment and the country's diverse array of plant and animal life. It evaluates and gives its blessing to activities that may have an effect on the environment.

V. Environmental Legislation and Agreements: Obstacles to Overcome and Opportunities to Seize

The Processes of Implementation and Enforcement:

The efficient and effective implementation and enforcement of environmental laws and agreements is one of the key difficulties that must be overcome. This frequently calls for cooperation across several government departments and at various levels of government.

Responsibility and Observance of the Law:

It can be difficult to ensure that companies, organizations, and governments comply with environmental standards. Mechanisms of accountability are absolutely necessary for both monitoring and responding to infractions.

Complexity and Many-sidedness of the Problem:

Environmental problems are frequently difficult to understand and intertwined. These complex problems require legal systems that can adequately address all of their facets.

The Changing Face of Legislation:

Legislation pertaining to the environment needs to progress in order to accommodate newly arising problems, which may include novel contaminants, advances in technology, or unanticipated environmental catastrophes.

Cooperation on a Global Scale and the Concept of Sovereignty:

Finding a happy medium between the competing demands of international collaboration and national sovereignty can be a tricky business. The task of ensuring that countries efficiently work while also preserving their own autonomy is one that never goes away.

VI. The Part That Stakeholders Play in Environmental Laws and Agreements

Agencies of the Government and Those Who Formulate Policy:

When it comes to the drafting, carrying out, and upholding of environmental laws and treaties, the primary responsibility is with governmental agencies and policymakers.

Civil society organizations and lobbying groups:

Civil society organizations and advocacy groups frequently take on the role of watchdogs, working to get stricter environmental regulations and to hold governments and businesses accountable for their actions.

Organizations and Commercial Enterprises:
Complying with environmental standards is one of the responsibilities of businesses, and they can also play a role in advocating for legislation that encourage responsible behavior and sustainable practices.

Institutions of Higher Education and Research:
Both scientific expertise and the creation of evidence-based environmental policies can be attributed to contributions made by research institutions and academic institutions.

People on their Own and in Their Communities:
Movements at the grassroots level, public pressure, and environmentally conscious lifestyle decisions are all effective ways for individuals and local groups to affect environmental laws.

VIII. The evolving landscape of environmental legislation and agreements

New and Evolving Technologies
Environmental monitoring and compliance enforcement will become easier to carry out as a result of technological developments such as remote sensing, artificial intelligence, and data analytics.

Problems That Cross Borders:
Environmental problems that extend beyond national boundaries, such as pollution of the air and water, will continue to call for international collaboration and the establishment of legal frameworks.

Environmentalism and a Sustainable Economy:
The establishment of legal frameworks will place an increased emphasis on the promotion of sustainability and the transition to economies that are environmentally friendly, circular, and efficient with their use of resources.

Young People's Activism:
It is expected that the evolution of environmental laws and accords will be influenced by the growing impact of young movements calling for climate action and environmental justice.

Both Adaptability and Resilience are Required:
It will be increasingly necessary for legal frameworks to handle adaptation to the effects of climate change as well as the construction of resilient communities and ecosystems.

Environmental laws and treaties demonstrate humanity's dedication to preserving the earth and promoting ecologically responsible growth. They supply the legal and regulatory tools that are required to address urgent environmental concerns, such as climate change and the loss of biodiversity, as well as pollution and the deterioration of habitats. These legislative frameworks provide optimism and a road map toward a more sustainable future, notwithstanding the ongoing difficulties associated with implementation, compliance, and the emergence of new environmental risks. It is absolutely necessary for governments, non-governmental organizations, enterprises, and private citizens to work together in order to achieve the objectives that have been outlined in these agreements and to make the world a safer, more ecologically sensitive place for future generations.

9.3 Public and Private Sector Partnerships

The term "public and private sector partnerships," more commonly abbreviated as "PPPs," refers to cooperative projects that are undertaken by government agencies and private companies or organizations. These partnerships intend to capitalize on the respective capabilities of both industries in order to accomplish shared objectives, which are frequently based on the provision of public services, the promotion of economic development, and the resolution of complicated societal concerns. PPPs have the potential to create innovation, efficiency, and sustainable growth across a variety of industries since they combine resources, skills, and capabilities.

In the framework of the development of infrastructure, public-private partnerships (PPPs) have played an important part in the funding and delivery of key projects, such as energy facilities, transportation networks, and public utilities. They make it possible for the government to draw on the knowledge and resources of the private sector, allowing the government to circumvent financial restrictions and speed up the delivery of essential infrastructure services. In the fields of healthcare and education, public-private partnerships (PPPs) have been significant in enabling the extension of services, improvements in service quality, and expansions in access to necessary facilities, particularly in areas that have been underserved.

In addition, public-private partnerships (PPPs) play an important role in driving innovation and technical progress across a variety of sectors. Governments have the ability to stimulate research and development activities, encourage entrepreneurial activity, and accelerate the adoption of cutting-edge technologies through the formation of collaborative partnerships with private businesses. The collaboration that occurs between the public and private sectors frequently results in the development of new markets, the creation of new job opportunities, and an increase in global competitiveness.

However, in order for public-private partnerships (PPPs) to be successful, there must be a crystal-clear knowledge of the objectives of each partner, as well as transparent governance structures and efficient risk-sharing systems. For partnerships to be long-lasting and profitable to both parties, it is essential to strike a balance between the competing interests and priorities of the two different fields. In addition, effective monitoring and evaluation mechanisms are necessary if one wishes to assure accountability, measure performance, and evaluate the influence of these collaborations on societal well-being and economic expansion. Partnerships between the public and private sectors have the ability to stimulate equitable development, foster resilience, and create lasting positive outcomes for communities and economies if they are well executed.

Chapter 10

The Future of Sustainable Tourism

There has been a paradigm shift in the way that we think about travel and the influence that it has on the environment, cultures, and economies over the past few decades, and one of the terms that has become increasingly important to discuss in this context is sustainable tourism. It is becoming more important than ever before for there to be sustainable tourism standards in place as globalization continues to increase the number of people traveling all over the world. The relevance of sustainable tourism is discussed in this in-depth article, along with its challenges, innovations, and potential future directions. We can obtain insight into how responsible and sustainable business practices will affect the travel and tourism industry in the years to come if we investigate the shifting landscape of the travel and tourism industry.

1. **The Importance of Ecotourism in the Tourism Industry**
   The Meaning of the Term "Sustainable Tourism"
   The notion of sustainable tourism, which is also sometimes referred to as responsible tourism and ecotourism, is one that places an emphasis on reducing the adverse effects of tourism while simultaneously elevating the sector's beneficial contributions. Its goal is to encourage travel that is sustainable from an economic standpoint, gentle on the environment, and fair to all parties involved.
   The Influence of Tourism on the World:
   Tourism is a massive sector that operates all over the world and helps economies, as well as providing opportunities for people to interact culturally with one another. On the other hand, concerns have been voiced over its effects on the environment and on society as a result of its rapid expansion.
   The Importance of Environmental Stewardship:
   As the earth is confronted with an increasing number of difficulties, such as climate change, the loss of biodiversity, and the erosion of cultural traditions, the demand for environmentally responsible tourist practices has become an

absolute necessity. The practice of sustainable tourism is one way to protect the health of our planet and the people who live on it over the long term.

2. **Obstacles and Difficulties in Achieving Sustainable Tourism**
Excessive tourism:
The increase in the number of tourists visiting certain locations has resulted in congestion, the destruction of the natural environment, and disturbances to the local culture. The difficulty of managing excessive tourism while ensuring that local communities benefit from it continues.
Pressures from the Economy:
The pursuit of profits in the near term might be detrimental to efforts made toward sustainability.
Maintaining a healthy equilibrium between economic interests, environmental concerns, and social concerns is a continuing struggle.
The principles of Inclusivity and Equity:
It can be difficult, particularly in underdeveloped places, to ensure that every person of a community is able to benefit from tourism and has a voice in the development of the industry.
Influence on the Environment:
The tourism industry is responsible for a significant amount of environmental damage, including the production of carbon emissions and garbage as well as the disruption of ecosystems. To achieve sustainability, it is necessary to reduce these consequences as much as possible.
Protecting Our Cultural Heritage:
The upkeep and maintenance of regional customs and practices in the face of globalization and increased tourist traffic is an ongoing struggle. The goal of sustainable tourism is to preserve cultural diversity while also celebrating it.

3. **The Development of Responsible Tourism: Recent Trends and Upcoming Innovations**
Ecotourism and Other Forms of Tourism Based on Nature
The sector of tourism known as ecotourism, which centers on encounters with native flora and fauna, is continuously gaining ground. Initiatives for the conservation of wildlife and encounters with animals that are conducted in a responsible manner are examples of innovations.
Tourism that is based on local communities:
Local communities are brought into the tourism sector through the practice of community-based tourism, which gives them the opportunity to take part in and benefit from the economic prospects that the tourism industry offers.
Technologies that are good for the environment and eco-friendly lodgings:
The use of environmentally friendly technologies, eco-friendly building materials, and environmentally responsible architectural designs are all on the rise in the hospitality industry.

The Digitization of Everything:
The use of technology to promote sustainable tourism is expanding, with mobile applications, internet platforms, and blockchain all playing important parts in the process of enriching the experience of travelers while also boosting the industry's ability to avoid negative environmental impacts.

Tourism centered on health and wellness:
Experiences that are more focused on wellness and health are becoming increasingly popular among travelers. This trend creates chances for wellness tourism programs that are environmentally responsible.

4. **The Role of Tourism Policies and Regulations in Ensuring a Sustainable Future for the Industry**

Agreements and Initiatives on a Global Scale:
Global agreements and initiatives are being aggressively promoted by international organizations such as the United Nations and the World Tourism Organization in an effort to promote tourism that is environmentally responsible.

Regulations at the National and Local Levels:
Many nations are in the process of enacting laws and guidelines that will support sustainable tourism practices. These rules and policies include things like environmental standards, fiscal incentives, and mandatory community engagement.

Programs for Accreditation as well as Labeling:
Certification systems, like as EarthCheck and Green Key, are extremely important when it comes to recognizing and promoting businesses who are committed to providing environmentally responsible lodging and tourism experiences.

Collaborations between the public sector and the private sector:
Collaborations between governmental entities, commercial sector stakeholders, and non-governmental organizations are required in order to effectively implement and enforce policies pertaining to sustainable tourism.

The acronym "DMO" stands for "destination management organization"
The Destination Management Organization (DMO) industry is evolving to take on more prominent roles in the stewardship of destinations and the management of sustainable tourism.

5. **The Global Context, With an Emphasis on Climate Change and Its Effects**

Tourism and the Changing Climate :
Because of its impact on weather patterns, sea levels, and natural attractions, climate change represents a substantial risk to the tourism industry. It is essential for the continued success of the sector to find ways to accommodate these shifts.

Transportation that is Kind to the Environment:
The contribution of the transportation industry to the overall carbon footprint of tourism is significant. The development of environmentally friendly modes of transportation, such as enhanced public transportation and electric vehicles,

is an absolute necessity.

Resilience and Preparedness in the Face of Adversity:
Destinations have a responsibility to take precautions in light of the fact that climate-related disasters, such as hurricanes and wildfires, are becoming more frequent and severe.

Action on Climate Change and Sustainable Tourism:
By decreasing emissions, supporting sustainable practices, and raising awareness about the effects of climate change, the tourism industry has the potential to play a significant part in the fight against climate change.

6. **Important Observations and Recommended Procedures**

    Participation in the Local Community and the Distribution of Benefits:
    It is a fundamentally important best practice to involve the local communities in tourism and to ensure that they profit from it.

    Management of Resources in a Sustainable Manner:
    For sustainability over the long term, it is imperative to practice responsible management of the world's ecosystems and natural resources.

    Education and a Consciousness of the Facts:
    It is essential for the development of sustainable tourism to educate travelers on the need of responsible travel and cultural sensitivity.

    Impact Evaluation and Evaluation of Measures:
    It is essential to have robust monitoring and evaluation mechanisms in place in order to track the impact that sustainable tourism activities have.

    Cooperation Between the Public and Private Sectors:
    Collaborations between the public and commercial sectors, in which the respective advantages of each are capitalized on, are frequently necessary for the development of sustainable tourism.

7. **Innovations, Collaborations, and Other Factors Driving Change**

Technologies of the digital age and environmentally responsible tourism:
Change is being driven by digital technologies such as blockchain, which enables transparent
supply chains, and artificial intelligence, which enables individualized environmentally responsible travel.

The acronym "DMO" stands for "destination management organization"
Destination management organizations (DMOs) are playing increasingly important roles in destination-specific marketing and sustainability initiatives.

Tourism that is based on local communities:
There has been a shift toward a greater emphasis on community-based tourism, with an increase in the number of destinations working toward the goal of including local residents in tourist-related decision-making and revenue distribution.

Resilience and Preparedness in the Face of Adversity:

To protect tourism assets in the face of climate change and other risks, tourism policy are increasingly focusing on building resilience and being prepared for disasters.

Increase in Tourism That Includes Everyone:

The idea of inclusive tourist development is gaining traction, which highlights the requirement for equitable sharing of economic advantages and opportunities.

VII. Policies and Regulations to Encourage Environmentally Responsible Tourism

The Sustainable Development Goals (SDGs) of the United Nations are as follows:

The Sustainable Development Goals (SDGs), in particular Goal 8 ("Decent Work and Economic Growth") and Goal 12 ("Responsible Consumption and Production"), are applicable to the concept of sustainable tourism.

The Global Sustainable Tourism Council, or GSTC, is an organization that:

The Global Sustainable Tourism Council (GSTC) is responsible for establishing standards and criteria for environmentally responsible tourism. This provides a framework for both destinations and businesses.

The United Nations World Tourism Organization, sometimes known as UNWTO:

Through its research, recommendations, and capacity-building programs, the UNWTO encourages tourist practices that are environmentally responsible.

Zoning and other municipal regulations:

Tourism is being managed by local governments, and sustainability is being ensured, through the implementation of zoning restrictions. These regulations include guidelines for short-term rentals and land usage.

Programs for Professional Accreditation:

Businesses and destinations can get assistance in adopting environmentally friendly procedures by participating in one of the many certification programs available, such as the Travelife Sustainability Certification or the Green Destinations Certification.

IX. Initiatives on a Global and National Scale

The Sustainable Development Goals (SDGs) of the United Nations are as follows:

The United Nations World Tourism Organization works to encourage tourism that is ethically sound, environmentally conscious, and open to all. It offers standards and information for use by corporations, government agencies, and individual travelers.

The Global Sustainable Tourism Council, or GSTC, is an organization that:

The Global Sustainable Tourism Council (GSTC) is a global initiative that sets criteria for sustainable tourism. It provides certification programs for enterprises and places of interest.

Initiatives for the Nation's Tourism Industry:

Numerous nations' sustainable tourism projects have been put into motion, and they frequently comply with the Sustainable Development Goals (SDGs) and other international accords.

Partnerships and Collaborations on a Global Scale:
worldwide efforts to make tourism more sustainable are being driven by public-private partnerships, worldwide alliances, and projects such as the 10YFP Sustainable Tourism Program (10YFP STP).

Initiatives Regarding Tourism and Conservation:
Several organizations dedicated to the protection of wildlife, such as The Nature Conservancy and the World Wildlife Fund (WWF), are hard at work developing tourist initiatives that are environmentally responsible and contribute to the economic well-being of local communities.

X. The Importance of Stakeholders in the Movement Towards a More Sustainable Tourism Industry

Governments and Those Who Formulate Policy:
The formulation of tourist laws, regulations, and incentives that are environmentally responsible largely falls under the purview of governing bodies.

The Private Sector and Individual Companies:
The practices of sustainable tourism are significantly impacted by the commercial sector, which includes establishments such as hotels, tour operators, and airlines.

The acronym "NGOs" stands for "non-governmental organizations"
Nongovernmental organizations (NGOs) play a significant role in the development of sustainable tourism initiatives, the promotion of change, and the execution of community projects.

Communities Close to Home:
It is essential for the success of efforts promoting sustainable tourism that local communities are actively involved and given agency in the process.

Visitors, Passengers, and Vacationers:
Travelers have the ability to shape the industry by the decisions they make and the firms they support in terms of responsibility and sustainability.

XI. Upcoming Developments and the Changing Face of Tourism in Sustainable Destinations

Integration of Technology with Responsibility:
Technology will continue to play an important part in the promotion of sustainable tourism, from digital platforms that make responsible travel choices more accessible to blockchain technology that makes supply chains as transparent as possible.

Tourism based on natural phenomena and adventure travel:
The ever-increasing demand for ecotourism and other forms of adventure travel will reshape the tourist sector to place a greater emphasis on environmentally conscious policies and procedures.

Destinations that are Sustainable and Tourism That Regenerates:

It is expected that the idea of regenerative tourism, which goes beyond the concept of sustainable tourism to actively contribute to the restoration of ecosystems and communities, will gain acceptance in the coming years.

Resilience in the Face of Crises and Adaptation:

The development of resilience to calamities, such as those brought on by climate change, as well as public health emergencies such as pandemics, will become an increasingly important emphasis of sustainable tourism.

Tourism that is Beneficial to the Climate

There will be an increase in the prevalence of a shift toward climate-positive tourism, with firms and destinations trying to offset emissions and make a net-positive impact on the environment.

The future of environmentally responsible tourism will be one in which people's lives are enriched, cultures are preserved, the environment is protected, and local communities are benefited. The tourism industry has the potential to become a potent driver of positive change if it adopts more ethical business practices, capitalizes on innovation, and complies with both international accords and local rules. It has the ability to generate economic growth, safeguard natural and cultural assets, and contribute to a more sustainable and inclusive global society. All of these things could be accomplished thanks to its potential. It is possible that the vision of a world in which tourism is a catalyst for positive change can become a reality if tourists, those with vested interests in the tourism sector, and governments continue to collaborate.

10.1 Emerging Trends and Technologies

The lightning-fast pace of technological progress is transforming the world as we know it, which will have enormous repercussions for society, industry, and life in general. The ways in which we interact, work, learn, and live are all being revolutionized as a result of developing trends and technology, which presents us with both unheard-of opportunities and brand-new obstacles. In this in-depth investigation, we look into the most significant emerging trends and technologies, analyzing their relevance as well as the possible benefits and ethical considerations associated with them. If we can get a grasp of these forces of transformation, we will be better able to traverse the complicated landscape of the future.

1. **The Importance of New Fashions and Technologies Currently in Development**

   The following are some examples of emerging trends and technologies:

   Emerging trends and technologies include innovations and advancements that are at the forefront of their respective sectors and often contain the potential to disrupt established industries and norms. These can be thought of as a combination of the terms "cutting edge" and "leading edge."

   The Rapidity with Which Things Are Changing:

   The advent of the digital age has ushered in a period that is characterized

by unprecedented levels of change and innovation. The rate of technological progress is quickening, which will drive the need for ongoing adaptation and change.

Influence on Culture and Manufacturing:
The way in which we communicate with one another, work, and live is being revolutionized by newly emerging technologies. They are having an effect on a variety of facets of society, including healthcare, education, and governance, as well as revolutionizing numerous industries, generating new economic prospects, and creating new economic opportunities.

2. **Artificial intelligence and machine learning will be discussed next.**
   The Role of AI and Automation:
   Automation, data analysis, and the capacity for prediction are just some of the ways that artificial intelligence (AI) and machine learning are causing a revolution in a variety of different industries. They have the ability to simplify procedures, cut down on error rates, and increase overall productivity.

   The Role of AI in Healthcare:
   Artificial intelligence is making huge advancements in the healthcare industry, helping with diagnosis, the discovery of new drugs, and the creation of individualized treatment programs. It has the ability to both enhance the results for patients and lower the expense of healthcare.

   Considerations of an Ethical Nature:
   Concerns about privacy and bias, as well as the loss of jobs, are raised by artificial intelligence. It is of the utmost importance to ensure transparency, justice, and responsible development of AI.

3. **Technology of the fifth generation and connectivity**
   The Revolution of 5G:
   The deployment of 5G technology is making it possible to have wireless connections that are both faster and more dependable. This is helping to foster the expansion of the Internet of Things (IoT) and fostering innovation across a variety of industries.

   Internet of Things with Smart Cities:
   5G is a driving force behind the rise of the Internet of Things (IoT), making it possible to build smart cities, driverless vehicles, and linked devices that improve both productivity and convenience.

   Privacy and protection of sensitive data:
   Concerns regarding data privacy and security are growing in tandem with the expansion of connectivity. It is crucial to ensure that adequate cybersecurity measures are in place.

4. **Technologies of the Blockchain and Distributed Ledgers**
   Trust that is not centralized:
   The blockchain technology provides a distributed ledger that cannot be altered,

making it ideal for secure data sharing and financial transactions. It has the potential to be applied in a variety of fields, including finance and management of supply chains.

The Cryptocurrency Market:

Blockchain technology is the foundation of cryptocurrencies such as Bitcoin and Ethereum, which have the potential to disrupt existing financial institutions. It brings up questions regarding regulation, taxation, and the security of the financial system.

Accountability and Openness to the Public:

The immutability and transparency of blockchain technology have important implications for transparency and accountability in a variety of businesses, including voting systems and food supply chains.

5. **The Combination of Virtual and Augmented Reality**

   (VR) stands for "virtual reality":

   Virtual reality (VR) transports people to computer-generated worlds and has potential uses in a variety of contexts, including gaming, education, and simulations of virtual travel.

   The acronym "augmented reality" (AR):

   Augmented reality (AR) superimposes digital content onto the physical world, making it possible to improve industries such as education, retail, and architecture.

   The Opportunities and the Challenges:

   Virtual reality (VR) and augmented reality (AR) provide prospects for creative learning and interactive experiences, but they also raise worries about addiction, privacy, and the influence on mental health that these technologies have.

6. **Biotechnology and Genetic Engineering**

   Editing of Genomes:

   Precision genome editing is now possible thanks to the development of technologies like as CRISPR-Cas9, which has uses in agriculture, medicine, and gene therapy.

   Recent Developments in Biotechnology:

   Innovations in biofuels, pharmaceuticals, and renewable materials are being driven by biotechnology, which has the potential to address issues relating to the environment and health.

   Ethical Contradictions:

   Concerns about designer babies, GM creatures, and invasions of privacy are all brought up when discussing the ethical implications of genetic engineering. It is of the utmost importance to find a middle ground between innovation and ethics.

7. **Computing on the Quantum Level**

   The preeminence of the quantum:

Quantum computing is a form of computing that uses the principles of quantum mechanics to do complicated calculations in a way that is far more effective than traditional computers. Cryptography and materials science are two examples of fields that could be significantly impacted by this innovation.

The Role of Cryptography in Security:
The development of cryptography that is resistant to quantum computing is required since the current methods of encryption could be compromised by quantum computing.

Discoveries Made in Science:
Quantum computing has the potential to speed up scientific research in a variety of domains, including the search for new drugs, the study of new materials, and the prediction of climate change.

8. **Biometrics and the protection of personal data**
   Authentication using Biometric Measurements:
   The use of biometrics for secure authentication in mobile devices and financial services is becoming increasingly common. Examples of biometrics include fingerprint and face recognition.

   Confidentiality and Permission:
   Concerns concerning privacy, security, and informed permission are raised in relation to biometric data, which then leads to discussions over regulatory frameworks and ethical use.

   Recent Developments in the Protection of Individual Data:
   New technologies are pushing new developments in the security of personal data, such as safe multiparty computation and homomorphic encryption.

9. **Technology for the Quantified Self and Health**
   Wearable Technologies:
   Wearable technology, such as fitness trackers and smartwatches, gives people the ability to monitor and take control of their own health and wellbeing.

   Remote medical monitoring and telemedicine:
   The advent of telemedicine and other technologies that allow for remote monitoring of patients' health is revolutionizing the delivery of medical treatment by making it more convenient and affordable.

   Privacy and the Protection of Data:
   Inventions in health technology create worries about the privacy and safety of individuals' sensitive health data, highlighting the importance of instituting stringent cybersecurity safeguards.

10. **The Transition to Renewable Technologies and Energy Sources**
    Resources d'énergie renouvelables :
    The shift toward cleaner and more sustainable energy sources, including solar, wind, and hydroelectric power, is being driven in large part by the reduction of reliance on fossil fuels.

The acronym EV stands for electric vehicle:
The development of electric vehicles (EVs) is helping to advance the electrification of transportation, which in turn helps to reduce emissions of greenhouse gases and dependence on oil.

Options for the Storage of Energy:
The dependability and sustainability of renewable energy sources are being improved because to developments in energy storage technology such as better batteries and grid-scale storage.

11. **Obstacles to Overcome and Ethical Factors to Consider**

    Privacy and the Protection of Data:
    Concerns have been raised regarding privacy, user consent, and the possibility of data breaches as a result of the growing gathering and exploitation of personal data by developing technologies.

    The "Digital Divide":
    Because not everyone has access to newly developed technology, a "digital divide" has emerged, which exacerbates existing inequalities in areas such as education, healthcare, and economic possibilities.

    Displacement from One's Job:
    Because of the potential for automation and AI to cause job losses in certain fields, it will be necessary to train workers to acquire new skills and update their existing ones.

    Concerning Bias and Ethical AI:
    Artificial intelligence systems can perpetuate biases that are present in the data that they use for training, which poses ethical concerns related to fairness, transparency, and accountability.

    Influence on the Environment:
    Because of the environmental impact of manufacturing and disposing of electronic gadgets as well as the energy usage of data centers, more environmentally responsible business practices are required.

12. **Prospective Trends and the Changing Terrain of Emerging Technologies**

    Computing at the Edge:
    Edge computing, which processes data closer to the source, is expected to cut latency and make it possible for real-time applications such as driverless vehicles and the Internet of Things (IoT).

    Enhancing the Human Condition:
    The line that separates humans and machines will continue to become more blurry as a result of emerging technologies, which will have applications in areas such as healthcare, accessibility, and communication.

    The term "decentralized finance" or "DeFi"

Decentralized finance, also known as DeFi, is a relatively new concept that makes use of blockchain technology to build decentralized financial systems and services. This reduces reliance on conventional banking institutions and other intermediaries.

The Circular Economy and Sustainable Practices:

New technologies will play a critical part in the advancement of sustainability and a circular economy, as well as the promotion of resource efficiency and the reduction of waste.

Exploration of Space and the Commercialization of Space:

In the years to come, one of the most noticeable trends that will emerge will be the commercialization of space. This will include activities such as space tourism and the mining of asteroids.

Emerging patterns and technologies are transforming society as well as industry, presenting opportunities and problems that have never been seen before. It is crucial to address ethical questions, encourage inclusion, and build responsible regulatory frameworks as we traverse the ever-changing world of innovation. By embracing new technologies and ensuring that they are used in a responsible manner, society may tap into the potential of these technologies to create a brighter, more sustainable, and more interconnected future.

One thing is certain despite the fact that we are continually adjusting to the ever-changing technological landscape: the voyage of discovery and innovation is not even close to being finished, and the future promises endless potential for the evolution of humanity.

10.2 The Role of Sustainable Tourism in Mitigating Climate Change

Through the promotion of responsible travel habits that lessen the toll taken on the environment by the tourist sector, sustainable tourism is an essential component in the fight to slow the progression of climate change. As the global climate crisis worsens, the tourism industry is coming under a greater amount of scrutiny for its role in the production of greenhouse gas emissions, the loss of habitat, and the accumulation of garbage. Recognizing that tourism can be both an economic driver and a force for the preservation of the environment is essential to the practice of sustainable tourism, which offers a comprehensive approach to addressing these challenges.

Bringing Down Emissions of Greenhouse Gases:

Reducing emissions of greenhouse gases is one of the most important aspects of climate change mitigation that may be accomplished through sustainable tourism. Sustainable practices include reducing carbon footprints as much as possible by advocacy for low-impact activities, promotion of environmentally friendly accommodations, and encouragement of energy-efficient modes of transportation. Travelers are strongly encouraged to take use of public transportation options, book flights that are nonstop, and sign up for carbon offset programs.

Increasing Energy Efficiency Through:

The use of energy-saving procedures in both lodging establishments and modes of transportation is a primary focus of sustainable tourism. Green hotels and eco-lodges make an effort to reduce their environmental impact by utilizing renewable energy sources, energy-efficient appliances, and water-conservation practices. Additionally, environmentally friendly modes of mobility are encouraged, such as electric vehicles and public transit systems.

Protecting and Maintaining Natural Habitats:

The preservation of natural habitats and ecological systems is a primary focus of sustainable tourism. Conservation efforts, such as the administration of national parks, the protection of wildlife, and the establishment of marine sanctuaries, have the dual goals of preserving biodiversity and storing carbon in ecosystems in their natural state.

Providing Assistance to the Neighborhoods:

Community engagement and equitable benefit sharing are both fostered by sustainable tourism practices. When tourists become involved in the lives of local people and lend their financial support to local businesses, they lessen the demand for environmentally destructive industries such as logging and mining.

Efforts Made to Reduce Waste and Pollution:

Initiatives promoting sustainable tourism work to reduce the amount of waste generated as well as pollution. Habits such as responsible consumption and recycling are included in these practices along with responsible waste management and programs. These measures help to lessen the harmful effects that tourist sites have on the surrounding ecosystem.

Promoting Policies That Are Environmentally Friendly:

Advocacy and support for tourist policies are necessary components of sustainable tourism. Responsible policies, such as controls on carbon emissions, wildlife preservation, and environmental conservation, are supported by organizations and travelers alike as a matter of public policy advocacy.

Bringing Things to Light:

Travelers that participate in sustainable tourism are incentivized to be culturally sensitive and environmentally conscientious. Through education and awareness campaigns, travelers are informed about responsible travel practices, which helps to reduce harmful affects on both the environment and society.

Utilizing Alternative and Renewable Energy:

In order to lessen their dependency on fossil fuels and cut down on the amount of carbon emissions they produce, many environmentally friendly hotels and vacation spots have installed renewable energy sources like solar panels and wind turbines.

Increasing Participation in Eco-Friendly Activities:

Hiking, bird watching, and animal safaris are examples of eco-friendly and nature-based activities that can be offered through sustainable tourism. These activities help reduce the amount of ecological harm that occurs and foster a greater respect for the natural world.

Participating in Activities That Offset Carbon:

Many times, sustainable tourism may urge both tourists and those who provide tourism services to engage in carbon offset programs.

These programs are designed to compensate for the emissions that are produced during travel by making investments in projects that either reduce or sequester carbon, such as afforestation and reforestation.

10.3 Building Resilience and Preparedness

Building resiliency and being prepared is of the utmost importance for individuals, communities, and nations in a world that is becoming increasingly uncertain due to factors such as climate change, natural catastrophes, pandemics, and shifts in geopolitical power. When we talk about resilience, we're talking about the ability to endure shocks, adapt to changing conditions, and recover quickly from disruptions. On the other hand, when we talk about readiness, we're talking about taking proactive efforts to limit risks and respond effectively to crises. These guiding principles, when used together, give communities the ability to withstand the storms of an uncertain future.

Adaptation to Climate Change:

The effects of climate change can be seen in a variety of ways, including more severe weather and higher than normal sea levels. Developing climate resilience requires making adjustments to infrastructure, agricultural practices, and urban planning in order to endure the effects of climate change and recover from their effects. It is also necessary to make measures to limit emissions of greenhouse gases in order to prevent the problem from becoming even worse.

Preparation for Emergencies:

The risk of natural calamities such as earthquakes, hurricanes, and wildfires should never be taken lightly. A comprehensive disaster plan, early warning systems, emergency response training, and emergency drills for the community are all components of preparedness. Communities can lessen the number of lives lost and the damage done to their property if they are well prepared.

Preparedness for the Pandemic:

Recent pandemics all around the world, such as COVID-19, have brought to light the importance of pandemic preparedness. In order to accomplish this, medical supplies need to be stocked up, effective vaccines need to be developed, and powerful public health systems that are able to react quickly need to be put into place.

Resilience in the Economy:

To be able to resist economic shocks such as recessions and financial crises, it is necessary to have strong economic resilience. Individuals and communities can better weather economic downturns by diversifying their economic activities, building up their savings, and increasing their financial knowledge.

Resilience of the Infrastructure:

In order for infrastructure to continue operating during and after a crisis, it needs to be robust. This involves taking precautions to ensure that buildings are built to survive natural disasters such as earthquakes and floods, and that electricity grids can withstand attacks from both hackers and harsh weather.

Safeguarding Both Food And Water:

For resilience to be achieved, it is essential to guarantee adequate and contaminant-free supplies of food and water. Food and water security can be maintained during times of crisis with the support of sustainable agriculture, the conservation of water, and supply chains that are resilient to natural disasters.

Healthcare Continuity and Recovery:

The planning of surge capacity, the training of healthcare staff, and the stockpiling of medical supplies are all necessary steps in the construction of a robust healthcare system. This guarantees that the healthcare system is able to handle the demands of a crisis without becoming overwhelmed by the volume of patients seeking care.

Resilience of the Community and the Society:

For someone to be resilient, it is necessary for them to have social cohesion, community engagement, and support networks. Communities that come together to support individuals who are vulnerable and work together to address difficulties are better positioned to do so.

The Resilience of Government and Policy:

The development of resilient communities is largely dependent on the policies, legislation, and resource distribution decisions made by national governments. The ability to effectively manage emergencies, provide adequate medical treatment, and set up social safety nets all contribute to overall resilience.

Education and a Consciousness of the Facts:

Individuals and communities can benefit from education and awareness campaigns because it helps them recognize hazards and how to prepare for them. It is imperative that people are aware of the importance of being prepared for natural disasters, pandemics, and climate change.In a world that is becoming more interconnected, finding solutions to global problems requires cooperation on an international level. The development of resiliency and readiness should not be viewed as a national or local enterprise; rather, it should be viewed as a global one. It is possible for nations to work together to combat issues such as climate change, pandemics, and other global challenges if they share their information, experience, and resources.

www.ingramcontent.com/pod-product-compliance
Lightning Source LLC
LaVergne TN
LVHW011938070526
838202LV00054B/4719